The standing of psychoanalysis

B. A. Farrell

The standing of psychoanalysis

Oxford New York Toronto Melbourne

OXFORD UNIVERSITY PRESS

1981

Oxford University Press, Walton Street, Oxford OX2 6DP

London Glasgow New York Toronto
Delhi Bombay Calcutta Madras Karachi
Kuala Lumpur Singapore Hong Kong Tokyo
Nairobi Dar es Salaam Cape Town
Melbourne Wellington

and associate companies in
Beirut Berlin Ibadan Mexico City

British Library Cataloguing in Publication Data

Farrell, Brian Anthony
The standing of psychoanalysis.
— (Opus).
1. Psychoanalysis
I. Title   II. Series
150'.19'5   BF173   80-40865
ISBN 0-19-219133-0
ISBN 0-19-289120-0 Pbk

Phototypeset in Great Britain by
Filmtype Services Limited, Scarborough

Printed in Great Britain by
Cox & Wyman Ltd,
Reading, Berks.

Contents

To a beloved daughter
Sheila Aitkenhead

Preface

Psychoanalysis is a notoriously controversial subject. In this volume I try to dig down to the roots of the controversy, and to elucidate some of the rational considerations that determine the standing and value of psychoanalysis. In doing this I have tried to handle the work of analysts, and their theorising, with sympathy and appreciation and yet also with ruthless Socratic detachment.

I have aimed to elucidate the subject for the benefit of the ordinary educated person. I have not aimed at elucidating it for those who are professionally engaged in psychodynamic and psychological work, or for my philosophical colleagues who are interested in psychoanalysis, though I hope that these two groups of people will also learn something from this book. My limitation of aim produces two difficulties.

(1) There is an immense popular literature on psychoanalysis, which is full of claims and counter-claims about the subject. It is easy to make such claims and counter-claims. But to dig down to the roots of the controversy about psychoanalysis, and to make assertions about it which can really stick – all this is a difficult and even tedious business.

So, when I address the ordinary reader, I invite him to undertake a journey which is quite tough going. I only wish that I could have made his journey in this book a shorter and an easier one.

(2) Psychoanalysis oozes technicalities with which the ordinary person, in all probability, is very unfamiliar. If we are to get at the sources of the trouble about the subject, we have to explain and discuss some of these technicalities. Moreover, I can only elucidate the controversy with the aid of a number of distinctions which are well known in philosophical circles, but with which, once again, the ordinary person is probably quite unfamiliar. All this increases the difficulty of the journey I am inviting him to undertake. However, it may encourage him a little when I add that I have tried to pitch my elucidation at a level which, I believe, he will be able to follow without any previous training in the disciplines involved. Indeed, I have tried throughout to be as simple as possible.

Given my limited aim, I trust that analysts will appreciate my difficulties in attempting to present their work fairly; and I hope that my philosophical colleagues will not become too irritated by all the occasions – and there are many – when I deal with issues in ways which, to them, will seem slovenly and superficial.

Though I have tried to dig down to the roots of the controversy, it is important to note that there are aspects of the subject which I underplay, or do not even mention. I underplay the relations of psychoanalysis to other psychodynamic doctrines and practice, and to contemporary developments and practices. I do not look at the work on child analysis and psychotherapy, and do not even mention longitudinal studies. I only touch on the large amount of work that has been done on development and conflict in animals.

In my experience psychoanalysis is a subject about which people are apt to like to hear, read and write what they *wish* to hear, read and write. The same applies, I have no doubt, to what I myself have written in this volume. What I say in it has also been affected by what I have wished to say. The discerning reader will probably be able to notice where my personal wishes and predilections have unwittingly and unfortunately influenced my judgement. But in so far as my judgement is a rational one – that is to say, in so far as what I say is determined by rational considerations alone – I fear that the reader may *fail* to find in the text of this book what he wishes to read there. Thus, the ordinary reader will not find support for any of the popular or fashionable views about psychoanalysis to which he may have succumbed. Psychoanalysts will not find in it 'a defence' of their subject, or some philosopher's magic which will enable them to abolish their own insecurities about their theories and methods. Non-analytic psychiatrists will not find what some of them might wish for – namely, a depreciation of the whole subject. Nor will they find what others among them might hope for – namely, armchair, high-powered confirmation of 'Freud's great discoveries'. Those readers who have been influenced by the natural sciences will not find that the book simply dismisses analysis as untestable and the method as valueless. So I advise the reader *not* to approach the book in the hope of finding in it what he would like to read. If he does, the chances are that he will be disappointed.

My obligations in writing this book are many. In my efforts to understand what analysts do, as distinct from what they say, my chief single obligation is to my friend, the late Dr. P. M. Turquet. For some years I observed him at work at the Tavistock Clinic, and I had the privilege of running joint classes with him at Oxford. In these classes he presented examples of his own work for examination and discussion. To all those who attended – undergraduates and graduates, philosophers and psychologists and others, from this country and from abroad – these classes were, I believe, a unique experience. We were all very conscious of our indebtedness to Turquet for his readiness – so rare in the psychoanalytic profession – to expose his own work to public view and scrutiny. In this volume I present and analyse some of his work. Honour should be paid where honour is due. I believe this is the place for me to record my gratitude to Turquet for the help which he has given us in the past, and which he gives us again posthumously in this volume.

I have benefited over the years from various discussions and conferences at the Tavistock Clinic and Centre. Recently I have been helped there by Drs. Robert Gosling and David Malan. Mr. Herbert Phillipson (one time Senior Clinical Psychologist at the Tavistock) gave essential help with the patient John (Chapter 5), for which I am very grateful. I have also benefited from discussion with Dr. Joseph Sandler (of the Hampstead child-therapy clinic, and the Institute of Psychiatry).

I have learned much from psychiatrists and clinical psychologists of various persuasions at different institutions, and, more especially, at the Warneford and Park and Littlemore Hospitals, Oxford. In particular, I have gained much from case conferences that were run there by Drs. McInnes and Skottowe, and from joint classes for undergraduates with Prof. Gelder, Dr. Letemendia and Miss Davidson.

From the psychologists at the Department of Experimental Psychology, Oxford, I have obtained an appreciation of what is involved in scientific inquiry. Their work has provided me with a constant reminder of what has to be achieved to obtain knowledge about human nature.

In the preparation of this book my chief obligation is to Dr. Neil M. Cheshire (Dept. of Psychology, University College of North Wales) for his scholarly aid in helping me in the final stages. I wish to thank Dr. Paul Kline (Dept. of Psychology, University of Exeter) for scrutinising Chapter 8 with the aid of his great knowledge of the field. I am very grateful to Dr. David Malan and to Dr. David Shapiro (at the Dept. of Psychology, University of Sheffield) for their help in commenting on Chapter 9. Dr. Joseph Sandler very kindly read and assisted me to improve the quality of Chapter 7. I am grateful, too, to the readers for the Oxford University Press, Drs. Weiner and Storr, for their comments.

I have benefited from discussions about Freud's case of Paul Lorenz (Chapter 4) with the late Dr. Michael Sherwood.

A number of other people have helped me in different, and smaller ways. I pick out for special mention: Sir Kenneth Dover, Dr. Peter Hodgson, Dr. Richard Passingham, Dr. Tony Harris, and Eveline Farrell.

I need hardly add that the responsibility for what I say is mine alone.

To Dr. Henry Hardy, of the Oxford University Press, I am very grateful for the kindness and patience he has shown me throughout.

I want to thank my college for the facilities it provided; and the librarians of the Radcliffe Science Library for their efficiency and endless patience in producing references for me. I also want to thank Miss Christine Sankey for her unruffled calm and excellent work at her typewriter.

Corpus Christi College,   B.A.F.
Oxford.

1 Introduction

In the early part of the nineteenth century, a very distinguished psychologist began one of her works with the following statement: 'It is a truth universally acknowledged that a single man in possession of a good fortune must be in want of a wife.' In offering us this generalisation about human motives, Miss Jane Austen made use of the commonsense psychology of her society at that time.[1] She used it, with characteristic irony, to give us insight into the virtues and limitations, the foibles and interests of the characters in the world she created for us. In so doing she helps us indirectly, no doubt, to obtain a better appreciation of ourselves. In the hands of a master craftsman, such as Austen, the psychology of common sense can yield considerable dividends. But, as a psychology, it obviously has very great limitations. Like Mr. Darcy, we do often overhear the conversations of others; our memories, like Mr. Bingley's, are frequently exact; and most of us – like Miss Elizabeth Bennet – have had the experience of changing our views and feelings about a person. But the psychology of common sense cannot say much about listening, remembering and attitude change. Indeed, there are large tracts of normal functioning which it cannot explain at all. What is more, its generalisations are vague; the evidence that supports them is uncertain; it is unsystematised and probably unsystematisable, since it appears to include generalisations that are mutually inconsistent. Moreover, though a skilful person, such as an Austen, can use common sense to make us picture and understand an *ordinary* person such as Mr. Darcy, it is doubtful whether even Austen could use commonsense psychology to throw much light on an extraordinary character, like Napoleon or Hitler.

It was also in the first half of the nineteenth century that the first steps were taken to improve upon the psychology of common sense and the reflections of philosophers. Methods were developed in Europe at that time to study certain aspects of conscious functioning, namely, the intensity of sensation. These methods were accepted as scientific in character; and this early work by Weber and Fechner led on – in the course of the next fifty years – to the development of objective and experimental psychology. When a student comes to a British university today to study psychology, what he studies is a psychology which is concerned to investigate the functioning of human and lower organisms by methods which are objective and experimental (with results that are reproducible), and which are, therefore, generally recognised and accepted as scientific. It is characteristic of this psychology that it investigates different *aspects* of human functioning – attention, memory, attitudes, emotion; that the evidence it looks for is *hard* and therefore indefeasible; and that its discoveries and theories are restricted in scope. What this psychology does not provide at present are established theories of human functioning *as a whole*, in an important sense of the expression. This, perhaps, is why the outside critic is apt to complain that the psychology one studies at universities does not help students to understand how human beings tick.

But at the very time that Jane Austen was introducing us to some very ordinary people, serious attempts began to be made to help and to understand some very un-ordinary people, namely, the insane. The introduction of more humane methods of caring for the insane, by Pinel and others, led to the observational study of human disorders by the medical profession, and to attempts to bring some sort of order out of the chaos they presented. From this work there emerged the branch of medicine known today as psychiatry. By the early years of the twentieth century, the work of a number of psychiatrists, and notably that of Emil Kraepelin, had produced a classification of human disorders, which was, and still is, substantially accepted and widely used.[2]

By the early part of the nineteenth century it was generally accepted in scientific circles that mental functioning was closely dependent on the workings of the body. The studies of physiologists and anatomists, such as Flourens and Broca, led on to the discovery of the sensory and motor areas of the brain, and to areas responsible (in some way) for speech and hearing, and so on. By the third quarter of the nineteenth century the hope had been raised that, by further careful exploration, it would be possible to uncover the neural basis of all our ordinary mental activity. This hope, in turn, gave rise to another, namely, that when a person was *not* functioning ordinarily, his disorder would be due to some injury to, or damage or lesion in, the relevant part of the nervous system. This hope encouraged all those concerned in the study of human disorders to hunt for the lesions responsible for them.[3]

This hunt was not without some initial successes – for example, in establishing the syphilitic origin of general paresis of the insane. But the search for lesions soon ran into difficulties. One of these was produced by the type of disorder where the malfunctioning bore no relation whatever to any identifiable underlying neuropathology. For example, the man who complained that he could not stand up or walk, but who had nothing physically wrong with him. The clinical neurologists of the time were uncertain what to say about patients like these. Did the patient really have an illness – even though it did not make neuro-anatomical sense; or was the patient not ill at all, just shamming? The distinguished French clinician Charcot then found that he could induce in a patient the very same sort of paralyses and motor disturbances by the use of hypnosis. His demonstrations were witnessed by, among others, Pierre Janet and Sigmund Freud; and both were convinced that the patients were not shamming. Freud also witnessed demonstrations by the clinician Bernheim, which showed how post-hypnotic suggestion could make a person behave in a certain way (for example, open an umbrella indoors), and yet leave him quite unaware why he was doing so. Freud's colleague Breuer then used hypnosis on a patient with a paralysed arm to try to discover why she was keeping her arm paralytically inactive. The technique appeared to work, in that the patient then reported what she accepted as her motive with its connected emotion, and in so doing was apparently cured of her paralysis.[4]

The subsequent history is well known. When it was found that hypnosis had great limitations as a therapy, Freud moved on slowly to drop hypnosis, and to substitute what is known as 'free association' – as the means (he believed) of uncovering unconscious material from the patient. He found himself exploring the disorders that are known today as the neuroses. It was therefore the work of Charcot, Janet, Breuer and Freud which, in particular, led psychiatrists to give the neuroses a firm place in the neo-Kraepelinian classification of mental disorders.[5]

At the turn of the nineteenth century and in the early years of the twentieth, Freud went on to develop a psychology of mental functioning and neurotic disorder, and to elaborate and practise a method which seemed to be an application of the theory. The method was regarded both as a tool of research into human functioning, and also as a technique for the treatment of mental disorders. So, by the first decade of the twentieth century, there had emerged a new psychological theory and therapy, which Freud called 'psychoanalysis'. By the end of the 1930s, it had become a recognised speciality inside psychiatry in a number of countries. After the Second World War it proceeded, in effect, to 'take over' the psychiatric profession in the United States of America – in the sense that the profession became psychoanalytically oriented. In Western countries in general, except for the Soviet empire, the large and growing profession of mental healers and counsellors of all sorts adopted many psychoanalytic concepts and generalisations, and borrowed from psychoanalytic method in a variety of ways. At the present time, therefore, the influence of psychoanalysis in the relevant professions is immense and world-wide in its extent.

But this is only part of the story. At the end of the nineteenth century the educated public was already familiar with the notion that part, or much, of our mental life may be unconscious in character.[6] But it had no idea how to explore the unconscious. Freud then offered a method which, it was claimed, enabled us to do this very thing; and which, moreover, cured us of our neurotic difficulties in the process. On top of this, when psychoanalysts used the method to explore the unconscious, they claimed to have found that we are all moved – as children and as adults – by unconscious wishes of a very surprising sort. (For example, all little boys have an unconscious wish for sexual intercourse with their mothers.) These surprising claims had their place inside a theory of very great scope, a scope which covered many aspects of human life and activity – dreams, forgetting, slips of the tongue, religious belief, art, human development, the varieties of human character, and so on. It was no wonder, therefore, that psychoanalysis caught the attention of the public and produced the excitement that it did. In the course of the next half century Freud came to be accepted as a psychologist of genius, a Darwin of the human mind, who had made discoveries about human nature of fundamental and lasting significance. During this period psychoanalysis revolutionised the popular view of human nature in much of the West, and penetrated into almost every nook and cranny of our culture. It was quite natural, accordingly, that on Freud's death Auden should say:

> To us he is no more a person
> Now but a whole climate of opinion.[7]

II

What are we to make of the professional and the popular standing of psychoanalysis? Is it justified? This is the question I shall examine in this book.

The question arises quite unavoidably out of the paradoxical situation which psychoanalysis occupies at the present time. No matter how high its popular standing may be, no matter what its prestige is among certain professions in some parts of the world, the fact is that the whole subject is beset by continuing controversy and uncertainty. Freud's psychological theory has been criticised on the ground that it is untestable and therefore unscientific in character. A large number of the generalisations of his psychology have been subjected to searching investigations; and it has been claimed that, over all, these generalisations are poorly attested, or have been found wanting. The method of analysis has been criticised for being quite unreliable as a tool of inquiry or research. The therapy of psychoanalysis, and of related psychotherapies, has been the subject of intensive scrutiny; and it has been claimed that the upshot shows the therapy to be, at best, of unproven utility. According to Medawar, 'the opinion is gaining ground that doctrinaire psychoanalytic theory is the most stupendous intellectual confidence trick of the twentieth century: and a terminal product as well – something akin to a dinosaur or a zeppelin in the history of ideas, a vast structure of radically unsound design and with no posterity.'[8]

What made, and what has continued to make, matters worse for Freud's work, and the psychoanalytic tradition connected with him, was the emergence, in the first and second decades of the century, of other different and rival psychoanalytic theories and generalisations – notably those associated with the names of Adler and Jung. These other psychoanalytic psychologies not only differed from Freud's, but actually contradicted Freud's stand in important places; and yet the analysts were unable even to begin to settle their mutual disagreements by rational means. These divergent developments, and others closer to the Freudian tradition itself, continued to grow and flower down the decades of the century. All this generated fundamental doubts as to whether psychoanalytic method was really a sound way of uncovering the truth about human beings, and therefore whether *any* psycho-analytic doctrine is worthy of acceptance on the strength of what analysts tell us about their patients. So this growth of divergent analytic doctrines has been mutually self-destructive.

It is well known that analysts have tried hard to protect themselves personally, from the surrounding storm of critical uncertainty, by ensconcing themselves behind the defensive barriers of their own special training institutes and professional in-groups. Common sense alone should have told them that this policy was self-defeating. Indeed, this policy has not been enough to prevent what seems to be a widespread sagging of morale among analysts at the present time, even in the United States. The inquiring outsider may even gain the impression that analysts of all traditions have almost got to the point of admitting that it may be reasonable to ask for the justification of their work, and reasonable to question the very existence of their whole profession.

III

The fundamental problem, therefore, that psychoanalysis raises is this. What place does psychoanalysis really occupy on the map of knowledge and belief? To state the problem is quite easy; but to try to answer it satisfactorily runs us into some very special difficulties.

(*a*) There are three generally recognised uses of the word 'psychoanalysis': a wide, a narrow, and a restricted use. On the wide use, the word covers the whole family of psychoanalytic doctrines – Freud's own and all those that have grown out of his original work. On the narrow use, the word covers only the doctrine of Freud himself, and of those that are recognisably Freudian in character. On the third and restricted use, the word refers to the thought of Freud alone. To prevent confusion, I shall from now on replace the word psychoanalysis in the wide use by the word 'psychodynamic'. I shall employ the expression 'Freudian psychoanalysis', or some cognate, for 'psychoanalysis' in the second narrow sense. I shall use the word 'psychoanalysis' itself to refer to Freud's own thought. This is a decision that would probably have won Freud's own approval. When therefore I examine the standing of psychoanalysis, we shall be looking into the standing of Freud's own theoretical contribution.[9]

However, when I speak of 'psychoanalysts' or 'contemporary psychoanalysis', and so forth, I shall be speaking in line with the second sense of the word 'psychoanalysis' above, and be referring to those analysts who are working within the Freudian tradition, and to their doctrines. In addition, and this is important, when I speak of 'psychoanalytic method' or 'psychoanalytic treatment', I shall not confine myself to Freud's practice, but shall be referring to that which is used in the Freudian tradition. Those working in other psychodynamic traditions seem to employ procedures that are akin to psychoanalytic method and treatment. What, therefore, we find out about the latter may well be relevant to the procedures employed in all psychodynamic exploration and therapy.

Still, these linguistic decisions bring out at once that we will not be doing justice to the non-Freudian traditions. We also run into a fashionable objection from psychodynamic quarters, namely, that Freud is pretty *passé* nowadays and really only of historical interest. These disadvantages are regrettable but not serious; for the other traditions of psychodynamics grew out of psychoanalysis and explain themselves by reference to their *fons et origo*. If we can determine the standing of psychoanalysis, we will also do much at the same time to determine the standing of the other traditions of psychodynamics.

Contemporary analysts may not be able to escape the fog of uncertainty merely by taking flight into new psychodynamic languages and declaring Freud to be *passé*.

(*b*) But to restrict ourselves to psychoanalysis still leaves matters unclear. Freud changed his views over the years on several very important issues. Moreover, he was not a systematic thinker, writing for the benefit of philosophers engaged in an obsessional hunt for clarification and precision. He wrote primarily to help himself and his associates to deal with current problems of psychoanalytic practice; and he wrote an enormous amount. Understandably, therefore, what he wrote was sometimes obscure and not necessarily consistent with what he wrote somewhere else. All this produces the inevitable problem of textual interpretation. But if we wish to get on with the job of determining the standing of his work, we have to sidestep this formidable preliminary hurdle. I shall do so by examining a *reconstructed* psychoanalysis. This will be reconstructed in a way which (I hope) will not be regarded as departing far in any important respect from what the textual critics will ultimately agree to have been Freud's later or mature position.

(*c*) But this psychoanalytic doctrine can be appreciated only by means of the material that set the whole development going, and by means of which the concepts of psychoanalysis are paradigmatically explained. This material is to be found in the sessions with patients who have been treated by means of psychoanalysis. But for obvious reasons it is difficult to obtain adequate access to this sessional, or case, material; and, when access is obtained, the material typically requires to be explained in its turn. I shall try to meet this difficulty by presenting and examining some excerpts from analytic case material.

2 Psychoanalytic theory

Let us begin our inquiry into the standing of psychoanalysis by reminding ourselves of the gist, or core, of Freud's view of human nature, as reconstructed.

I

Consider the new born infants, Joe, a boy, and Sue, a girl. The mind of each is powered by two basic forces or instincts – Eros and the Death instinct (or Thanatos). The instincts are manifested in the energy the mind displays. Eros is itself composed of two instincts – self-preservation and sexuality; and the energy of the sexual instinct is called 'libido'. The Death instinct manifests itself in the aggressive and destructive activity of the mind, including the wish to destroy oneself. No name is given in the theory to the energy of the Death instinct.

To begin with, the mind of Joe (or Sue) has no internal structure, and Joe goes into action, without inhibitions, to satisfy the demands of the instincts. In other words, his mind operates in accordance with 'the pleasure principle'. But little Joe soon finds that he has to wait, for example, for his Mummy to come to him, and even to give up demanding that she attend to him when (say) she has to go into hospital. That is to say, he soon discovers that it is better for him not merely to act according to the pleasure principle, but also to take the real world into account, and so act in accordance with 'the reality principle'. As he comes to act in this way, his mind becomes differentiated into two parts, or structures – the Id (which contains the instincts) and the Ego, which does the job of mediating between the demands of the Id and the demands of the real world. The Ego therefore works in accordance with the reality principle. When some threat looms up, Joe reacts with anxiety; and this is the danger signal that sends the Ego into self-preservative action to deal with the danger.

However, the differentiation of Ego and Id is only one change that happens quite early in Joe's life. Another is the development of his sexual instinct.

This instinct has its source in a process of excitation in an organ, namely an erotogenic zone of the body. The instinct has an aim, which is to obtain satisfaction by means of the appropriate stimulation of an erotogenic zone. It also has an object, which is the person to whom the sexual attraction is directed. The zone of the body which first predominates in Joe's life is the mouth. This is followed by the anus; and the anal phase or stage (or, more correctly, as we shall see below, the anal-sadistic stage) is followed in turn by the phallic stage. But little Sue does not possess a penis, and the excitations of this last stage come from her clitoris, which is the dominant erotogenic zone for her at this stage. From this point onward the sexual histories of Joe and Sue begin to diverge.

How does this divergence come about? As the Ego starts differentiating itself from the Id, the energy of the sexual instinct in Joe and Sue – their libido – is directed towards themselves. This is the stage of primary narcissism, in which the object of their sexual impulse is themselves. But the Ego soon starts to invest libido in, or to 'cathect', mental items that in some way represent other objects. Its first cathexis of other objects enables the child to become sexually interested in objects other than itself – first the breast, and then later the mother. The phallic stage in both Joe and Sue is contemporaneous with a period in which their early libidinal interest in the mother comes to dominate the scene.

The boy Joe becomes sexually attracted to the mother, wishes to have bedroom access to her and becomes sexually jealous of the father. In short, he develops the well-known Oedipus Complex. But he now takes in that his mother has no penis, unlike himself, and his fear grows (as the, result, for example, of masturbation prohibitions) that, if he pursues his interest in his mother, his penis too will be cut off. This conflict is resolved by repressing his libidinal interest in his mother; by his Ego absorbing, or introjecting, (in particular) the standards of the father, which prohibit incest; and by identifying himself with the father. All this has two results.

(i) His libidinal interests in his mother are transformed by being desexualised and inhibited in their aim – so that they now appear as affection for the mother. If Joe can sublimate his libidinal interests at this point, then he will be successful in destroying his Oedipus Complex. (See page 16 below for an explanation of the word 'sublimation'.)

(ii) By introjecting parental and, especially, paternal standards, and by identifying himself with the father, Joe's mind undergoes a further differentiation. It acquires a new structure, the Super-Ego, which serves to control his own activity by means, in particular, of the imperatives that issue from what we ordinarily call his 'conscience'.

The history of little Sue at this stage is very different. In her phallic phase, Sue, like Joe, develops a wish to give the mother a child. But then she comes to recognise that she has no penis and holds her mother responsible for this lack. So her strong early attachment to the mother begins to break down. She becomes ready to give up her clitoral interest, she develops 'penis envy', and turns to her father to satisfy her wish for a penis. The pets and dolls she has been playing with now fuse with the penis into a wish for a child-penis from the father. At this stage she enters upon her Oedipus Complex. Her mother becomes her rival for the father, and she remains Oedipally attached to the father for an indefinite period of her life. Because of this fact, the Super-Ego she acquires is not as strong and clear cut as Joe's.

After the drama of the Oedipal stage and at about the age of five, both Joe and Sue enter a period of relative libidinal calm – called the latency period. With the changes at puberty, the genitals now achieve primacy as the erotogenic zone, with Joe developing a new sex aim – namely penetration, and with Sue transferring her susceptibility to stimulation from her clitoris to the vaginal orifice. They both bring together the affectionate and sensual currents of their sexuality, and each directs them, with the normal genital aim of copulation, to one person of the opposite sex.

It is clear from this history that normal adult sexuality is not a 'simple' instinct, but is a sort of synthesis out of the component instincts, which, as we have seen, are at work from birth. In the course of development, the instinct may undergo a more or less serious failure to pass through some given stage. The instinct will then be 'fixated' at this stage, and this will have important consequences in later life. Moreover, the infant and child live in a particular family, with its own social milieu; and this setting can give the child experiences which produce – through the fixation of instinct – all manner of perverted sexual aberrations in adulthood.

The child's development is further complicated by hereditary and constitutional differences, in, for example, the strength or weakness of some component instincts, the sexual precocity of the child, or his (her) capacity to deal with excessive sexual excitation by sublimation. Moreover, and very important, it is quite misleading to distinguish Joe as a male and Sue as a female in the simple way we have done. For Joe's libido is also partly female in character, and Sue's partly male. That is to say, they are each bisexually disposed, the proportions and strengths varying widely between different children. We must also remember that this whole, schematically presented history is open to wide and subtle variations from child to child; and, in any case, an analyst may say, our knowledge of it is still incomplete and uncertain in a number of respects.

A still further complication in the development of the sexual instinct is produced by the role of our other fundamental instinct, namely destructiveness. This interacts with Eros and the growth of psychic structure in a number of ways and places. Thus, initially the libido neutralises the destructive impulses. The latter emerge strikingly in the anal-sadistic phase, when Joe's destructiveness comes out in his aggressive behaviour, and in the use to which he puts his excretory functions (by, for example, asserting his own will against the parents by defiantly refusing to part with his faeces). Joe's sadism, therefore, is a fusion of his libidinal and destructive impulses, and he comes to view the sexual intercourse of his parents as a violent and sadistic interchange. With the development of his Super-Ego, Joe becomes able, for example, to feel personally unworthy and useless (having failed to live up to parental standards); and hence his destructive impulse can now be directed against the Ego itself. Again, just as with Eros, the destructive impulse develops in ways that vary widely – depending on heredity and the family situation and social milieu of the child.

II

We have seen that the job of the Ego is to take account of reality. How, in outline, does it go about doing this? Suppose the mother of little Joe has great difficulties in breast-feeding him, and handles the whole situation somewhat ineptly. Suppose that for purely biological reasons Joe reacts very badly to his frustrations at this time, and develops great tension and anxiety about feeding. This anxiety may threaten to grow beyond the limits of what he can tolerate. Joe's Ego will then react by exerting counter, or anti-cathectic, energy to repress the impulses responsible for his growing tension. He may then begin to show lack of interest in feeding and the activity of the oral stage. This is an instance of 'primal repression'; and it is the way the child's Ego deals with the anxiety produced by all childhood traumas involved in the development of sexuality, including the resolution of the Oedipus Complex. Primal repression also works against anxieties produced by the destructive instinct, but only where the activity of the latter is associated with the sexual instinct, as, for example, in sadism.

In the post-Oedipal child, and in the adult, the Ego works in a somewhat different way. When the boy Joe comes to adolescence and adulthood, he is likely, for instance, to develop a wish to fondle and suck the breasts of Sibyl, his girlfriend or fiancée. But this wish may generate anxiety, because it threatens to reactivate the anxiety of the oral trauma he experienced as a child. Joe's Ego then exerts anti-cathexes on the idea of the wish; and this makes the wish an unconscious one for Joe. But this wish has all manner of associations – with ideas of his wishing to suck sweets, to chew gum, and so on. Most of us are able to recognise such wishes, should we have them, and partly, for this reason, they can be said to be 'preconscious' in character. But for Joe to have such wishes preconsciously (for example, that he would like to chew gum) is to retain dangerous links (for him) between his power consciously to recognise this preconscious wish and his unconscious wish to suck Sibyl's breasts. Therefore his Ego also withdraws sufficient energy from all such associations, or derivatives, as to make these unconscious. Joe cannot now recognise, by any ordinary means, that he wishes to suck sweets or Sibyl's breasts. When the Ego works in this way, it is carrying out 'Actual Repression' or 'Repression Proper'. Both types of repression, Primal and Actual, involve the constant expenditure of energy by the Ego. Furthermore, what is unconscious for Joe includes much more than what has been repressed. The Ego's way of controlling excitation which we have just described, namely repression, is itself unconscious to Joe.

However, repression is only one way, though a critically important one, of controlling the excitation to which the mind is subject. There are a number of other unconscious ways of doing so; and, along with repression, they are usually referred to as Mechanisms of Defence. Some of these are well-known. Thus, when Sue at seven runs into trouble at school, she may try to cope, in part, by regression – for example, by thumb-sucking and playing the role of a small child. Joe may try to deal with his guilt about some piece of misbehaviour by blaming his older brother for leading him on, and thereby projecting his guilt on to the latter. Some other well-known mechanisms are displacement, reaction formation, identification, destruction in the Id and sublimation. Most Mechanisms of Defence are unsuccessful, in that they do not eliminate the dangerous impulses, but only keep them at bay at the price of a steady, never-ending expenditure of energy. Some defences, however, are successful, not in the weak sense of producing temporary or uneasy stability, but in the stronger sense of ensuring that the dangerous impulse ceases to exist. Thus, when a boy begins to turn away from his Oedipal wishes, he uses repression; but in normal cases the child goes on to achieve the complete destruction of the wishes. Again, at the beginning of her latency period, Sue may deal with her pre-genital sexual impulses by sublimating them, that is, she may replace them altogether with one or more other impulses, with new aims, and ones which are socially acceptable – for example, a passionate interest in scientific discovery, or artistic expression.

Though we have listed and discussed some of the defences one by one, we have to remember that these mechanisms work jointly and in an interlocking way to enable the Ego to control the excitation affecting the whole mind of Joe or Sue. The single most important aspect of this activity of the Ego is the control by the unconscious Mechanisms of Defence of the relations between the mental structure containing unconscious items, and the structure containing preconscious ones. The mechanisms work, overall, so as to allow only such items from the unconscious through into the preconscious that each mind is in a position to tolerate. When, therefore, a person's mind is not in a position to tolerate recognising that he, or she, has a wish (say) to injure the married partner, unconscious defensive manoeuvres will be taken to keep this wish unconscious.

But in ordinary life the Ego is not wholly able to stop the unconscious getting through to consciousness. Where some derivative of the repressed material is sufficiently remote from the latter, or is sufficiently distorted by the Mechanisms of Defence, then the Ego does not recognise the true significance of the derivative, and it can emerge into the light of consciousness. It can come out in various, very familiar ways. Thus when Sue, as a child, had a dream, this was the undisguised expression of an unrepressed wish. But when Sue, as an adult, has a dream, it is in most cases the disguised revelation of a repressed wish. As the latter cannot get through directly in its real guise, it is transformed by the unconscious mechanisms, more especially condensation and displacement, into something unrecognisably different. This then gets past the censorship barrier, and appears as the manifest content of the dream; and this is what Sue reports. If Sue becomes aware of the real significance of her dream, she becomes aware of its latent content, and of her repressed wish, which came out in disguised form in the manifest content of the dream. It is no surprise, given the history of the sexual instinct, that in a great many dreams of the type we are considering, the repressed and disguised wish is sexual in character.

In a somewhat similar way the unconscious also gets through to consciousness in our daytime fantasies. The unconscious is also at work in an analogous way in humour and jokes with a point to them. Moreover, the unconscious is also operating in our lapses of memory, slips of the tongue and the like. These are not accidental events, but the manifestation of unconscious motives. Then, again, the unconscious also gets past the Ego in the quite different field of belief in God. When Joe grows into adulthood, he may develop the unconscious wish to have his strong and loving father with him to protect him always. Because he cannot keep his real and earthly father, he cathects the fantasy of a substitute father in Heaven. Because of the influence of his unconscious wishes here he comes to believe in this God, when in reality he is believing in an illusion.

III

Now let us look at the adult whose Ego has been able to deal fairly satisfactorily with the demands made upon it. Such an adult belongs to the vast majority. In him (or her) the genitals have primacy erotogenically; the components of the sexual instinct have been synthesised; and the affectionate and sensual aspects of sexuality have fused in the manner we have already outlined. In this sort of adult the Ego itself is strong, since the adult has developed normally; his Ego has not had to develop extensive defensive measures to dam up instinctual energy; and therefore the energies available to the Ego have not been greatly curtailed.

Of course, normal adults differ from one another in countless and subtle ways. Nevertheless, amid all these differences, one can discern some patterns of uniformity in certain types of character which they display. Thus when the individual as a child becomes fixated at a certain sexual stage, say the anal, he is liable to develop as an adult certain character traits, which reflect his difficulties in getting through the anal stage as a child. He is liable to exhibit the trio of traits – orderliness, parsimony, and obstinacy. Experiences at the oral stage may be such as to contribute to him developing into an oral character. Furthermore, the normal adult in the course of his development from the latency period will also have dealt with his sexual impulses by sublimating them, so that as an adult he may have a deep interest in, for example, science or art. But again individuals vary widely in their capacity for sublimation, for biological reasons about which psychoanalysis can say nothing.

However, even though he and she are quite normal human beings, it does not follow that they are free from conflict and contented. Rather the contrary. For in the course of their individual development, they have had to repress their sexuality and to restrict their innate destructiveness and aggression. They have had to do so in order to become members of a civilised community. It is only because this happens generally to the young that a civilised community is possible at all. But this process is liable to generate and maintain all manner of conflicts in individuals; and, in Freud's words,[1] 'the fateful question of the human species seems to me to be whether and to what extent the cultural process developed in it will succeed in mastering the derangements of communal life caused by the human instinct of aggression and self-destruction.' Will Eros be able to keep Death or Thanatos at bay?

IV

But what of the many adults whose Ego has not managed to deal fairly satisfactorily with the demands made upon it, and who therefore exhibit, or suffer from, some manifestly pathological condition? How does this come about? What has gone wrong in these instances? It follows very obviously from what has been said already that matters can go wrong in an indefinite variety of ways. On the other hand, this variety does exhibit – so it is alleged – certain patterns of regularity. Let us concentrate on the putative pattern which is central for psychoanalysis, namely that of neurotic disorder.

Consider again the adult Joe, who, we supposed, has had a history of oral difficulties as a child. Let Joe now have some experience (such as, for example, the death of his mother) that produces excitation which his Ego is not strong enough to master. Joe's Ego cannot master it, because in the course of his development the Ego has had to expend a great deal of energy on building and maintaining defences against Joe's impulses. This has left the Ego in a weakened condition. The reason the excitation has to be mastered is that it threatens to revive the anxiety of infantile and childhood traumas. Because the Ego cannot control the situation, Joe's experience (of his mother's death) precipitates a regression – that is to say, in this instance, instinctual impulses appropriate to an earlier stage of Joe's development are reactivated. Since the resolution of the Oedipus Complex is the climax of the infantile development of sexuality, Joe's impulse regresses to the Oedipal period. But, because of Joe's earlier oral history, his Oedipus Complex, far from being destroyed, was poorly resolved and influenced by his earlier difficulties. The fixation points in his sexual development are pre-Oedipal and pre-genital in character, and are to be found in the oral stage. Hence, under the impact of the precipitating experience of his mother's death, Joe regresses to fixation points in the oral stage. Joe is now threatened by the return of what he had repressed as an infant.

But if the ghastly anxieties of the infantile traumas were to get through to consciousness, Joe would be flooded and overwhelmed by agitation. Now, though the Ego has not been strong enough to prevent the threat arising, it still has the strength to resort to a variety of defences to stop the threat materialising – displacement, reaction formation, and so forth. Therefore, when the repressed material does emerge into consciousness, it does so in such a heavily disguised form that Joe does not recognise its significance. What emerges is a compromise between the unconscious material really present, and what the mind of Joe can tolerate in consciousness. This compromise constitutes the symptoms of Joe's neurotic disorder. Since Joe, on our supposition, suffered oral traumas, his symptoms will be some array characteristic of adults who had severe oral difficulties as infants. For example, feelings of depression, feeling that he is unloved and neglected, difficulties in eating anything, oscillating, perhaps, with bouts of gormandising which disgust him.

From all this it is clear that before an event (for example, the death of Joe's mother) can serve to precipitate a neurotic collapse, a whole complex set of predisposing conditions has to be realised. Thus, Joe's oral libido was strong and liable to get stuck at this stage; he was not good at 'taking' frustration; his early experiences with the mother and others were traumatically frightening, and he developed libidinal fixations; the Ego had to defend against the ensuing anxiety by means of primal repression at this stage, and also right through the Oedipal period, thereby leaving itself very weak. If Joe's oral libido had been strong and liable to get stuck at this stage, but if, on the other hand, he had been a placid baby, or if the mother had not been so frustrating, then his predisposition to neurotic disorder of the sort he showed would not have existed, or would have been less strong. Alternatively, if his capacity for sublimation after latency had been very great, then, in spite of his predisposition, his Ego might have been able to master the disturbance set up by the death of his mother.

Joe exhibits one specific type of neurotic disorder. There are other forms, and whether a person's collapse takes one form or another depends on a variety of other conditions. Thus, if a male infant fixates at the anal-sadistic stage and resolves the Oedipus Complex by, in particular, developing and repressing intense anger at the father, then he is predisposed to this extent to collapse into an obsessional neurosis. Or, again, if the infant libidinises some bodily organ or function excessively, and fixation occurs in respect of it, then he is predisposed, to this extent, to break down into what is called a conversion neurosis – one in which the central symptoms are physical complaints involving the organ or function concerned. On the other hand, if Sue suffers, not from excessive frustration as Joe did, but from overgratification of her impulses, at some stage or stages, then she will be disposed to exhibit a different pattern of disorder (for example, that of a spoilt immature individual who is incapable of standing on her own feet).

The different forms of disorder we have been considering go to constitute one pattern of neurosis which is standard and central for psychoanalysis. There are other patterns. For example, the Ego of a war-time bomber pilot may suffer, after a number of flying missions, from an inability to master the excessive excitation produced by the stress of his work; and he collapses into what is called a traumatic neurosis. It is important to note that in all the examples mentioned so far, the Ego *opposes* the regression that occurs. But if the Ego *accepts* it, then the person's disordered conduct will not constitute typical neurotic symptoms (which are 'desexualised'), but will be the manifestation of a perversion, which will help to bring about its own sort of sexual satisfaction and orgasm.

What goes wrong when a person suffers from a neurosis is different from what happens when he develops a psychosis. In the latter, the Ego splits into two – a part which is reality-facing, and a part which withdraws from reality completely. If the latter part is the stronger, then a necessary condition is satisfied for the development of psychotic disorder – whether schizophrenia, where the world of real objects is denied, or psychotic depression, where the person gives up altogether trying to realise his desires in the real world.

V

From the account we have given so far of psychoanalytic theory, it is clear that it falls into certain sections or parts, or sub-theories – the theories of instincts, psychic structure, development, defence, dreams, errors and lapses, and psychopathology. It is also clear that the theory is not a unified one, in the way that, for instance, the theory of Mechanics, or Mendelian genetics, are unified theories. However, psychoanalytic theory is more unified than our account so far may suggest. For the theory also contains what can be called a High Level theory, which is closely involved with the various sub-theories we have sketched above, and which serves to unify them to some extent. This High Level account contains what analysts refer to as 'Metapsychology', and can be sketched as follows.

What psychoanalysis as a theory is fundamentally about is the way in which the mind works. The mind consists of a set of 'elements' in very complicated interrelations. An element is a mental presentation, and, in their mutual interrelations, the elements go to constitute what can be called a psychic or mental system. Now a mental element has a charge of energy attached to it, and it may also have an 'idea' or 'ideational presentation' attached to it. Hence, the system as a whole contains a quantity of excitation, coming both from the instincts (in the Id) and from the external world. The system controls this excitation in accordance with certain interconnected principles. In particular, it functions so as to keep the total quantity of excitation in the system as low as possible (the principle of inertia), and also (under other circumstances) so as to keep the quantity constant (the principle of constancy). Consequently, when little Joe, or Sue, wants the breast, the mental system seeks to discharge the tension or excitation by feeding, and thereby keep the quantity of excitation as low as possible. But when little Joe's frustrations over feeding generate excitation that the system cannot tolerate, then the latter works to keep the quantity of excitation constant, and therefore stable and within tolerable bounds. It does so by exerting force against the mental presentations involved, thereby primarily repressing the impulses responsible for the threat of excessive excitation. Later in life, when Joe develops a 'dangerous' wish, the system exerts a counter-force against the ideational aspect of the mental element involved, and withdraws energy from the ideational aspects of all derivative elements – thereby actually repressing the wish, as we saw above. The part of the mental system that does this work is the Ego, which is sometimes aided and sometimes hindered by another part, the Super-Ego. What the Ego has to do, in particular, is to keep away from consciousness those mental presentations, whose recognition by the person would raise excitation to an intolerable level. As we have seen above, the different ways in which the Ego achieves this result are known as the Mechanisms of Defence. When the adult system is faced by a threat to its defensive position, excitation is generated, which serves as a signal of danger – called anxiety – and this feeds back to set going protective measures. It is orthodox to say, following Freud, that the unconscious part of Joe's mind is regulated by 'primary processes', which are mainly concerned to discharge energy; whereas the preconscious part is governed by 'secondary processes', which only allow for discharge in ways that are consonant with the capacities of the Ego and the nature of the real world.

In psychoanalytic theory, therefore, the mind of a person is a self-regulating control system. The specific form the system takes, and how it actually works in the case of any given individual, Joe or Sue, depends on a very large number of conditions. Its specific form and manner of functioning is the outcome, in particular, both of biologically given material and the experience the system has undergone, especially in its early years. This experience comes to the system through its own family, and the way this functioned during the early years of the system. The family, in turn, is the important agent by which the community exerts its influence on, and control over, each individual mental system, and so enables the person concerned to grow up and function as a member of the community to which it belongs.

VI

So much for an outline of Freud's mature position as reconstructed. In order to examine its standing, it is necessary to take note of the other main traditions in psychodynamics.

As we saw (Chapter 1), two of Freud's early associates to break away were Carl Jung and Alfred Adler. Jung argued[2] that the concept of libido should be widened to cover all forms of psychic energy, not merely the sexual; he presented a view of development which differed from Freud's; he made important use of the concept of the Collective Unconscious (which embraced items common to all mankind, because they are biologically inherited); and he used the concepts of the Unconscious and the Ego in new ways. He also offered his own account of psychic structure, which led on to a complex differentiation of personality types. Though he regarded the psyche, like Freud, as a self-regulating system, this worked for him in a non-Freudian sort of way (for example, with a different concept of repression); and he had non-Freudian views about treatment. Adler took a very different stance from both Freud and Jung.[3] He appeared to offer no theory of instincts, no biologically fixed stages of development, no concept of libido or psychic energy, and little about psychic structure. He concentrated on the ways the individual child and person adapts to the problems of living, and the relative success or failure of these modes of adaptation. The child begins from a state of helplessness, for which it strives to compensate; the way it does so becomes its 'life style'. If the child develops Oedipal difficulties and castration fears, for example, these are evidence of failure to adapt brought about by defective personal relations within the family. Neurotic difficulties in the adult are the outcome of early failures, which have produced a life style that no longer works.

Jung began the tradition in Psychodynamics known as 'Analytical Psychology', Adler began 'Individual Psychology'. This happened before the First World War. Between the wars new psychoanalytic doctrines and traditions developed vigorously, more especially perhaps in the United States.

One such development took an Adlerian-like stance, rejected Freud's libido theory, and emphasised the importance of the inter-personal environment and the task of the child and adult in having to deal with it. This development is associated, in particular, with the names of Horney and Sullivan.[4] In contrast, there were others who kept the libido theory and developed Freud's own later emphasis on the Ego, in order to develop what is known as 'Ego-Psychology'. The chief names associated with this development are Anna Freud and Heinz Hartmann. The latter concentrated on an effort to incorporate the Ego functions (for example, thinking and perception) within a Freudian type of scheme.[5]

However, there were still other analysts who modified the Freudian theory in quite different ways. Thus, Melanie Klein[6] pushed the story back to the very first experiences of the infant at the breast, when it mentally splits the breast into the good, feeding one, and the bad, frustrating one, and develops a world of unconscious fantasies about the part and whole objects it encounters. Otto Rank[7] had previously pushed the story even further back, namely to the trauma of birth and the related problem of separation. In great contrast with these trends Wilhelm Reich[8] was concerned in his early years with an attempt to bring together or reconcile Freudian and Marxist theory – an attempt which led him to reject what he took to be Freud's views about the repression of sexuality as a necessary condition for the growth and maintenance of a civilised culture. Later on, Erich Fromm[9] applied a Marxist-oriented sociology in an endeavour to explore the interactions between psychological forces within the individual and different kinds of social structure – interactions that issue in different types of personality.

After the Second World War, Western countries – and especially the United States – witnessed a boom in psychotherapies of various kinds, psychodynamic and non-psychodynamic in character, with their connected doctrines. During this period the West also saw the development of therapies and theories which concentrated on the behaviour of patients and its modification. These post-War theories are too numerous to outline here.

VII

It is obvious that our glance at the history of psychodynamic theories is so sketchy as to be very arbitrary. For this history is full of contributions from a large number of analysts, and our sketch has only named a few of them. It is also clear that these contributions, from Freud onwards, present collectively a great variety of different views.[10]

It is important, however, that these differences should not be exaggerated. For behind them lie, in most instances, certain common themes which these views all share, and which unite them as specifically psychodynamic in character. These common themes are not open to precise formulation; different analysts would probably state them somewhat differently; and analysts make use of them in dissimilar ways.

Still, it is very necessary to state these themes and to bear them in mind.

1. Psychic Determinism. No item in mental life and in conduct and behaviour is 'accidental'; it is the outcome of antecedent conditions.

2. Much mental activity and behaviour is purposive or goal-directed in character.

3. Much of mental activity and behaviour, and its determinants, is unconscious in character.

4. The early experience of the individual, as a child, is very potent, and tends to be pre-potent over later experience.

We do not need to ask whether these common themes actually form part of psychoanalytic theory and other psychodynamic theories. For, irrespective of whether they do so or not, it is clear that they do serve as principles to regulate or guide the thought and work of analysts. It is by the use of these themes, in conjunction with the theories, that psychodynamic psychologists claim to be able to make sense out of much of human functioning that was previously inexplicable. If, when we examine the validity of psychodynamic theories, we find that they are weak and poorly supported, then *ipso facto* we also throw doubt on the value of these four themes as guides to research and to the truth about human nature. Conversely, the better supported we find the theories to be, the more do we establish the value of these themes, or Regulative principles.

3 The standing of the theory: psychoanalysis and science

What are we to make of psychoanalytic theory?

Let us bear in mind that the roots of the controversy about this subject are likely to go off in contrary and contradictory directions. Consequently, when we explore in one direction, we may be inclined to think that psychoanalysis is a sound and respectable subject; when we explore in another that it is fit only for the rubbish dump. We must be prepared to meet these differing pressures that psychoanalysis may exert upon us. It is only by facing up to them, and by working through them carefully that we can dispel our confusions, and arrive, perhaps, at a clearer and rationally more secure view of the subject than we had at the outset.

I

Many of us have our favourite story about a relative, friend or acquaintance, who, it is said, has been damaged or 'messed about' by a psychoanalyst.[1] These stories tend to add up to an unflattering picture of the profession. As individuals, psychoanalysts can be difficult or even impossible people. As a group, they are full of dissension and personal rivalries, striving for recognition from the learned world, and yet pathetically on the defensive against criticism from the outside. All in all, they may appear to the professional man (or woman) riding on the Clapham omnibus to be a group of somewhat unsatisfactory people with whom he would prefer to have nothing to do. Moreover, it has also been argued, psychoanalysts are not really interested in the evidence that bears on the truth and falsity of their psychology. For they are committed to a faith; and psychoanalytic theory functions for them as a statement of this faith. Hence, there is no need for us to bother about its place on the map of knowledge.

This short way of dealing with, and dismissing, psychoanalysis will obviously not do. Even if we were to suppose that analysts, in their lives and professional practice, are a group of distasteful con-men and women, this fact would have no bearing on the nature of psychoanalytic theory. Even if the theory does formulate what is, for analysts, their faith about human nature, it is quite possible that the theory should also embody important truths about fact, and be of great scientific relevance. Clearly, the attitudes of analysts towards the theory tell us little, or nothing, about it. We can only determine what it is really like by examining it.

What, then, are we to make of this theory?

II

It is tempting to argue that there is no point in examining psychoanalytic theory, since it contains a built-in self-protective device. This takes the form of the generalisation that 'All criticisms of the theory represent so much resistance to it'; and this warrants the analyst in disregarding any criticism. This argument must itself be disregarded. The theory contains *no* such built-in self-protective device. Freud and some other analysts may have sometimes rejected criticism as resistance; but they were in great danger of being untrue to their own theory in doing so. For the *mere* fact of criticism is not sufficient to show that the critic is resisting. To suppose that it is sufficient is to apply the concept incorrectly. If we are to be justified in describing some piece of criticism as a manifestation of resistance, then what matters is *how* the criticism is offered – for example, its strident tone, its obsessional and over-done character, and the like, going along, perhaps, with an apparent absence of careful study of the theory and the method. The claim, therefore, that a particular critic is resisting in offering a certain criticism is a very complicated assertion, which requires specific support to make it worthy of assertion and attention.

If one comes to psychoanalytic theory from a background in the Natural Sciences, the first response one is tempted to make is to say that the theory is obviously not a testable one. If one has been influenced here by Popper, it is tempting to argue that the theory is not testable because it is really a pre-scientific myth: 'And as for Freud's epic of the Egos, the Super-Egos and Ids, no substantially stronger claim to scientific status can be made for it than for Homer's collected stories from the Olympus.'[2]

This argument will not do. The theory may be untestable but not for these reasons. If the theory were a pre-scientific myth, then it would be a closed story, not open to modification under the impact of new facts. But the history of psychoanalytic theory up to the mature version presented in Chapter 2 makes it quite clear that over the years Freud changed and extended his views on several quite central matters. For example, on Narcissism, on the first instinct theory, on the Oedipus Complex, on character development, on personality structure. He did all this – so it would appear – under the influence of empirical fact, in one form or another. Now it is difficult to see where the logical differences are between the *earlier* versions of the theory and the later version (of Chapter 2) – differences in virtue of which the former are open in character and the latter closed and a myth. The latter (in Chapter 2) would seem to be as much open to the influence of empirical fact as the former. Moreover, to compare concepts such as the Ego with Homer's concepts of the Gods of Olympus is to fail completely to appreciate how they function in psychoanalytic theory, and the way in which the theory works as a whole. Freud was attempting, quite manifestly, to offer us what today is called 'a psychological model' of how the mind functions (as we shall see). Quite manifestly too, the model Freud offered us is very defective (as we shall also see). But however serious its defects may be, it is quite misleading to compare Freud's account of psychic structure with Homer's tales of the Gods.

III

'Very well', the man at the laboratory bench may say, 'this type of argument for untestability is no doubt a bad one. Still, when I look at Chapter 2, and I think of the typical theories I deal with in my laboratory, I find the story in Chapter 2 so vague and so poorly constructed that I cannot imagine how anyone could possibly set about validating it empirically – let alone validating it so as to decide between it and any of its rivals. In other words, it does not seem open to confirmation or disconfirmation, and hence it is untestable. But if this is so, we can settle at least one thing about the theory. It is not a scientific story, and we don't have to bother to fit it into any curriculum of scientific studies in this university!'

This reply from the laboratory man is very natural. But is it sound?

It is widely accepted that a scientific theory contains two sorts of concepts: (*a*) those whose instances are observable – in an important and standard sense of this word; and (*b*) those whose instances are not observable. For example, in genetics up to recent decades, it was generally accepted that instances of the concept of chromosome could be observed down a microscope, whereas instances of the concept of gene could not be observed. Likewise, it is accepted today that, whereas instances of atoms can be observed, or are close to observability, with the help of X-ray photography, instances of an electron are not observable, and in the nature of the case will remain so. Concepts of this second sort are generally called 'theoretical'.

These two sorts of concepts differ from each other in important ways, and the generalisations of the theory in which they appear also differ from one another. Thus, and obviously, if the generalisation 'All As are Bs' contains no theoretical concepts, that is, if 'being an A' and 'being a B' are concepts whose instances are observable, then the generalisation can be supported or refuted by observing instances of As and Bs, and noting whether all observed As are also Bs. But if being an A (say) is a theoretical concept, then we cannot confirm or disconfirm the generalisation by direct observation. We will have to resort to indirect ways of doing so; and these are apt to be complicated and uncertain in their results.[3]

Does psychoanalytic theory contain non-theoretical and theoretical concepts and related generalisations? Yes, it does. Consider the generalisation: 'The organ or zone of the body in which the male infant is first interested is the mouth, then comes the anus, and next the genitals.' It is plausible to say that in this example the concepts, including that of being interested, are non-theoretical in character. The generalisation can be regarded as being on the ground floor; for it is quite obviously open to straightforward observation or support or disconfirmation, in the ways that Arnold Gesell was, perhaps, the first systematically to exploit.[4] But psychoanalytic theory also contains the generalisation: 'The interest of the male infant in these zones of the body is in part libidinal in nature, in that it is also a manifestation of his sexual instinct.' Clearly, the concepts of sexual instinct and its energy (libido) are theoretical in character. We cannot confirm or disconfirm this generalisation merely by looking for observable instances. The same applies to the generalisations about the Oedipus Complex and related stages of development. Thus, psychoanalytic theory contains propositions expressible in the statement that: 'At and after the phallic stage, all boys tend to show an interest in having body access to the mother, and to treat their father as a rival.' It is plausible to argue that this generalisation is a ground-floor one, being open to observational confirmation or disconfirmation. It contrasts with the generalisation: 'All boys of this age – from three to five (approximately) – are sexually attracted to the mother and sexually jealous of the father.' This latter statement is one of the standard ways of expressing the generalisation about the Oedipus Complex in psychoanalytic theory. It is not open to observational confirmation or disconfirmation; for it contains theoretical concepts, and therefore embodies what we would ordinarily call an interpretation or explanation of the boy's observable behaviour, for example, in wanting to get into the mother's bed, and so on. Obviously it is open to an Adlerian to use different theoretical concepts and generalisations and to offer a *different* interpretation and explanation.

The behaviour of the boys, he can say, is the manifestation of their feelings of inferiority and their wish to compensate for these by keeping up with father. So the Oedipal generalisation can offer us an interpretation or explanation of observable behaviour, in virtue of the fact that the concepts of the boy being sexually attracted and sexually jealous are not observational but theoretical in nature. Similar considerations apply, *mutatis mutandis*, to other generalisations of the Oedipal story, for example about castration fear in boys and penis envy in girls.

It is evident, also (see Chapter 2), that the theory contains a large array of theoretical concepts. For example, Ego, fixation, repression, anxiety as a danger signal, unconscious mental elements. An analyst can make use of his theoretical concepts and the generalisations containing them, to do two things: (i) to describe systematically what happens to, for example, castration fears and penis envy in the development of the child; and (ii) to explain how these early events influence later conduct, and how they may contribute to later neurotic disorder. Thus, he can say, for example, 'the boy resolves his castration fears by, *inter alia*, introjecting parental standards and identifying with the father'; and 'adult males with sexual difficulties are apt to be threatened by a reactivation of their castration fears and traumas.' In speaking like this, the analyst brings out that the theory contains concepts and generalisations which can be used to order and to explain, in a strong sense, what we would all agree to call the observable behaviour of people, and so explain the ground floor generalisations about them.

IV

So far analytic theory seems to work like a very respectable scientific one. But in recent years it has been argued that this appearance is a delusion. Psychoanalytic theory does *not* really work like a respectable member of the scientific establishment. The differences are great and of quite critical importance.

It is generally accepted that the argument can be stated as follows. For a theory to be scientific, it must be open, at the very least, to empirical validation and invalidation. For this to be the case, the theory must satisfy two requirements.[5]

(*a*) At least *some* of the theoretical concepts of the theory must be linked with observable fact in a way which enables observers to decide objectively whether the concept applies in any given instance. That is to say, some of the theoretical concepts must be 'tied down to fairly definite and unambiguously specified observable materials by way of rules of procedure which have been called "correspondence rules", or "coordinating definitions", or "operational definitions".[6] Thus (and to simplify the whole matter), if a bio-chemist is to make his usual determinations, he has to be able to assert that, for example, when he performs certain operations in the laboratory, the data then collected show objectively that DNA was present on that occasion. These operations give him 'an operational definition' of the concept. Without such a rule, or definition, for the concept of, say, a DNA molecule, he would be unable to determine, in his usual and accepted way, whether or not certain data provided him with evidence that DNA was present. If this requirement (a) is not met, a theory will have no determinate consequences about matters of fact. Being empirically indeterminate, we will not know what matters of fact will support or upset it. Hence, it will not be open to empirical validation or invalidation.

(b) It must be possible to deduce determinate consequences from the generalisations of the theory containing the theoretical concepts. If this is not possible, then we cannot tell what observable consequences to expect from the postulation of this or that theoretical concept. Unless, therefore, the theory satisfies this second requirement, it can be said to be logically indeterminate and without definite content.[7]

Consider the first requirement, (a). Is analytic theory empirically indeterminate?

Let us look at an example of a theoretical concept. Take regression. It is clear that this concept is not linked to fact by any correspondence rule, or operational definition; no such rule or definition seems to be available in the psychoanalytic arena. On the other hand, the concept has *some* links with observable fact. What are they? And can they be used to achieve such a rule or definition?

Consider the adult Joe, who goes into a clinic suffering from a neurotic collapse. According to analytic theory, Joe will have regressed to an earlier stage of libidinal development. In the absence of information about Joe's early development the analytically orientated Registrar who examines Joe on intake at the clinic will expect his regression to be manifested in any one of an indefinitely large and wide variety of ways – which cannot be summarised in any rule or definition, but to which his professional training has nevertheless alerted him. Therefore, the Registrar does not approach Joe with some operational definition on hand for the concept of regression. It would be quite out of place to expect him to do so. However, in his interview with Joe the Registrar may uncover a history of early feeding difficulties, and personality tests may suggest that Joe is very much of an oral character (see Chapter 2). The Registrar's expectations will then be restricted to, and directed along, certain avenues. *Inter alia*, he will then expect that

Joe's regression will manifest itself in ways that he regards as characteristic of patients with oral difficulties.

What are these ways? If challenged, the Registrar will probably point to a pattern of behaviour that forms part of the total pattern he would point to if asked to indicate the symptoms of Joe's disorder. Analysts would be ready to agree, in general, on the pattern of symptoms, and therefore of regression, which is characteristic of Joe's type of disorder. Characteristically (as we noted in Chapter 2), Joe will have feelings of depression, feel that he is unloved, and so on, he will have difficulties in eating, which perhaps will vary with bouts of compulsive gormandising that disgust him.

Can this pattern of (alleged) manifestations of regression be used to construct an operational definition for this concept? It is very doubtful indeed; for the pattern involved is far too loose and unbounded. A historian of art may be able to work with the family likeness that constitutes the Hapsburg face, and work sufficiently well to pick out correctly the next, alleged Hapsburg face presented to him in a portrait. But we cannot transform this family likeness into an operational rule for identifying the Hapsburg face. Likewise, the Registrar examining Joe is working with a pattern of behaviour that constitutes a family likeness for instances of regression in a case with oral difficulties. He uses this family likeness to pick out the regression in Joe's particular case. Clearly, we cannot transform this family likeness into an operational definition for the concept of regression in this type of case. If we were to attempt such a transformation, we would fail because the concept, so defined, would then be too tight to do the job that analysts want it to do. Similar difficulties would arise if we were to try to ensure that our proposed operational definition is objectively applicable.

What is true of Joe and his regression seems very generally true of everyone else, and the regression they may exhibit. Furthermore, what is true of regression is also true of the large number of other theoretical concepts of the theory. No doubt, these concepts differ logically from one another in various ways. But, in one respect, they do all resemble the concept of regression we have examined. None of them can be tied to observable fact by operational definitions or correspondence rules. Accordingly, when we use analytic theory to assert that the Ego, or repression, or an unconscious mental event, or some other theoretical concept applies here or there, there is no set of accepted and objectively determinate observations we can make to confirm or to upset our assertion. The theoretical concepts of psychoanalytic theory do seem, therefore, to be empirically indeterminate, and to function very differently from their counterparts in science.

V

What of the second requirement, (b)? Is analytic theory logically determinate? The argument for saying that it is not can be set out and explained in the following way.

Consider one important part of the theory, namely, the Mechanisms of Defence. This part is specifically concerned to cover the ways the individual deals with, and so adapts to, the excitations that affect him from within and without. Now the generalisations in this part of the theory are not typically universal in character. Thus, we do not find repression or identification functioning here in generalisations of the form: 'All individuals, when frustrated, will regress (or identify) in such and such a way.' Rather, they appear in generalisations of the form: 'All individuals, when frustrated, tend to, or are liable to, or may regress (or identify) etc.' These are generalisations which state that the concept may, or is likely to, or is apt to, or tends to apply. In other words, these concepts function, typically, in generalisations which assert unquantified likelihoods or tendencies.

This fact has serious consequences. It means that we cannot use a generalisation of this type about (say) regression in the standard deductive way to infer, and so predict, that some particular group of individuals will regress when frustrated. Nor can we infer, and so predict, in the standard way that Joe (or Sue), when frustrated, will regress. This means, in turn, that, if we investigate and find that the particular group being studied, or that Joe, do not regress under frustration, we do not invalidate the original generalisation. Negative findings, therefore, do not appear to invalidate the relevant generalisation of the theory. Hence, this part of analytic theory – that concerned with the Mechanisms of Defence – does seem to be logically indeterminate. In so far as the theory as a whole relies on this part, to that extent is the whole theory infected with similar indeterminateness.

What is more, it can be maintained, this conclusion is far from being the whole, or full, sad story. The difference between psychoanalytic theory and a scientific one is much greater and more serious than this conclusion suggests. The fact is that analytic theory is really logically indeterminate in a way that makes it empirically empty or vacuous. For it is not possible to derive *any* observable and testable consequences whatever from the theory. Consequently, the theory is not even open to indirect empirical validation. Some psychologists claim to have investigated the theory by deriving observable consequences from it. But this claim (it is said) is a mistake. No such observable consequences can be obtained from the theory; and the objective investigation of analysis by psychologists will have to be justified in some other way.

We can best explain the objection of vacuity by looking at a couple of examples of such putative derivations.

Consider the theoretical concept of repression. Suppose we argue that repression serves in most of us to keep emotionally disturbing or emotionally toned words out of consciousness. Next, we propose the hypothesis (of Bruner and Postman)[8] that if we present to Sue, and others, words such as 'whore' and 'shit' visually in a tachistoscope, they will take longer to recognise them than they will comparable but undisturbing words. That is to say, the perceptual threshold will be higher for these disturbing words. It is now tempting to say that what we have done here is to infer from the psychoanalytic theory of repression that, if adults are presented with emotionally disturbing words, they will take longer to recognise them than undisturbing words. Accordingly, it is tempting to claim that we have now tested in a small way the psychoanalytic theory of repression.

But it is simply not right to say this without serious qualification. When we argue that repression serves to keep emotionally disturbing words out of consciousness, we are not asserting the major, or any other, premise of our inference. Our major premise appears to run something like this: 'If people are disturbed by certain words (like 'whore'), then they will take longer to recognise them.' And this says nothing about repression. If the concept of repression *were* to appear in a suitable premise, the latter would have to take a form of which the following would be a specific type: 'Emotionally disturbing words A to J have repression strengths 1 ... N associated with them' (generalisation R). This premise would then, perhaps, put us in a position logically to infer that 'If these words are presented tachistoscopically, recognition of them will be delayed by a corresponding scale of milliseconds, 1 ... N.' That is, we could infer that the perceptual threshold will be raised by a corresponding scale of 1 ... N milliseconds. But psychoanalytic theory contains no such generalisation R about repression or any other of the required forms. Hence no such inference is possible. What we can say is that the psychoanalytic theory about repression *suggested* to Bruner and Postman that they carry out this piece of experimental work. But we cannot rightly describe it as testing or validating analytic theory in any straightforward way (cf. page 45).

The second example is a little different. Consider one study by Hall on dreaming.[9] It is plausible to say that Hall inferred from the Oedipal generalisations that, *inter alia*, there will be more male strangers in male dreams than in female; and that there will be more aggressive encounters in male dreams with male than with female strangers. Hall then tested and confirmed these (alleged) consequences by analysing reported dreams from large samples of different age groups. But where is the Oedipal generalisation from which these conclusions can be inferred? Perhaps it is the generalisation, G: 'Boys, unlike girls, go through a period of being jealous of their fathers.' From this, along with some other premises, it may then be possible to infer that related wishes and fears will be manifested in certain ways in dreams (proposition p). But if our observation confirms p, do we thereby confirm the Oedipal story, and refute, say, the Adlerian one? The answer is no; for an Adlerian would be happy to accept generalisation G and the inference p from it, and he would explain generalisation G by saying that, in respect of their fathers, boys have greater feelings of inferiority and a greater need to compensate than girls. Suppose, then, we try again – by dropping G and adopting the obvious alternative. Suppose we adopt, as our premise, generalisation H: 'Boys, unlike girls, go through a period of being sexually jealous of their fathers.' From this along with other premises, we may then attempt to infer the same consequence p, as before. Generalisation H does state a central proposition of the Oedipal story, namely, that the behaviour of boys at the time is libidinal in character – that it is the manifestation of the sex instinct. However, it is not obvious how p is to be inferred from H, and it is quite clear that we *do not need* generalisation H to obtain p. We can infer the latter equally well from generalisation G, which makes no reference to the sexual instinct. So it is very misleading indeed to say that conclusion p is derived from the Oedipal generalisations of psychoanalytic theory. But it is generalisation H, not G, which contains the relevant theoretical concepts of analytic theory, namely sexual energy and instinct. Nothing observational, therefore, has been derived here from this part of the theory.

What is the reason for these failures to derive observable consequences? The answer seems to be that nothing observable *can* logically be derived from the theory of repression or of sexuality. For it is logically possible to do this only if we ascribe some *intrinsic* properties (a notion we explain below) to the working of repression, and to the sexual instinct and energy – properties with the help of which we can derive observable consequences. The latter may then enable us to determine whether Freud or Adler or Jung were right about the way the mind works and about sexual development. But at the present time psychodynamic theory does not offer us, in either of these two examples above, intrinsic properties that will generate observable consequences for us.

What applies to the two examples we have just considered – repression and the Oedipus Complex – applies to *all* the theoretical concepts of psychoanalytic (and psychodynamic) theory. It is not possible to infer observable consequences from the generalisations of the theory in which they function, and for the reason just given. The same applies to that part of psychoanalytic theory in which the mind is viewed as a self-regulating control system. This part also ascribes no intrinsic properties to the psychic system from which observable consequences can be drawn.

We can appreciate the sort of properties which are required if we contrast, briefly, this part of the theory with the stock, and therefore very familiar, example used in almost every textbook on the philosophy of science. The example is the kinetic theory of gases.[10] It is well known that, when physicists got to grips with the behaviour of gases, they constructed a model in which they supposed that a molecule of a gas was a very small particle of matter, whose elasticity was infinite. They then used their knowledge of the behaviour of small particles to infer that the molecules of a volume of gas in a container would collectively exhibit certain observable properties. Therefore, it was the behaviour of particles of matter – with certain properties – which formed the source of this model.[11] No doubt Freud speaks in many places in physical and electrical terms about the mind, but what he says is vague and insufficient. Psychoanalytic theory ascribes no intrinsic properties of the sort required, and hence really has no source for the model of the self-regulating control system which the theory contains. Hence, unlike the model used by the kinetic theory of gases, no observable consequences can be derived from the model in analytic theory. We are forced to conclude, therefore, that the theory is logically vacuous.

This has a critical consequence for psychoanalytic theory. It means that it would make no difference to the observable world if the theory were to be dropped. The empirical facts about patients and people would remain the same as before. Psychic energy, the Ego, the Unconscious, and all the rest of the apparatus (set out in Chapter 2) could be thrown on to the rubbish dump, and human nature and the human world would be logically unaffected. For the theory is factually empty. (Here psychoanalysis contrasts sharply with the kinetic theory of gases with its particle model. For if we were to throw out this model and to suppose that gas molecules do *not* behave, in the relevant circumstances, like particles of matter, with certain properties, then we would have some reason to claim that the observable world would have to be different from what it is; and this would make it necessary for us to find an alternative explanation of the facts.) If we believe that our unconscious wishes play an important part in our lives, our belief has content in so far as we use the concept of unconscious wish to classify ways in which we do behave in respect of our wishes – for example, failing to recognise in ourselves what other people can see quite easily. But in so far as our belief leads us to the claim that, in addition to our behaviour, some unconscious mental events or states actually exist 'in the mind' or 'psychic system', then our belief is vacuous. This whole way of speaking, so characteristic of analysts and so essential to psychoanalytic theory, can be eliminated without loss.[12]

VI

Is this criticism of psychoanalytic theory (in IV and V) sound? Is it safe to describe the theory as empirically and logically indeterminate, and hence not open to validation or invalidation? The answer is: No it is not. It is very misleading indeed simply to assert that the theory cannot be validated or invalidated, and that it is therefore untestable. Why is this?

As soon as we look into the details of how the generalisations and concepts of the theory actually work, it becomes clear at once that we have to distinguish between, what can be called, two parts of the theory – the High Level Theory (see Chapter 2) and the Low Level one. The latter contains generalisations such as the following:

(a) All young boys are sexually attracted to the mother and sexually jealous of the father;

(b) When a person suffers frustration, he is liable to regress to an earlier stage of development;

(c) When an adult patient exhibits fears about sexuality, this goes along, typically, with a recognition later that he was afraid because his adult sexuality threatened to revive the fears aroused by traumatic sexual experience in childhood, which he had forgotten (that is, repressed).

The High Level theory, on the other hand contains generalisations, and concepts, such as these:

(i) The mind contains mental elements, each of which has two aspects, an ideational presentation and an affective charge of energy;

(ii) When the emergence of a mental element into consciousness would produce excitation too great for the system to bear, then energy is withdrawn from the mental element concerned;

(iii) There is a strong tendency in the psychic system to keep the quantity of excitation as low as possible.

From these examples it is obvious that the High Level theory gives us an account of the way the mind works as a whole. It postulates certain machinery and functioning, which go to explain the low level generalisations of the theory; and, along with the latter, also explains the observable conduct of people – the ground floor generalisations about them. The generalisations of the Low Level part resemble those in the High Level one in also containing theoretical concepts (for example regression and repression). They differ from them, however, in not being concerned to use analytic concepts to spell out the details of the way in which the psychic system goes about its business. They are concerned, rather, to bring some order into the conduct, thought and so on, which analysands present to them.

It is customary for psychoanalysts themselves to distinguish between the High Level part of the theory – what is known as the 'Metapsychology' – and the rest by saying that the former is concerned to handle mental phenomena in terms of the concepts of the psychic apparatus, in contrast with the rest, which does not do so. But this customary way of distinguishing High Level theory is confusing, and will not do for the purposes of analysts. Though there are some concepts which belong exclusively to the High Level theory (for example, mental element, withdrawal of energy), there are a large number of others, which function in important ways in *both* High and Low Level parts of the theory. The reason for this is that the concepts of the Low Level theory are typically Janus-faced in their functioning. They look towards the machinery of the psychic apparatus or system; but they *also* look towards the bewildering panorama of human conduct, thought, etc., and to ways in which this can be given some pattern and order. When the ordinary analyst is in his working clothes and uses these concepts in a standard way, then he does *not* use them to spell out the details of the machinery of the system. The analyst in his working clothes is not interested in the details of the machinery; he is interested in ordering the material produced by his patients. Here these concepts are functioning in the Low Level theory. But when the analyst dons his theoretical clothes, he uses these concepts to help spell out how the psychic system of a patient, or person, works to deal with the problems facing it. Here the concepts function in the High Level theory.

Thus, the concepts of regression and repression function in generalisations (*b*) and (*c*) above (page 37) in the Low Level theory, to help to state generalisations which bring order into the case material; and, thereby, to explain the material in the weak sense that such patterned ordering achieves. But, if an analyst is concerned to explain why and how this sort of material is produced at all, then he will use regression and repression to help him to specify and describe the states of affairs in the system that these concepts are referring to. They then function in the High Level theory. If, for instance, he is interested in spelling out the process and state of affairs that the concept of repression is about, then generalisation (ii) above (page 37) from the High Level segment will help him to describe and to explain this process and state of affairs. Chapter 2 makes it clear that analytic theory is a close interweaving of both High and Low Level theories.

There is nothing disreputable about the fact that so many concepts of analytic theory are Janus-faced in character – that they function in both its Low and High Level parts to do two different jobs. Something similar is true of a number of the concepts used by the man on the omnibus about himself and his fellows. For example, suppose he says of Smith in some standard context: 'Oh, he's an honest man'. Here he uses the concept of honesty to order Smith's conduct, and in a weak sense to explain it. But he does not say anything about the state of affairs which is somehow 'inside' Smith, and in virtue of which Smith does conduct himself honestly. If challenged to tell us about this state of affairs, he would not know what to say. He would not know how to spell it out; and he would not be in the least interested in doing so. He is quite happy to speak about Smith's honest disposition without being interested in, or knowing anything about, the internal state of Smith in virtue of which he has, and manifests, this disposition. However, a theoretical psychologist of personality could be interested, and in the future will have to be interested, in the relevant internal state of Smith, which underpins his honest conduct. This psychologist would then use the concept of honesty in the same Janus-faced way in which psychoanalysts use a number of their concepts.

Now when the working analyst deals with his patient Joe (or Sue), he will be concerned to order and so (in a weak sense) to explain the material they produce. In so doing he may well find himself using the concepts of regression and repression, and generalisations (*b*) and (*c*) above, or ones of the same logical type. He may not be interested at all in filling out what these concepts and generalisations are pointing to in the psychic system. What is really going on 'inside' Joe (and Sue) when regression or repression takes place may be of no, or little, concern to him. He will then be happy to speak dispositionally about Joe, without being able to spell out what he is really referring to in his dispositional use of the words 'regression' and 'repression'. Moreover, he may well be able to develop a psychodynamic account of Joe's (or Sue's) condition, which is good enough for his purposes, but which makes little use of the High Level part of analytic theory.

What is the logical relevance of the distinction between Low and High Level theories? It draws attention to one important way in which analytic theory is not a simple homogeneous affair (which the criticism of non-validation supposes), but a very complex, differentiated one, whose functioning is very involved indeed. This fact suggests at once that the different parts of the theory are likely to be related to empirical fact in different ways; and this makes it necessary for us to look at the theory afresh.

VII

It is evident that, in so far as the Low Level theory makes use of the concepts of defence – regression, repression, and so on – to that extent does this theory remain logically indeterminate in character. It does seem to be true that we are debarred from using the generalisations containing these concepts to infer, and predict, in the standard deductive way in which negative results invalidate. But the fact that the theory can generate no inferences of this sort does *not* mean that it can generate no inferences at all about observable conduct, and the like. Thus, for example, from the generalisation of the theory that 'All people, when frustrated, are liable to regress', we are entitled to infer that some specific class of people (say, the members of small therapeutic groups) are liable to regress, when frustrated. We are also entitled to infer that Joe, when frustrated, is liable to regress. Again, we are entitled to argue as follows, for example:

All people, when frustrated, will tend to regress;

Joe is frustrated at present.

Therefore, we have some reason to assert that

Joe will regress.

In this case, we do not derive the conclusion from the two premises. The relation between premises and inferred conclusion is not that of logical implication, but one of providing rational support. We are arguing that the premises give us some ground for inferring, and so predicting, that Joe will regress. And this argument is quite legitimate.[13]

Now these two types of inference occur with great frequency in psychodynamic discourse. Indeed, they play such an accepted role in the work of analysts, psychiatrists and others that all these professionals are apt to be quite unaware that they are employing them. Naturally, these inferences produce their own peculiarities and limitations – arising from their use of tendency statements. But we need not pursue this matter here. The fact that analysts can use the concepts of the Mechanisms of Defence in legitimate forms of inference is sufficient to show that it is very misleading to speak, without qualification, of the Low Level theory as being logically indeterminate in character.

In so far as the Low Level theory does not make any, or much, use of the Mechanisms of Defence, the theory seems to be, or approximate to, a logically determinate account. Thus, the theory contains important generalisations about human development, character formation, and psychopathology, which seem to generate observable consequences in the standard, determinate way. For example, since the Oedipal generalisation is a universal one, it seems possible to infer that, if boys are very close to their mothers in certain cultures, the adult men in these cultures will exhibit certain specifiable sexual disturbances (for example a fear of menstruation). In view of the role which the Oedipal period is alleged to play in development, it seems possible to infer that children who have suffered early parental loss should subsequently exhibit certain related difficulties. Even when we pick out an unconscious item (for example castration fear), it seems possible to infer that, in observable situations which (*a*) are analogous to those in real life where castration fears are felt, but which (*b*) are also sufficiently different from actual ones to allow displacement to occur, we should find castration fears being manifested in such situations. We cannot settle in advance how sound these inferences are, and whether the theory is really determinate here or not. We can only settle this by going into the details and actually trying to infer observable consequences (see Chapter 8).

But is there any virtue in the Low Level theory being logically determinate in certain respects, if the concepts involved in it cannot be operationally defined? Can we really set about validating the generalisations of this theory if the concepts it contains are *empirically* indeterminate? The man from the laboratory may still feel inclined to think that the concepts are so vague as to make validation a hopeless enterprise.

In discussing the concept of regression (above pages 31–32), we saw that the Registrar acquired it with the necessary aid of his clinical experience and case material. Because of this the concept can be said to be clinically based. When the Registrar applied it to Joe's difficulties, we also saw that he put it to what we have called a dispositional use. Does the fact that this concept of regression is not operationally defined entail, or in any way have the consequence, that no matters of fact can bear logically on the truth or falsity of the generalisations in which the concept functions – for example, (*b*) above (page 37)? Inspection makes it obvious that no such dire consequence follows at all. Moreover, as soon as we take a look at the ways the case material and theory actually work, it is apparent that there are, indeed, close evidential relations between the case material and the generalisations of the theory (see Chapter 7). This is consistent with the widely accepted view that the chief support for the generalisations of the Low Level theory – such as (*a*), (*b*) and (*c*) above (page 37) – come from the case material. The fact, therefore, that theoretical concepts in the Low Level theory are without operational definitions, and so empirically indeterminate, does not mean that we cannot give a use to these concepts – a use which is based on clinical or case material, and which allows the generalisations containing them to be empirically confirmed or disconfirmed.

Of course the degree of support which the case material does provide, is surrounded by the usual qualifications that go along with all evidence from clinical sources. What is more, the case material of psychoanalysis may itself be infected by doubts that are peculiar to analytic material. The extent and seriousness of these doubts is a matter for special inquiry (see Chapters 4 and 6 below). But what we are not justified in doing is to dismiss the Low Level theory as not open to empirical validation *just* because its concepts are not operationally defined. In any case, if we do dismiss it for this reason, we seem obliged to go on to dismiss much of clinical medicine itself. And this consequence would be too horrific for most of us to contemplate.

What of the High Level theory? What follows from the fact that this part of analytic theory is logically indeterminate, and therefore factually empty or vacuous? It is tempting for the man from the laboratory to conclude that, in the light of this feature, the High Level part is a story of no scientific interest or importance or value whatever, and that we need pay no attention to it at all for research or teaching purposes anywhere in the vast mansion of the scientific enterprise. For the defects of the theory seem to make it plain that it contains no genuine knowledge at all. It is just a tale told by a very clever man, full of much sound and furiously good intentions, signifying nothing.

Do these conclusions follow? Let us look at a piece of history. In 1704 Newton published his *Opticks*; and in the second edition, at the end of Book 3, he added a number of 'Queries'.[14] Now one problem that troubled the natural philosophers of the seventeenth and eighteenth centuries, as it had troubled others before them, was a problem quite fundamental to any theory of matter. How do we explain the solidity and cohesion of material things? Why is it that an apple or a stone stays together as one, and does not fall apart? In Query 31, Newton addressed himself to this central problem.

> The Parts of all homogeneal hard Bodies which fully touch one another, stick together very strongly. And for explaining how this may be, some have invented hooked Atoms, which is begging the Question; and others tell us that Bodies are glued together by rest, that is, by an occult Quality, or rather by nothing; and others, that they stick together by conspiring Motions, that is, by relative rest amongst themselves.

Let us now remember what could be said to be the essence of Newton's achievement in the *Principia*. He had used the concept of an attractive force, had extended the concept from falling bodies on the surface of the earth to the large bodies of the Solar system, and had calculated the strength of this universal attractive force. In Query 31 he sets out to explain the cohesion of material things by extending the concept of attractive force in the other direction – to cover the very minute bodies that make up observable material things:

Have not the small Particles of Bodies certain Powers, Virtues, or Forcés, by which they act at a distance, not only upon the Rays of Light for reflecting, refracting and inflecting them, but also upon one another for producing a great Part of the Phaenomena of Nature? For it's well known, that Bodies act one upon another by the Attractions of Gravity, Magnetism, and Electricity; and these Instances shew the Tenor and Course of Nature, and make it not improbable but that there may be more attractive Powers than these...

The Attractions of Gravity, Magnetism, and Electricity, reach to very sensible distances, and so have been observed by vulgar Eyes, and there may be others which reach to so small distances as hitherto escape Observation; and perhaps electrical Attraction may reach to such small distances, even without being excited by Friction.

I had rather infer from their Cohesion, that their Particles attract one another by some Force, which in immediate Contact is exceeding strong, at small distances performs the chymical Operations above-mention'd, and reaches not far from the Particles with any sensible Effect.

And thus Nature will be very conformable to her self and very simple, performing all the great Motions of the heavenly Bodies by the Attraction of Gravity which intercedes those Bodies, and almost all the small ones of their Particles by some other attractive and repelling Powers which intercede the Particles.

These quotations give us the gist of Newton's theory. He used his concept of atomic particle and the concepts of attractive and repelling forces operating between particles to explain the cohesion of material bodies, and also to suggest an explanation of a variety of other natural phenomena – not only a large range of chemical interactions but also why water rises between two sheets of narrowly separated glass, and why 'Flies walk upon the Water without wetting their Feet.'

Let us now suppose that we are living in the 1730s, and we apply the acids of logical scepticism to Newton's theory in Query 31. We could then argue as follows: 'It is clear that no observable consequences can be derived from Newton's theory of cohesion. It is therefore not open to empirical validation, and hence untestable and vacuous. The concepts of the theory are not genuinely theoretical, and therefore it would make no difference at all if the theory were just dropped. It is therefore not a scientific theory at all; it is of no scientific interest or value; and, indeed, contains no genuine knowledge at all about material things.'

It is evident that this sceptical attack, in the 1730s, on Newton's theory is very misleading. If we use the words 'empirical validation', 'vacuous', 'makes no difference', and 'scientific' in the way we have been doing, then it is correct to conclude that Newton's theory is unscientific, vacuous and makes no difference. But it is also manifest that this description and judgement are quite wrong. For it is agreed that Newton's idea of forces operating between atomic particles had a significant role in the subsequent history of scientific inquiry into the nature of chemical reactions and matter. It played an important regulative and heuristic function. Chemists in the next hundred and more years were greatly influenced by Newton, and his theory of cohesion, far from being vacuous, was pregnant with possibilities. We are safe in saying that, if Newton had not produced this theory, its absence would have made a considerable difference to the subsequent history of scientific thought and work in this field. Consequently, though it is true to claim that Newton's theory of cohesion was not open to validation, was untestable and vacuous, this is a trivial claim; and not one from which any important sceptical conclusions can be drawn.

The logical parallel with psychoanalytic theory is obvious, and surprisingly close. Newton offered us a vague model of attractive and repulsive forces between the unobservable atoms of material things. One of the features of the model which made it so powerful was that Newton used it to explain a wide range of otherwise disparate phenomena. Likewise with Freud. The latter has given us a vague model about forces operating on and between unobservable mental elements; and he used it to explain a wide variety of phenomena, as we have seen (Chapter 2) – phenomena that were not previously covered by any one psychological theory.

Moreover, just because analytic theory is vacuous in the same sense as Newton's, it does not follow that analytic theory is vacuous and makes no difference in the important heuristic sense, which made Newton's theory so influential in the history of science. Far from it. For, though the theory has plainly not played a heuristic role in the history of science at all comparable to Newton's, it has played, and still is playing, a role of some interest and importance in the development of psychology. It plays this role for a reason that is easy to understand. Though it does not generate determinate observable consequences, it contains suggestions about observable matters of fact. These suggestions stem, in part, from the metaphors, analogies and vague pictures, which are contained in the High Level theory. Psychologists can then set about discovering whether these suggestions hold or not.

Thus, we saw (page 34 above) that Bruner and Postman did not, and could not, infer any observable consequences from the psychoanalytic theory of repression. But it is clear that what they *did* do was to extract from the theory the suggestion that, if any words are subject to repression, then there will be a delay in perceptually recognising them. In other words, they had the idea that a delay in perceptual recognition could be used as observable evidence of repression at work. Their argument can be schematised as follows:

All words that are subject to repression will exhibit recognition delay.
Emotionally disturbing words (for example, 'shit', 'whore') are subject to repression.
Therefore, these words will exhibit recognition delay.

This inference is quite legitimate, and, if the prediction is confirmed, then the findings of Bruner and Postman are consistent with the vague theory, or model, of repression in psychoanalytic theory, and do a little to support it. If the prediction is not confirmed, then this negative result does something to invalidate the hypothesis that emotionally disturbing words are subject to repression, and can be used as evidence of this mechanism at work. To the extent that suggestions contained in the High Level theory of repression are upheld in this sort of way, to that extent is the theory supported, and filled out. (*Mutatis mutandis* for Hall's work on dreaming.)[15] Generalisations such as (i), (ii) and (iii) (page 37 above) are open in this way to empirical support, modification or rejection. So empirical fact can do something to sustain, or to upset, the rough and vague picture, or model, of repression, of dreaming, and of the mind in general, which is contained in and suggested by the High Level theory (cf. Chapter 8 below).

The fact, therefore, that the High Level theory is logically vacuous, and, in this way, empirically empty, is not *in itself* a lethal defect in psychoanalytic theory. It is certainly not enough by itself to establish that the theory is of no scientific interest. Indeed, the sceptic's argument against Freud today may turn out to be just as ridiculous as his argument against Newton in the eighteenth century.

VIII

What is the general upshot of these doubts about psychoanalytic theory?

It is evident that its logic is very different from that of an advanced natural science. It is infected with empirical and logical indeterminateness. But these differences do not mean that it has no evidential connection with empirical fact – that the latter cannot be used to support or upset the theory. In spite of all the defects we have considered, it is still possible logically, and it also seems possible in practice, to bring empirical evidence to bear on the theory in ways that have an important bearing on its truth. It also seems evident that the theory is internally very complex, and that the relevant matters of fact come from two different sources at least, namely, case material and objective scientific inquiry. This strongly suggests that the evidential connections between the theory and the facts are likely to be very complex also; and all attempts to impose on the theory the strait-jacket of the two concepts – empirical and logical indeterminateness – are just simple minded and inappropriate.

Of course, if the sceptic in the laboratory restricts the adjective 'scientific' to those studies and theories which satisfy the criterion of empirical and logical determinateness, then analytic theory becomes untestable and unscientific by definition. But by now this has become a rather boring consequence, which in itself throws no further light on the standing of psychoanalysis. Our sceptic may be unwise enough, at this point, to take the further step and to maintain that, because analytic theory is unscientific on his criterion, it is not worth discussing. This step is unwise, because it presupposes that, if a study is not scientific on his criterion, it is not a rational enterprise. And this presupposition is an elementary and egregious mistake. The scientific and the rational are not co-extensive. Scientific work is only *one* form that rational inquiry can take: there are many others. The man in the laboratory may be tempted, in his wilder philosophical moments, to identify the rational with the scientific. But we must on no account allow ourselves to be bludgeoned, or unwittingly induced, into doing the same, and hence into accepting his criterion of intellectual respectability.

Accordingly, when considering the standing of analytic theory, we would be wise *not* to concentrate on its determinateness or its testability. Such concentration is liable to mislead. We would be wiser to raise other questions. What rational grounds, or considerations, are there for accepting the theory, and for querying or rejecting it? How believable or credible is it? Are some parts or segments of the theory better grounded than others? What is the strength of the support from the case material? How much has scientific inquiry done to support or upset the theory? What connection, if any, is there between the theory and the therapy? What is its standing in relation to connected disciplines? What does its future seem to be? Answers to these questions will help us to decide what place to give psychoanalytic theory on our map of knowledge and belief.

4 The support from the case material: the argument from intelligibility

I

We must clear away a current and fundamental doubt standing in our path.

When we ask: 'How credible is psychoanalytic theory?', we presuppose that it is coherent. But this presupposition has been challenged in recent years on various grounds. The challenge is associated, in particular perhaps, with the names of the philosophers Sartre, Habermas, and Ricoeur.[1] If this challenge is justified, if the theory is indeed incoherent, then obviously it is pointless to try to determine the degree of rational support the theory can muster. There is no need for us to go on to bother about its credibility.

The challenge has several central strands. Analysts, we are reminded, are especially concerned to explain the thoughts, emotions, dreams, and so on, of their patients. These events have significance or meaning; and can only be understood by analyst and patient when the significance or meaning is understood. But analytic theory is concerned to outline the machinery and functioning of a psychic system. The theory does not embrace the significance or meaning of the mental events that the analyst is actually concerned with. Moreover, as Sartre for one argues, it is logically impossible for the theory ever to embrace the significance or meaning of mental events. Likewise, psychoanalysts are concerned in their practice with the motives, intentions, and purposes of people. The theory, however, is concerned with causes, and how these work in the system to produce human conduct, and difficulties, and so on. But man is a free agent, not a psychically determined puppet. Motives, and the like, are quite different from causes, and cannot be embraced within a theory of the type Freud proposed.

It is, therefore, the challenge goes on, a complete mistake for Freud himself, and for anyone else, to suppose that what he is doing resembles a scientific inquiry. He is not building a body of scientific knowledge, and it is quite wrong to regard his theory as an account of such, supposed, knowledge. What he is doing is engaging in historical and hermeneutic studies. For psychoanalysis is an interpretative discipline – one of the historical studies which seeks to understand the reasons behind human actions and the significance of our experience. It is not, and cannot be, a psychology of behaviour; and hence it is a mistaken waste of time to try to determine its credibility as if it were a candidate for scientific truth.

Now it would be comforting if we could set psychoanalytic theory on one side and forget about its credibility. But the challenge from Sartre et al. to the coherence of psychoanalysis is not strong enough to provide us with this comfort. On the contrary, the challenge seems to be very weak indeed. What is quite true is that analytic theory does not embrace reasons, meanings, motives, and so on, in a way which is theoretically satisfactory. This is also true of analytic theory when elaborated by Hartmann (Chapter 2) so as to allow for a conflict-free, Ego-sphere in the psyche, where reasons and thought operate. No version of analytic theory spells out how to map our ordinary discourse about reasons, meanings, and so on, into the discourse of the theory, as a first step towards the incorporation of the former into the functioning of the psychic system. The challenge from Sartre et al. draws our attention to, and emphasises, this great theoretical lacuna in all psychoanalytic and psychodynamic theories.

But the existence of a lacuna is one thing; it is quite another to show that it is *logically* impossible ever to fill it. The fact is that the problems produced by the relations between ordinary discourse about human nature, and scientific discourse about it are very difficult. They have been the subject in recent years of intense inquiry by professional philosophers, and they are still unresolved.[2] It is true, therefore, to say that philosophers would *not* generally accept that Sartre et al. have already shown it to be logically impossible to fill the lacuna in analytic theory; and have, therefore, established their case against the theory. On the contrary, many philosophers would probably regard the challenge from Sartre et al. to the theory as feeble and unacceptable. For example, many would say that it is very doubtful indeed whether the principle of psychic determinism, which analysts use, really does entail that the ordinary concept of a freely willed action is a delusion. Whether determinism really is incompatible with the freedom of the will is very doubtful, and this topic is still the subject of close investigation. In short, the whole problem of the relations between ordinary discourse about human nature and scientific discourse about it is still an open and unsettled one.

In these circumstances, we would be very ill advised to dismiss psychoanalytic theory as incoherent, and one into whose credibility, as a body of putative empirical knowledge, we do not need to inquire. We must, therefore, put on one side the challenge from Sartre et al. We can accept that the theory is incomplete, on account of the lacuna it contains. But we must also take the theory at its face value as a coherent construction of enormous importance. Psychoanalysts would be well advised to do the same; and for the present to go along with Freud in regarding his construction as a psychological theory about matters of fact.

Of course, it is necessary in practice that analysts should treat their patients in *ordinary* language. But there is nothing illegitimate in them then going on to *explain* the aetiology and pathology of their patients' states in a technical discourse of a scientific type, such as analytic theory. No doubt, it is interesting and important that no one can satisfactorily relate these types of discourse at present, and hence that there is a corresponding lacuna in the theory. But there is no need whatever for analysts to be frightened or troubled by this fact.[3] For it seems to have no *practical* consequences for them in their therapeutic work. They can safely leave the problem to others (such as professional philosophers), who are equipped to deal with it, while they stick to their lasts and get on with their job.

II

Since psychoanalytic theory presents us with a view of human nature, we can only determine its credibility by discovering how well or badly it accords with the empirical facts about human nature. If a psychoanalyst is challenged to justify why he talks as he does, his first move, perhaps, in answer to this question may run something like the following: 'I speak in the way I do because, to me, analytic theory contains a good account of the facts of human development, human difficulties, and so on. Of course, it is not a perfect theory – no theory is. But psychoanalytic theory seems to me to give on the whole the best account available of the facts; and I find it the most helpful one to use in my work.'

Where are these supporting facts to be found? Because the theory is very wide-ranging, the facts can be found, no doubt, in almost any department or aspect of human life. But the chief and critical place is the psychoanalytic session. This is the place where a psychoanalyst uses psychoanalytic method to analyse patients, or trainee analysts, or others who just wish to go through the experience for one reason or another. Over the last three quarters of a century psychoanalytic method has produced in these sessions a great deal of material. It was this material that got the theory off the ground in the first place, and that has been its chief support ever since.[4] Now, it can be argued, this material supports the theory largely in virtue of the fact that it, the material, can be ordered and explained by the theory and so made intelligible by means of it. It is by postulating that we have the fundamental drives of Eros and Death, that we go through certain stages of development and psychic differentiation, and that we meet our difficulties and fail to meet them in various ways under different conditions (as sketched in Chapter 2) – it is by postulating this complex theoretical story, and by supposing that human nature is really what the story makes it out to be, that we can order and explain the puzzling material produced in the psychoanalytic session, and so make it intelligible. Without the theory, the argument continues, the material is likely to remain puzzling. For it is difficult to see how it can be ordered and explained by any theory other than the psychoanalytic. In virtue of all this, it is reasonable to claim that the theory gives a good account of the facts of human nature.

How are we to assess the strength of this argument from the analyst? How are we to examine the weight that the sessional, or case, material bestows on the theory?

An analyst may be tempted to object that our enterprise is an impractical one. For he may fall back on an old and well-known claim (which Freud himself seems to have accepted at one time), and argue that no one who has not been personally analysed is in a position to appreciate and to assess the weight that the case material bestows on the theory. Hence no unanalysed person is able to assess the strength of this, the strongest support for psychoanalytic theory. This old claim from analytic quarters would seem to be a mistake. There is no need to belittle in the least the importance and relevance for other purposes of a personal or training analysis. There is no need either to deny that it may be an advantage to have had an analysis before setting out to examine the weight which the case material bestows on psychoanalytic theory. For, at the least, what an analysis would give one, which is of relevance, are examples from one's own life and experience, to which the concepts and generalisations of the theory apply. Such personal demonstration may well be more illuminating and convincing than demonstrations on third parties.

But an analysis is not a necessary condition of our inquiry. For personal demonstration in analysis is manifestly not the only way in which one can come to understand the meaning of psychoanalytic concepts and generalisations, in a way which is enough to enable us to examine the logical question that we have raised. Nor is a personal analysis a sufficient condition. This may leave the individual so convinced of the truth of the theory as to debar him from appreciating the problem of the logical relations between the case material and the theory, and the strength of other psychodynamic theories. So analysts would be well advised *not* to trundle out this old war-horse of an argument against the sceptical outsider. Happily, they seem, in general, to have buried this war-horse long ago. Those who resurrect it today are apt to be the critics of psychoanalysis, more concerned perhaps to fight over old battles, or to erect Aunt Sallies, than to examine the problem in front of us.

The important obstacle we face in our inquiry is something rather different. In the course of his clinical training, the medical student spends many weary hours doing his ward rounds in the various departments of hospitals. For it is generally accepted that he needs to have the experience of seeing and studying very many cases of all sorts before he can hope to appreciate the clinical material he will face as a doctor, to acquire necessary diagnostic skills, and to appreciate the force and point of theoretical considerations which are clinically based. Now there is, prima facie, a close analogy in one respect between the position of the medical student and the position we are in in examining psychoanalysis. Just as the former needs to have experience of a large and varied range of cases in every field of medicine, so we need to be presented with the material from a large and varied range of psycho-analytic cases. Without this range of material it is very difficult, if not impossible, in practice to appreciate the force of the case material – its strength, its limitations, and its peculiar qualities.

It is not easy to satisfy this condition in the case of psychoanalysis. Even the trainee analyst is probably not as close to his material as the ordinary medical student is to his. But it is quite clear that there is almost nothing we can do here to overcome this practical obstacle, and to put ourselves in touch, in a satisfactory way, with the rich and enormous range of case material that (allegedly) serves to support psychoanalytic theory, and psychodynamic doctrines in general. The only helpful step we can take here is to look closely at a single example of psychoanalytic case material.

Since we are examining analytic theory, the obvious material to use is some which Freud himself has given us. I shall try to present a sample of his material as persuasively and forcefully as I can. But no matter how successful I am in doing this, I shall naturally be wholly unable to convey the persuasive impact produced by the mass of material in this whole field. In this respect, we cannot do justice to the work of Freud and others in psychodynamics; and we must never lose sight of this fact in the course of our subsequent examination of psychoanalytic theory and its rivals.

III

The sample chosen is from Freud's report on Lorenz, 'the rat man'. This is to be found in 'Notes upon a Case of Obsessional Neurosis', and in Freud's notes on the case made at the time, which were posthumously published under the title: 'Original record of the case'.[5] The treatment lasted eleven months, and Freud claimed that the patient's mental health had been restored by the analysis. The disadvantage of choosing this case, methodologically speaking, is that Freud's treatment is much more didactic than that which came to be approved later by analytic orthodoxy. The disadvantage of this case, theoretically speaking, is that it is early Freud, in that he had not yet formulated his later views about the anal sadistic phase of sexuality and its role in character formation (see Chapter 2). Freud also appears to admit that his own account of the case is not complete. However, the great advantage of choosing this case is that it is one of the best of the very few case reports he did publish. Freud's report is full; he described the first seven sessions on the basis of 'notes made on the evening of the day of treatment'; and he has left us his notes covering the first three and a half months of the treatment. Let us concentrate on the central difficulties the patient exhibited, and ignore the minutiae of his obsession. This will enable us to highlight the logical relations between the case material and psychoanalytic theory.

Freud begins his account of the case history as follows:

A youngish man of university education introduced himself to me with the statement that he had suffered from obsessions ever since his childhood, but with particular intensity for the last four years. The chief features of his disorder were *fears* that something might happen to two people of whom he was very fond – his father and a lady whom he admired. Besides this he was aware of *compulsive impulses* – such as an impulse, for instance, to cut his throat with a razor; and further he produced *prohibitions*, sometimes in connection with quite unimportant things. He had wasted years, he told me, in fighting against these ideas of his, and in this way he had lost much ground in the course of his life... Altogether, he said, his sexual life had been stunted.

At the second session next day, Freud gave him the rule of analysis, namely to say everything that came into his head. After some preliminaries (about male friends), the patient L. said that 'his sexual life began very early'. He reported incidents of sex play at four or five and six, and at seven, with two young governesses, and a great curiosity to see the naked female body. He had the morbid idea that his parents knew his thoughts, and that, in wishing to see girls naked, he had the uncanny feeling that something must happen, which he had to prevent – for example, that 'his father might die'. Fears of his father's death still occupied him, though the father had actually died some years previously.

In the third session, he reported the events leading him to seek Freud's help. During a halt on army manoeuvres he lost his pince-nez, and a Czech captain told him about a horrible punishment on criminals used in the East. Freud reports that, after great difficulty, L. described the punishment as consisting in turning a pot containing rats upside down on the buttocks, and the rats gnawing their way into the anus. L. went on to say that he had the idea this was happening to the lady he admired (called Gisela), and also to his father in the next world. He went on to tell how the pince-nez was returned, with charges to pay on it, and how he then had the thought that he should *not* pay them, or else the fantasy of the rats would be realised on Gisela and his father. This third session was occupied with L.'s turmoil about paying the charges on the pince-nez. He ended the session as though 'dazed and bewildered'.

In the fourth session L. spoke at length about his father's last illness and death. He had happened to be taking a nap when his father died; he had deeply reproached himself for not being present at the death; and for a long time he had not taken in his father's death. Freud intervened here by pointing out that the intensity of his self-reproaches and connected emotions seemed to be exaggerated. Session 5 was largely occupied, apparently, by Freud doing the didactic job of explaining the workings of the Unconscious and of repression.

Session 6 began by L. saying how, at twelve, he had been in love with a little girl, and the idea had occurred to him that she would be kind to him if some misfortune should befall him, for example if his father were to die. He had the same thought six months before his father's death, and the idea that the death of the latter might make him rich enough to marry Gisela. These thoughts had surprised him very much, and he said forcibly that he was quite certain he could never have desired his father's death, but only feared it. Freud then did some explanation, and offered the interpretation that his fears about his father corresponded to a wish that he should die, which he had repressed. This interpretation disturbed him and left him incredulous. Freud then suggested that something had produced a hatred of the father, but his intense love prevented this from becoming conscious – which L. agreed was plausible but which left him unconvinced.

L. went on to say that he had stronger sensual wishes in childhood than during puberty, and that he had not felt sensual wishes about Gisela. Freud offered the interpretation that the source of his hostility to the father derived from interference by the latter with his sensual desires as a child, and that, when Gisela stirred up his erotic desires, the early childhood situation was revived and his hostility to the father reappeared.

In Session 7, L. took up the theme of wishing to get rid of his father. He reported a criminal act in which, at eight, he used a toy gun in order to hurt his younger brother; and he also reported being aware of having vindictive impulses towards Gisela. Freud suggested that his indefinite mourning of his father was abnormal.

At the end of this expository portion of the treatment, Freud went on to select some topics for report from the other sessions. He sketched L.'s suicidal impulses, his fastidiousness, and his obsessions about Gisela. Thus, L. developed an obsession to protect her and made up special formulas to do so. For example, on a day she was due to leave, he knocked his foot against a stone in the road, and was *obliged* to put it out of the way at the side of the road, because the carriage taking Gisela away might come to grief against it. Yet a few minutes later he was *obliged* to replace the stone in its original place. He reported that Gisela had refused his proposal of marriage some years before, and since then he was aware of having passed through alternating periods of loving her intensely, or feeling indifferent to her.

L. offered further reports about his father. After his father's death, his mother told him that one of her wealthy relations was ready to allow L. to marry into this family when he had finished his education. L. was faced with a choice of doing so, or of marrying the poor girl Gisela. This conflict was the same as one that (he knew or suspected) had faced his own father before his marriage to his wealthy wife. L. then became incapable of working, which postponed the completion of his education for four years.

Several years after the father's death, L. had sexual intercourse for the first time, and 'the idea sprang into his mind: "This is glorious! One might murder one's father for this!"' Shortly after his father's death his masturbation revived, he proposed to Gisela, and he developed the fantasy that his father was still alive and might reappear at any moment. Late at night, after he had been working hard, he would open the door of his flat, as if the father were just outside, and then, coming back inside, would take out his penis and look at it in the mirror. His symptoms subsequently became more severe, his religious piety revived, and he began compulsively praying for his dead father. In the light of this and other material, Freud offered the interpretation that, when L. was 'a child of under six he had been guilty of some sexual misdemeanour connected with masturbation, and had been soundly castigated for it by his father'. The patient then said that his mother had repeatedly described to him an occurrence of this kind, of which he had no recollection. About three or four he had done something naughty (his mother said he had 'bitten' someone), and his father had given him a beating. L. had flown into a terrible rage, in which he had screamed childish abuse at his father. After the emergence of this scene in the analysis, the patient was prepared to consider that he had in childhood been furiously angry with the father he loved so much. He then went on to heap abuse on Freud and Freud's family, and it was only after this period (of transference) that L. was ready to accept that his father had had a violent temper and that L. had a double attitude to him – of hate and love.

Following on this it then became possible to deal with the complexities of the rat obsession, via his identification with his father who had seen many years' military service, and whose experience had made L. unconsciously hypersensitive about certain topics, which hypersensitivity had been stirred up by the Czech captain's remarks.

IV

I have now offered an incomplete summary of Freud's account of his sessions with L., based almost entirely on his published 'Notes' on the case. It is natural for an analyst to claim that this summary presents some of the material which L. offered to Freud in the course of his analysis. (In our subsequent discussion, I shall rely almost wholly on this material, and not on that which was posthumously published – for two reasons. Freud's argument for his explanation of L.'s problem was based on the published material; and the posthumous material hardly affects the logic of the argument.)

The material Freud has presented to us is likely to be very puzzling and confusing to an outsider. This is partly due, no doubt, to the fact that I have stated it in a very abbreviated form, and that the chronology of events is itself a very confusing one. But what is *chiefly* responsible, almost certainly, for the outsider's bewilderment is the fact that the material is so unintelligible. Why on earth should L. be afraid of his father's death years after it had happened? Why should he fuss so much about protecting Gisela? Why should he go through the ritual leading up to looking at his penis in the mirror? And why the fears of the rat punishment being inflicted on Gisela and the father? And so on.

At this point it is open to, and natural for, an analyst to claim that the material can be made intelligible by the application of psychoanalytic theory. By using the latter we can explain it, and so understand L. and his difficulties. Let us consider this claim by taking the core of the material, chronologically, and looking at Freud's own explanation of it.

As a child L. had a strong sexual impulse – he was sexually precocious and very curious. He also did not take easily to the frustration of his wishes, as seen, for example, in his great fury when beaten by the father. The material showed that the father was a very kindly man, and L. came to love him deeply. But, we are forced to suppose, the boy also developed a very strong hatred of the father, arising from – Freud suspected – interference with his libidinal interests. L. arrives therefore at the Oedipal period with a severe unresolved conflict in respect of the father – a conflict between great love and hate; and L. deals with the excessive excitation of this conflict by repressing his hatred and connected wish to get the father out of the way.

This resolution is not wholly successful. The boy has worries that the parents know his thoughts, and that if he has his wish to see little girls naked, his father might die – worries which are clearly a disguised manifestation of his wishes and fears. Moreover, his now unconscious hatred of the father and unconscious wish to get him out of the way are so strong that he has to take counter measures to keep them at bay. He develops an intense love for the father, of which he is very much aware. But this defensive position is unstable. For, when the father does die (a death made more traumatic by his happening to be asleep at the time), what he really wanted all the time has now come to pass, and this threatens to make him realise that he had wanted this very thing to happen. So, to help to keep his real unconscious wish and feelings at bay and out of consciousness, he refuses to accept the death of his father. But when this defensive denial crumbles later on, he tries to undo the father's death by making him very much alive in the next world. And he does defy the father a little, for example, by resuming masturbation, by showing him his penis in the hall of his flat, by proposing marriage to Gisela. Yet, because his unconscious hatred and anti-paternal wishes are still there and threatening even more to come through into consciousness, L. is forced into a never-ending round of sterner and sterner defensive measures. His guilt and self-reproaches about his father, and fears that something terrible will happen to him all increase. He starts compulsive prayers for him, and believes that if he marries Gisela something terrible will happen to the father in the next world.

Since L. came to adulthood with a severe Oedipal conflict, his sexual impulses were naturally impaired, and, indeed, seriously blocked. For to marry would be to disregard and to injure the father whom he dearly loves. The situation was aggravated by his father's disapproval of Gisela when he was alive; and by the fact that to marry her would be to marry a poor girl, so again rejecting what the father had done himself. Gisela's rejection of L.'s proposal of marriage greatly disturbed him; and he repeats with Gisela the pattern he produced with the father. He now also hates her unconsciously for doing what the father had done, namely, frustrating his sexuality. At first his anger is directed at himself, in the form of destructive suicidal feelings, while believing that he is just indifferent to Gisela. Then his obsession and obsessional rituals begin and worsen. His mother's marriage plans for him precipitate his collapse, and he becomes incapable of working. After Gisela's second refusal of marriage, his ambivalence of love and hate towards Gisela is intensified. His anger at her does emerge (in fantasies of revenge), and he is ashamed of his anger. He then develops an obsession about protecting her – in order to keep his own anger at bay (hence the incident of the stone).

The rat obsession is a ramification of his obsessional state. The root of this obsession lay in L.'s unconscious identification of the Czech captain with his father (for causes which we need not describe). His anger against the father took a displaced outlet in imagining that the latter was being given the rat punishment. Likewise for his anger against Gisela. This fantasy was distressing and frightening to L. just because it aroused his unconscious anger against them, and because he really did have the unconscious wish that they *should* be punished in this way.

In short, therefore, the kernel of L.'s whole trouble lay in his deep unconscious anger and hostile wishes against the father, which were repressed at the cost of a perpetual threat that this unconscious matter would emerge – which, in turn, resulted in a never-ending struggle to keep the matter at bay.

V

We have now been given an example of the material of some psycho-analytic sessions. We have also been given a narrative which, it could be claimed, puts into order and explains that material. Clearly, the narrative represents an application of analytic theory to the material. Hence it is by means of analytic theory in the particular case of L. that it is possible to arrive at a specific narrative, which can order and explain the material of L. What is possible for L., we are told, is possible generally. By means of analytic theory it is possible to arrive at narratives, like the one offered about L., which will order and explain the material of analytic sessions.

How good is this argument for the justification and credibility of psychoanalytic theory? Let us ignore the difficulties that are special to the case of L. (which we mentioned above, page 55). These difficulties can be ignored, since they do not stop us using this case as a way into the *general* problem of justification and credibility. We have spoken, in orthodox fashion, of Freud presenting us with 'the material of the case'. But are we right to speak like this? Is this what Freud did? Let us remember, to begin with, that for the first seven sessions he tells us he took notes on the evening of the day of treatment, and kept notes of the analysis for a little over the next three months. All this was admirable and very helpful, and no doubt very laborious. But no such notes are, or ever could be, anything like a *full* account of what happened. Reference to the posthumously published notes shows us that these were very far from being a full account. They were to a large extent abstracts from and summaries of what had happened. Moreover, Freud's notes were liable to have suffered from his own unavoidable misrememberings, emphases, unwitting selections, and the like. Consequently the report of the case, based on these notes, would inevitably be a reconstruction of the sessions. All this means that the report Freud presents of the first seven sessions, and of the rest of the treatment, cannot be accepted as a reliable and adequate account of what happened in the analytic sessions with L. If we wish to appreciate the force of this criticism of Freud's notes and reports on L., all we need do is to compare them with the full recordings which have been made in recent years of some analytic and psycho-therapeutic sessions.[6] It is clear, therefore, that we cannot say, *simpliciter*, that Freud presented us with the material of the case. Freud, therefore, did not do what the young Registrar does in a neurological ward when he presents his report of the clinical material produced by a new patient to the consultant in charge. When one looks at the material presented in the case reports of analysts in general, it seems clear that the same is true of them. They also do not present material in the way the Registrar does in the neurological ward.[7]

This difference is important. For it exposes Freud to the contention that, in going through the whole business of selection, emphasis and reconstruction involved in framing his report of the material on L., he did so under the overriding influence of his own theory at the time. In other words, Freud viewed patient L. through the spectacles of his own theory. What appears as the material of the case is a fusion of the contribution that L. made and the theory Freud imposed on this contribution to order and describe it. Likewise for the material presented by analysts in general. Of course, this contention does not mean that Freud's theory sprang fully formed from his head before he started analysing any patients whatever. We know very well that this was not so. Nor does it mean either that Freud was uninfluenced theoretically by L. We have good reason to believe that he was influenced, since L. was the first case of this type that he had met; and we have already noted (Chapter 3) that psychoanalytic theory is not a closed story, but one open in some way to the influence of empirical fact. But all this does nothing to gainsay or qualify the contention that, when an analyst presents the material of a case, what he offers us is a fusion of the contribution of the patient and his own theoretical stand at the time about him – vague, shifting, ill-developed and barely formulated though this may be.

This contention, it is interesting to note, gains strong support from Freud's relevation of his own conduct of L.'s case. For example, he reports that he 'took the opportunity of urging his case' (that is, his view of the situation at the time) on L.; he says that 'he promised to prove it [that is, an interpretation of Freud's] to him', L.; and Freud's whole didactic style is very evident. Added to all this, there is a widely reported fact about Freud's personality. We are told that he was a man who had strong convictions about the rightness of his own views, and could be very resistant to ideas coming from others.[8] This could hardly fail to influence how he saw a patient in the analytic situation and how he reported on him afterwards.

But the contention we are considering is independent of Freud's personal revelations and his personality, and has quite general application. It rests on the consensus that seems to have developed over the years among students of psychotherapy.[9] When we put on scientific spectacles and try to account for the report produced by a psychotherapist on a patient, we are obliged to pick out, *inter alia*, the contribution of the therapist. He brings to psychotherapy, among other things, some theoretical orientation or perspective; and in his efforts to understand the patient, to get things moving in a helpful and controllable way, he looks at the patient and the whole situation through the mesh of his own orientation or perspective. For it is not possible in practice for him to get to grips with a case in psychotherapy and report on it, unless he does view it in this way. What applies to psychotherapy in general applies equally to psychoanalysis as a special form of it.

This conclusion has certain consequences. It follows that what the analyst reports as the material of the case is a fusion of the contribution from the patient and the orientation or theory of the therapist. This fusion is sometimes very evident in case conferences, or in papers in the journals, when it is clear that the particular case has been presented in such a way that it may be difficult, or impossible, to provide an alternative account of it. For 'the facts' or 'the material' in these cases have been so worked upon, or doctored and tailored that they fit naturally into the theory of the analyst in charge, and cannot be fitted easily into any other. Since 'a case' *has* to be viewed in practice from the perspective of *some* psychodynamic theory, it follows that when once it has been presented from a particular perspective, it may be difficult, if not impossible, in practice to view it from any other.

The position is very different from that facing, for example, the student of history. If the latter is interested in, say, the life of Napoleon, and is presented with a hostile, H. A. L. Fisher type of narrative about him,[10] it is possible, and indeed desirable, that he should consult other narratives which look at the life of Napoleon from different perspectives. Moreover, it is possible for him to go to the sources for himself and arrive at an account of Napoleon's life which he deems better, or closer to the truth, than the others on the market. Nothing like this is possible in practice for the reported cases that purport to supply the material which goes to support psychoanalytic theory. (This consideration should be sufficient to make us hesitate to follow Habermas, and others, and to regard psychoanalysis as a historical inquiry.)

From this it also follows that, if the material from the patient L. had *not* been the outcome of any doctoring at all, then the fact that it could be accounted for by analytic theory would be very impressive. But since the material we are given, in Section II, is doctored by analytic theory, the fact that it can *then* be accounted for by analytic theory is less impressive. Obviously so. Therefore we have to be cautious about placing much weight on the fact that, by applying analytic theory, we can make the material of the patient L. intelligible.

An analyst is liable to resist this conclusion very strongly. For the impact which a patient makes on him is typically so great and so immediate that it strikes him as absurd and downright ignorant to suggest that, in his reports, he is 'doctoring' or 'filtering' or 'reconstructing' what the patient is giving him. This response from the analyst is a very tempting one to make; but, in view of what we know today about the difficulties of observing and recording what happens in the group of two, or dyad, of psychotherapy, it is advisable that the analyst should not be so naive and unsophisticated as to fall for this temptation. It may help us to appreciate how the doctoring can happen if we look again at Freud's report on L.

Given the material in Section II above, it is obviously difficult to construct an alternative narrative (about the material) which is the application of some psychodynamic theory *other* than psychoanalytic theory. But it is not impossible to do so for a critical *part* of L.'s problem. Let us recall what L. said about his 'sexual' interest in girls and so on, and about his father beating him. Freud presents all this as supporting his theory of sexuality and the Oedipal conflict. But it is also very evident to common sense that, if we are to go along with Freud and accept L.'s reports of his early upbringing as true, then L. was abused as a child by the adult women around him, in the interests of their own sexuality. In consequence he developed an intense, and yet guilty and conflictful, interest and excitement in the sexual organs of women, and in his own pleasurable bodily feelings. When he betrays what can be reasonably interpreted as some manifestation of this exaggerated interest of his, the father interferes and beats him. All this suggests that L. was not a casualty of his sexual needs and development; but the victim of his corrupt upbringing, which saddled him with the problem, as a helpless child, of how to cope with his helplessness and justified anger at the father and the surrounding adults for their maltreatment of him.

It is evident that what we have just offered is an example of an Adlerian narrative about L. It is evident therefore that we *can* construct a narrative about some of the L. material, which represents an application of Adlerian theory. If we now suppose that Freud had listened to L. with Adlerian theory in the forefront of his mind, instead of the one he did use, it is not too difficult to imagine that his report of the material of L. in Section II would have read very differently. It would have been 'doctored' to fit in with an Adlerian theory, not with psychoanalytic theory.

It is tempting, no doubt, to try to defend the analyst at this point by arguing that the Registrar in the neurological ward is in just the same troublesome boat as the analyst. For is not the material he presents also, in practice, a fusion of the contribution from the patient and the whole theoretical orientation of contemporary neurology? Perhaps it is. But, let us note, the orientation used by the Registrar is the generally accepted one; and if a visiting neurologist is doubtful about the Registrar's report, or does not accept some particular variant of the accepted orientation which (let us suppose) the Registrar is using, then the visitor can observe and describe the patient for himself. So it is relatively easy in practice to separate the contribution of the patient from the particular orientation of the Registrar, and to look at the case afresh through different spectacles. Nor can we defend the analyst by arguing that nowhere in science or in medicine can one *logically* escape fusing 'the facts' and the orientation one uses to take note of, and to order, 'the facts'. This argument does nothing by itself to save the analyst. For in science and in ordinary clinical medicine there are accepted and fairly successful ways of safeguarding ourselves against the dangers that may ensue from fusing the contribution of 'the facts' and the theoretical contribution of the observer-cum-reporter. The trouble with psychoanalytic work is that in it there seem to be *no* accepted ways of successfully safeguarding ourselves against the dangers of fusion.

The upshot, then, is that the argument from intelligibility is not as impressive as psychoanalysts would like to think. It is clear, moreover, that in so far as the argument serves to support analytic theory, it also serves equally well to support any other psychodynamic theory. If a Jungian analyst, for example, uncovers material from a patient X, he is liable to claim that *his* material can be made intelligible by a narrative that applies *his own* theory. So what is sauce for analytic theory is sauce for other psychodynamic theories. To appeal to intelligibility, therefore, is insufficient to settle disagreements among analysts of different brands. Indeed, the argument is mutually self-frustrating as between different psychodynamic theories; and it may even be the case that the explanatory narratives of one theory are as good, or as poor, as those of any other theory, as Popper has implied.[11]

VI

Nevertheless, though the argument from intelligibility is weak, it is not as weak as the outsider may be inclined to imagine. We must be careful not to exaggerate the objection based on the fact that the patient is seen and described from a certain perspective – that the material reported is, among other things, a piece of doctoring, a fusion of input from the patient and analytic orientation. For this objection underplays the contribution of the patient. The material reported is a fusion of *what comes from the patient* and what the analyst supplies. No doubt it has been argued that the material also contains a manufactured, or artefactual component; and we shall come to this point later (Chapter 6). But, at the very least, the material does contain a large component that is supplied by the patient himself. Furthermore, the material reported in Section II – this joint product of patient and analyst – cries out for orderly description and explanation. Admittedly, the narrative by Freud about L. is incomplete – it does not account for everything. But, this apart, it does succeed in large measure in meeting our appeal for description and explanation. No doubt, the fact that the material in Section II has been doctored by Freud makes it easier to fit it under psychoanalytic theory. But this does not make it logically inevitable that the material can be explained by the theory. Hence, to make the material of L. intelligible by means of the theory is not an empty achievement.

Furthermore, in describing and explaining L.'s condition, Freud's narrative brings out how the material in Section II does *illustrate* certain psychoanalytic concepts, generalisations and regulative principles. For example, the concept of repression (to keep the wishes and the emotions out of L.'s consciousness); the concept of reaction formation (for example, overstressing his love for, and strenuously denying any hatred of, the father); the concept of sexual impulses in childhood; the principle about the potency of early experience, and its causal influence on the present in ways of which L. was quite unaware; and, by supposing L. to have certain unconscious wishes in respect of the father (for example to get rid of him), and certain unconscious emotions (of anger and hate in respect of the father and Gisela), it is possible to explain the core of L.'s behaviour. The fact that these and other concepts of analytic theory serve to make the material in Section II intelligible does lend *some* weight or support to these concepts and connected generalisations – even though the material was doctored through the filter of analytic theory itself. We can appreciate this if we imagine that we were to reject analytic theory as totally mistaken. We would then be faced with the large problem of having to explain the material of Section II, and other analytic material of the sort that analysts report. The critics who reject psychoanalysis entirely are apt to overlook both the need to explain this material, as well as the explanatory force of analytic concepts and generalisations, and the support that the case material brings to them.

Similar considerations hold for the other psychodynamic theories. The fact that the argument from intelligibility is insufficient to settle disagreements among analysts of different brands does not mean that the argument has no force; or that it may not help, along with other considerations, to adjudicate between rival narratives and theories (Chapter 10).

VII

So far, however, we have been looking at the argument from intelligibility in respect of particular psychodynamic theories – psychoanalytic, Adlerian and so on. At the end of Chapter 2 we noted that psychodynamic theories have certain themes in common. These were: psychic determinism, the purposive character of human functioning, the importance of the unconscious, and the importance of early experience. If a theory uses these common themes, it can naturally be said to be a theory of the psychodynamic type. Suppose, now, an analyst argues that theories of this type do make a great mass of material intelligible; and hence that this material does go *to support theories of this type*. Whatever the material may or may not do for particular psychodynamic theories, it does show that theories of this type have to be taken seriously as pointing to the truth.

How good is this argument? It is stronger than the related claim about psychoanalytic theory, or any other particular psychodynamic theory.

The reason is obvious. When we are offered a psychoanalytic narrative about, for example, L., it may be possible in practice to think up some other, and apparently equally good narrative about L., in spite of the fact that the material of L. has been doctored by Freud in the interests of psychoanalytic theory. But when we are offered a narrative of the psychodynamic type about a standard case, like L., it is much more difficult to think of an alternative narrative of a *non*-psychodynamic type, which will make the material intelligible. Indeed, if we ignore what are known as Behaviour Theories (Chapters 6, 10), then we may sometimes, or often, find it impossible. If, for instance, we try to explain L.'s conduct by the use of our knowledge of genetics and heredity, or our knowledge of neurophysiology, or both, and with *no* reference to L.'s early psychological history and unconscious motives, and so forth, then we are unlikely to get very far. Our present stock of scientific knowledge in these fields is quite insufficient to help us.

At this point, no doubt, a non-psychodynamic and sceptical psychiatrist may retort that we *should not try* at the present time to make sense of L.'s obsessional conduct, and of the other standard 'supporting' material which analysts produce for us. If we do try, we just commit ourselves to using unproven, bizarre theories of the psychodynamic type, and commit ourselves to spinning speculative psychodynamic narratives of patients and others.

But, unless the sceptical psychiatrist can find better reasons than this for refusing to try to make sense out of L., and other cases and material of the standard sort, his scepticism is unlikely to be generally persuasive. No doubt, a psychiatrist working in a large British mental hospital inside the National Health Service, is liable to be overwhelmed by the enormous intake of psychotic patients; and he is likely to be much concerned to maintain a high satisfactory rate of throughput of these patients. Accordingly, he will have no, or little, professional interest in trying to make their behaviour intelligible. He may naturally come to view all such attempts with some contempt as a sheer waste of time and effort. In contrast, a psychiatrist or counsellor at a University clinic trying to help students to cope with living and work problems may find it necessary, for the help and therapy he offers, to try to arrive at accounts of students' difficulties which make these intelligible.

Now such differences in professional interests and work are apt to be important. For they are likely to make it difficult, or impossible, to find reasons which will persuade professionals *in general* that they are wrong to try to use a theory of a psychodynamic type to make sense out of cases like L., and others of the standard sort. Presumably, the only way of persuading them all of this would be to show that the type of professional assistance given at places like the University clinic – assistance which may make it necessary to arrive at psychodynamic understanding and narratives – is itself an enterprise without justification, and should be shut down. But this avenue of argument takes us far away into other thorny fields, where the protagonists do battle over the therapeutic value of psychoanalysis and psychotherapy (Chapter 10).

It seems, then, that the argument from intelligibility is stronger in respect of theories of a psychodynamic *type* than it is in respect of any *one*, particular psychodynamic theory.

VIII

This brings us to a problem of quite a different sort. The argument we have considered so far in support of psychoanalytic theory rests on an appeal to intelligibility, and not to truth. The material of analytic sessions is alleged to support the theory in virtue of the fact that, by using the theory, in the form of descriptive and explanatory narratives, we can make the material intelligible. But if a narrative about a patient makes sense out of the material, it does not follow that it is true. At most intelligibility is a necessary condition for truth, and therefore a consideration which supports a truth claim. This distinction between intelligibility and truth lies behind all discussion in contemporary psychopathology; and comes out strikingly in those case conferences where the material on a puzzling patient is so presented that two, or even more, good explanatory, but incompatible, narratives can be put upon the material.

Some analysts try, in effect, to escape the problem of bridging the gap from intelligibility, or sense, to truth by taking the sort of view which is associated with names such as Habermas and Ricoeur. These analysts maintain that *all* that they do is to make sense out of the patient's conduct, choices, symptoms, and so on. What they do in particular is a semantic job – of uncovering the 'meaning' of the symptoms, since these are disguised communications from the patient.[12] Unfortunately, this defensive move seems to debar analysts from claiming to arrive at any truths about human nature, and from claiming, therefore, to contribute to our knowledge of it. And this deprives psychoanalysis of most of its interest – leaving it no more interesting, perhaps, than Yoga or Scientology. On the other hand, it is difficult to see how an analyst can logically make sense of, and so arrive at, the 'meaning' of symptoms without having, and applying, some putative knowledge of the ways in which unconscious wishes, etc. do reveal themselves symptomatically.

But the analyst has to justify these claims to knowledge. It is difficult to see how he can do this without going beyond 'intelligibility' or 'sense' or 'meaning', and without claiming that the accounts he gives of his patients are also true, or approximations to the truth. In short, this defensive move seems *either* to make the work of the analyst uninteresting, *or* to land him in incoherence.

The distinction between intelligibility and truth arises in respect of all theories of a psychodynamic type. The fact that we can make material intelligible by spinning a narrative of such a type is not sufficient to show that this type of theory and narrative points to the truth. It may not be true that, for example, L.'s early experience gave him some unconscious motives which accounted for his conduct. Some other, alternative and quite different type of account may be true instead about L., and about patients with neurotic disorders. Thus, the truth about the psychopathology of, for example, the conversion neuroses may turn out to be very different from what analysts and psychodynamic workers generally appear to believe. That we and they have difficulty in thinking of accounts which are different from those current in psychodynamics may merely reflect the limits of our scientific imagination and knowledge at the present period in the history of science. It may also be due, in part, to the success of psychoanalytic propaganda in making it difficult for us to envisage explanatory narratives other than those of the psychodynamic type.

There is nothing surprising about all this. Ptolemy gave us a theory which enabled us to make the motions of the planets and the sun intelligible. In the early eighteenth century, Phlogiston theory made the phenomena of combustion fairly intelligible. In the first half of the nineteenth century, Phrenology succeeded to some degree, perhaps, in making intelligible certain aspects of human functioning. But none of these theories is true. Accordingly, we must be on our guard against supposing that, because psychoanalytic theory does make some case material intelligible, it is therefore true. It may not be true at all. It may really be 'something akin to a dinosaur or zeppelin in the history of ideas' – as Medawar suggested. Similarly for the other, competing theories of psychodynamics. Similarly for any theory of the psychodynamic type.

Can we do anything to show that psychoanalytic theory is true or false? Can we appeal to further considerations, which will enable us to break out of the confines of intelligibility claims, and show that the theory really does accord with the facts of human nature?

5 The support from psychoanalytic interpretations

I

Let us recall that, in his account of L.'s case history (Chapter 4), Freud tells us that he intervened at various places by offering L. what are known as 'interpretations'. Thus, he said to L. (page 53) that L.'s fears about his father corresponded to a wish that he should die, a wish which he had repressed. Again, he said to L. that the source of the hostility to the father derived from interference by the father with his sensual desires as a child. We have no reason to doubt that Freud offered to L. a large number of interpretations throughout the course of the treatment. For it is a necessary and important part of psychoanalytic method that the analyst should present to the analysand interpretations of the latter's conduct in the course of the analysis. Now, though the word 'interpretation' has become a technical term in the discourse of analysts, it remains very vague indeed. It covers a wide variety of remarks, both in form and content, made by the analyst. But this vagueness does not matter for our purposes, because there are certain types of interventions that all analysts would agree to call 'interpretations', and which are central to the attempt to establish the truth of psychoanalytic claims. The two examples we noted above from Freud would be universally accepted as interpretations, and they are clearly ones which are central to the logic of the problem. In our subsequent discussion, we shall concentrate on examples of this type.

It is important, however, not to confuse this use of the word with other current uses. Thus, when a clinical psychologist has studied the performance of a patient on (say) the Rorschach (ink blot) test, he may then go on to offer a report on the patient's performance. This report can be said to contain 'interpretations' of the patient's responses. This use of the word is very different from the one we are employing – if only because we are concerned with remarks made in the context of an ongoing psychoanalysis, which is a very special situation. Because of this difference, the logical character or nature of psychoanalytic interpretations may be quite dissimilar from the nature of interpretations offered by a clinical psychologist. Again, when Freud gave us his account of Leonardo da Vinci, he offered a large number of 'interpretations' of

Leonardo's work and of items and episodes in his personal history.[1] This is a well-known and recognised use of the word 'interpretation', but it is not the one which we will employ. The one we have chosen for our discussion is logically the central or important one for our purposes.

How, now, can interpretations – remarks offered in the course of analysis – be used to establish the truth of psychoanalytic theory? The argument and the answer can be presented in the following way.

It is possible in practice to establish the truth or falsity of an interpretation, p, by reference to the conduct of the analysand which follows the presentation of p to him (or her). For it is possible in practice to apply to this subsequent conduct certain criteria, which, if satisfied, establish or confirm the truth of p, and which, if not satisfied, will falsify, or disconfirm p. By applying these truth criteria, therefore, over the course of an analysis of an analysand, it is possible to pick out those interpretations which are true of him. When an analyst constructs a narrative to order and explain the material coming from the analysand, it is these established or confirmed interpretations which he uses to build up the narrative about the material. It is these that go to form, at the least, the main and essential part of the narrative he constructs to make intelligible the material coming from the analysand. Since these confirmed interpretations are true, he has good grounds to believe that the main and essential part, at least, of the narrative about the analysand is true also. For example, Freud's interpretation that L. had an unconscious wish that his father should die. If this interpretation is confirmed, Freud can then use it, as he did, along with other confirmed interpretations to construct a narrative about L. Freud will then have good grounds to believe that at least the main part of this narrative about L. is true.

This applies to analysands and to psychoanalytic narratives in general. On the basis of these true narratives, analysts are justified (the argument goes on) in offering us the generalisations about human functioning which were mentioned in Chapter 2 – generalisations about human development, about defence against stress, about pathology, and so on. They are then obviously entitled to go on to construct a higher level theory which is sufficient to order and explain these lower level generalisations about human nature. We have good reason, therefore, to believe that the narratives analysts produce do not only make the material intelligible, and hence understandable, but are also substantially true or a good approximation to the truth. Hence, (the argument concludes) we have good reason to believe that the psychoanalytic theory, both Low and High Level, which is constructed on the basis of these true narratives must also be taken seriously as an approximation to the truth.

II

This argument is built upon the concept of truth criteria. What are these criteria, by means of which we can confirm or falsify an interpretation, and which thereby enable us to distinguish between true and false interpretations? And how are they to be applied in practice?

There seems to be no agreed list of criteria which analysts accept. Different analysts seem to favour different criteria. Typically, an analyst has his own special favourite, which he is ready to defend. Moreover, where a criterion is widely favoured, there seems to be no generally agreed formulation of it. In these circumstances the best that the student can do is to pick out some criteria which analysts would accept as good examples; and to try to formulate them in ways that analysts have done themselves, or that they would accept.

The criterion of acceptance

Consider the core of the account of what a very distinguished psychoanalyst, Fenichel, calls 'criteria for the correctness of interpretations.'[2] He says that 'a patient's yes usually is accepted as a confirmation, and that under certain circumstances, a no is not regarded as a refutation'. But, just as the confessions of an accused person in Court may be false, so too may the 'Yes' of the analysand; and a 'No' may represent an unconscious concealment of the truth. 'Hence,' he continues, 'neither a yes nor a no in reply to an interpretation is a final criterion of its validity. It is rather the manner in which the yes or no is expressed'. He states that 'there are various signs' which betray that a patient, 'immediately after uttering his no', 'has been inwardly affected by the interpretation, and feels that what the analyst has called to his attention really exists within himself'. However, Fenichel goes on at once to add: 'But in general one can say that an interpretation to which the patient objects is wrong', not necessarily in content but in timing. What gives the answer about the correctness of an interpretation is 'the patient's reactions in their *entirety* . . . not his first yes or no'.

What does the criterion of acceptance amount to after all these qualifications from Fenichel? Obviously very little. For what constitutes a genuine acceptance (or non-acceptance) is not a 'Yes' (or a 'No'), or indeed any verbal response or responses, but rather 'the manner' in which the 'Yes' or 'No' is expressed. However, Fenichel tells us hardly anything about this manner, or the circumstances of this verbal response; and certainly nothing anywhere near sufficient to give us a reliable way of determining whether the patient accepts in the 'right' manner or not. In any case, it is by reference to the patient's reactions 'in their *entirety*' that the analyst has to decide whether the patient has accepted an interpretation, and hence whether it is true or not. But this requirement makes the criterion unusable. For, taken literally, it means that the analyst has to wait until the end of the analysis before claiming that any, and therefore, every interpretation offered in the course of the analysis is true. This is absurd and manifestly misrepresents how analysts do think about and use acceptance by the analysand. But, if we are *not* to take the expression 'the patient's reactions in their entirety' literally, it is unclear how we are meant to take it.

Now an analyst may be disposed to agree that Fenichel's formulation is unsatisfactory, and that no reformulation of it is likely to be any better. Nevertheless, he may claim that he does regularly judge the reactions of the analysand and distinguish between those that are evidence of acceptance or of non-acceptance; and that he uses these judgements to guide him in subsequent course of his work with the analysand. This claim about his own behaviour as an analyst may be quite correct as a matter of fact. But by itself this claim does little, if anything, to help to establish that any interpretation p, which the analyst judges has been accepted, is true, and that any interpretation q, which has not been accepted, is false. For an interpretation p may be true, even though the analysand fails to accept it; and if the analysand does accept it, it is quite possible that he does so for reasons which have little to do with the truth or falsity of the interpretation. For example, he may have been persuaded, by the enormous and subtle pressures of the special analytic situation, into accepting it. This is not, prima facie, an implausible explanation; and unless we have good grounds for ruling out this alternative explanation of his acceptance of p, we cannot place much weight on this acceptance.

Freud's account of L. helps to make this clearer. Let us recall that when Freud first offered the interpretations that L. wanted his father to die, and that, as a child, he had been very angry with the father, L. did not accept them. But this did not make Freud withdraw them as false. Indeed Freud does not appear to mention any interpretations which he withdrew. Analysts follow him in this practice. They tend not to mention interpretations which the subsequent conduct of the analysand had led them to withdraw. However, Freud does tell us that it was only in the course of developing the emotionally disturbing involvement with Freud, and Freud's family, known as transference, (cf. page 98), that L. was able to accept Freud's interpretations about L. and his father. It is very evident that Freud uses this acceptance as very good, if not conclusive, evidence that his interpretations were true – that, for example, L. did have a double attitude of love and hatred towards the father. Now, Freud's interpretations here *may* be true, but it should be obvious to common sense that L.'s acceptance of them is far from constituting good or conclusive evidence that they are true. When an unhappy adolescent or young person from a Christian background, full of guilt perhaps about his sexuality, finds himself caught up in the tea parties and group meetings of Moral Rearmers, he will probably come to accept all manner of convictions about his present and past. For example, that his past masturbation has done him great harm. But his acceptance does not constitute sufficient evidence for the truth of these convictions. When we remember that L., in transference with Freud, was in an emotionally disturbed state, and that he was caught up with and subject to the great presence of Freud, we would be very rash to claim that there were no pressures on him to accept the interpretations that Freud offered him. On the contrary, common sense leads us to say that his acceptance was the outcome, in part, of the pressures of the analytic situation. Hence, unless we can find good grounds to assert that L.'s acceptance was *not* the outcome of these pressures, we cannot say that L.'s acceptance of the interpretations constitutes conclusive or good reason to claim that they are true.

The conclusion, in short, is that the criterion of acceptance is a feeble one. It is not strong enough logically to give analysts good grounds for claiming that an interpretation is true.

The criterion of movement

It is a familiar experience of analysts that sometimes an interpretation sets off a stream of associations, and opens up topics that have not been mentioned or explored before. The analyst and analysand may have reached some temporary impasse, so that the 'movement' characteristic of fruitful therapeutic work has come to a halt for the time being. Then, suddenly, some interpretation, or a set of them, seems to achieve a break-through and to get things moving again. Accordingly, the suggestion has been made that, when the presentation of an interpretation is followed by responses of this sort, the interpretation is true. Let us call this the criterion of movement.

It runs into serious difficulties at once.

(i) It can *only* apply to interpretations which do release the characteristic responses of movement from the analysand. Moreover, there are some patients who are so cautious and inhibited that they do not often indulge, at least for the long opening phases of the analysis, in the spontaneous release required by the criterion (see next section for such a case). At best, therefore, the criterion is of limited use.

(ii) If an interpretation *p* served as a releaser, then – on orthodox psychodynamic theory – this may not be 'due to' the fact that it states the truth about the patient, but because it represents some distant and distorted version of the truth about the patient's psyche, and, in virtue of this fact, serves as a releaser at that moment.

(iii) Consider the interpretation Freud gave to L. (in Session 6), namely that the source of his hostility to the father derived from interference by the latter with his sensual desires as a child. Analysts would almost certainly agree that this interpretation did in fact produce some movement, especially in the next session. Now interpretation p is an application of the Oedipal generalisations of psychoanalytic theory, and so serves to explain the subsequent movement responses that L. made. But, it could be argued, L.'s subsequent movement in response to p can *also* be explained fairly well by some *other* theory than the psychoanalytic. It could be explained by an Adlerian theory, according to which (as we have seen) L. had feelings of inferiority and resentment at the father, not feelings of an Oedipal character. Hence, the fact that p was followed by movement does nothing to support or confirm p, or the psychoanalytic theory of which p is an application.

The criterion of restricted response

It is clear that the criterion of movement just will not do. If we are to rescue it, it looks as if we have to characterise the subsequent sequences of the analysand in such a way that we can distinguish between the subsequent responses which *do* support the antecedent interpretation from those which do *not*. Can this be done?

Consider the following courageous and clear-headed suggestion. 'An interpretation p is true if and only if the production of p is followed at once by a sequence q, which is such that q can only be explained by the theory of which p represents the application'.[3] This amounts to saying that on this criterion an interpretation by Freud to L. is true if and only if L. produces at once a response sequence which Freud's theory can explain, and no other. This is an important suggestion, if only because the formidable objections it raises bring out how difficult the whole matter really is.

What is to constitute the subsequent response sequence q? How much of the subsequent material is to count? Can q be a *part* of the total subsequent response sequence? Obviously, the notion of a subsequent response sequence q is vague. But, putting this on one side, it is clear that the criterion is only applicable where q follows p *at once*. This greatly restricts its utility, since analysts want to say that subsequent responses may occur a little later on in the session, or in the next session, or later still. Freud gave some examples of such delayed movement responses in his account of L. But these examples would not count on the criterion we are examining, and hence do not go to show that *p* is true.

What is worse, *q* has to be explainable on the basis of the psychodynamic theory of which *p* is the application, and only on that basis. This is a very strict requirement, which psychodynamic theories may not be able to satisfy. Firstly, the requirement appears to demand that we have to explain *q*, in the sense of *deducing q* from the interpretation *p* and the relevant generalisations of the psychodynamic theory the analyst is using. But it is very doubtful whether psychodynamic theories can be used in this way to explain a particular occurrence, namely the production of *q* by the analysand. It is difficult enough to achieve this sort of explanation in the physical world with the full armoury of the Natural Sciences and their technology at our disposal. It is manifestly beyond psychodynamics at the present time. Secondly, suppose, *per impossibile*, we had an undisputed example available of a *q* which can be explained by the theory (say psychoanalytic theory), of which *p* represents the application. Before we can claim that *p* is true, *q* must be such that it can be explained by *psychoanalytic theory alone*. In Chapters 2, 3 and 4 we have seen how loosely constructed and woolly psychoanalytic theory and other psychodynamic theories really are. Given their parlous condition, can we ever be in a position to claim that a particular response sequence, *q*, can *only* be explained by *one* psychodynamic theory, say psychoanalysis, and by no other? Are we justified, for example, in claiming about some sequence which L. produced for Freud that this can be explained only by psychoanalytic theory? It is a bold Freudian or psychodynamic analyst who will say 'Yes' with confidence at this point.

In short, it is very doubtful whether what we have called the criterion of restricted response will give analysts what they want – an instrument they can use with confidence in their clinical assessments to distinguish interpretations that are true from those that are not.

The criterion of analogy

Suppose we had challenged Freud to defend his interpretation that the source of L.'s hostility to his father derived from interference by the latter with his sensual desires as a child. Freud could have defended himself (in principle) in a characteristic way: 'Given the material which L. has already produced so far in his analysis, and given our past experience with similar cases and material about father hostility, it is clear that this interpretation is very probably true. At the least, we have very good grounds to believe that it is.'

This criterion and defence appeals to the analogy between L.'s material and past analytic experience; and the trouble about it stares one in the face. Let us suppose that Freud would be right to claim that L.'s conduct in analysis is analogous to previous cases. What grounds have we to believe that, in these previous cases, the source of hostility to the father derived from interference with the child's sensual desires? Clearly, we can now only support this interpretation in L.'s case by showing that a similar interpretation was true in past analogous cases. And how are we to do this? By itself, therefore, the criterion of analogy is of no help. The same problem simply breaks out one step further back. Indeed, it is clear that the criterion of analogy really begs the root question with which we are now concerned: when we use psychoanalytic method, do we really arrive at the truth about the analysand? In other words, is psychoanalytic method a valid method of discovery? The criterion of analogy merely presupposes that it is.

Analysts tend to make considerable use of this criterion, but its use is so deeply embedded in their work that they are apt to be quite unconscious of the fact that they are using it at all. Thus, Freud draws our attention at one important place to the insufficiency of the plain 'Yes' or 'No' from the patient as evidence of the rightness or wrongness of what he calls 'constructions'. He goes on to write as follows:[4]

It appears, therefore, that the direct utterances of the patient after he has been offered a construction afford very little evidence upon the question whether we have been right or wrong. It is of all the greater interest that there are indirect forms of confirmation which are in every respect trustworthy. One of these is a form of words that is used (almost as though there were a conspiracy) with very little variation by the most different people: 'I've never thought (or, I should never have thought) that (or, of that).' This can be translated without any hesitation into: 'Yes, you're right this time – about my *unconscious*'.

Freud's argument in this passage simply will not do. In the first place, analysts cannot take the expression 'I've never thought of that' (and its cognates) as in every respect trustworthy'. They cannot do so any more than they can take every 'Yes' from the analysand as trustworthy, and for like reasons. In the second place, and this is the relevant difficulty here, *how* does Freud know 'that there are indirect forms of confirmation which are in every respect trustworthy'? How does he know that the utterance 'I've never thought that' can be translated without hesitation into: 'Yes, you [Freud] are right this time about my unconscious'? Would he accept that, when one of Rank's patients says 'Yes, I've never thought of that' – namely of wishing to return to the womb – that this can be translated without hesitation into the statement: 'Yes, you [Rank] are right this time about my unconscious'? What good reason has Freud for saying this about the remarks of his *own* patients in analysis, and *not* about Rank's or Jung's? It is difficult to find in Freud any explicitly stated reason or reasons for this assertion. All this naturally raises the suspicion that Freud is *taking it for granted* that his analytic method does in general get at the truth about people, and does so specifically when the analysand responds verbally in the way just mentioned ('I've never thought of that'). Of course, in the historical and epistemological circumstances of the period, it is understandable that Freud should have taken for granted the validity of his method. This helps to explain why he was not particularly interested in the truth criteria of interpretations, and seems to have been as confused about the problem as everyone else.[5]

The truth criteria we have examined are not the only ones which have been canvassed.[6] But they do all seem to run into serious troubles of one sort or another, and they fail logically to give the analysts the means of distinguishing, in his clinical judgements, between interpretations that are true and those that are not. The narrative he spins about a patient may make the material intelligible and therefore understandable. It may even be interesting and exciting. But he cannot use truth criteria for his interpretations to give us reasonable grounds to believe that his narrative is a true one.

III

So far our discussion of truth criteria has been very abstract. We have considered no actual examples of interpretations, apart from some that Freud offered to L., and our discussion of these was necessarily confined to the material that Freud reported. We have already noted some of the limitations of Freud's report, and of reports like his, which are based on notes made by the analyst. Can we do any better than this? Would the argument from truth criteria become any stronger if we were to examine some actual examples of interpretations from the records of an analytic session?

There is little doubt that we have lost for ever the data (from past analytic work) which may have been of the greatest value to analysts, and everyone else, in helping to determine the truth of psychoanalytic narratives and theory. This data is to be found in the actual interchange between analyst and analysand in the dyad of the psychoanalytic session. Of course, it was only after the Second World War that it became possible in practice (with the advent of magnetic tapes) to obtain records of the oral interchange in analysis. It was still later that it became possible in practice to record the visual material as well. But in spite of these developments in engineering technology, video and/or oral records of sessions by analysts which are available for public inspection are still rarities.[7] What we obviously need at this juncture are some such records, to which we can apply the truth criteria to see what support they can provide for interpretations; and whether the argument from truth criteria then becomes any stronger. Fortunately, we do happen to have at our disposal one of these recorded rarities. I shall now go on to describe this case and to examine a very small section of the taped record.

The case is that of a boy, whom I shall call John, a patient of the late Dr. P. M. Turquet.[8] John was approaching seventeen years of age when he was sent to a clinical psychologist for vocational guidance. The difficulty was that he was quite uncertain what career to take up. His school reports stated that his work was uneven – sometimes he did good work and expressed himself well, on other occasions his spelling and expression were poor; and the reports stated repeatedly that he was disappointing in examinations. He was due to take eight 'O' (or Ordinary) level subjects (of the General Certificate of Education) at the end of the academic year; but his showing at school suggested that entry to University would be difficult or late. He was the youngest child of a family of three, the others being sisters aged thirty and twenty-seven. These had university careers, and the father was a successful company executive. When the boy John was nine years old, the father was given an appointment abroad and the boy went to live as a boarder in a public school. It became apparent, both from the boy himself and from his elder sister, that he had found adjustment in his school very difficult in the first two terms and had missed his parents considerably. However, the parents thought that John had subsequently developed well at school. He was good at sport, and took part in the social life of the school. But he made less progress educationally, was late in attempting the G.C.E., was in the second stream form, and the Headmaster had doubts about his capacity for sixth-form work. On psychological examination it was found that intellectually John had quite outstanding abilities – well up to good G.C.E. 'A' (Advanced) level and University work – but that he was making use of them poorly and inefficiently, especially in any test requiring self-expression. The way he attempted the tests revealed a great fear of making mistakes and of things getting out of control. In short, the immediate problem John presented was one of intellectual under-functioning. In the light of the total picture he revealed, it was thought that he might benefit from analytic treatment. This was begun, when he was sixteen years ten months old, with three sessions a week. There were various interruptions, owing to illness and school holidays. In the course of the next eighteen months, he had eighty sessions of treatment, of which seventy-seven were taped and transcribed.

Now the analyst, Turquet, had a Kleino-Freudian orientation; and this, in the light of the clinical report on John, led him to have certain views and expectations about the boy. He thought of him as having suffered the childhood trauma of parental desertion, as one who lost touch in the past with mother and father, who was emotionally deprived in consequence, and as a result has an unconscious fantasy in which mother and father and family are idealised, who is now really greedy for their love and attention, and who is also at the same time Father and Super-Ego dominated. Hence, John really wishes to rejoin Mother and Father – to be with them; and yet when he does join them in reality, he is still out of touch with them; his fantasy about the delights of being with them does not come true, and he is disappointed.

For our purposes it makes little difference, in my judgement, what session, or part of a session we select from Turquet's treatment of John. For the lessons we can draw from one session are much the same as the lessons we can draw from any other. I select the first half (approximately) of Session 5. This was the first session, perhaps, in which John started to reveal some 'genuine' responses to the analyst; but, being a very early session, he cannot yet be said 'to be under the analyst's thumb'. (In what follows a few very minor and obvious errors of transcription have been corrected.)

Session 5

John 1. I was just wondering, hm, how will I get on in the exams? We just have finished a whole week and I have only done three, but –,

Turquet 1. When did you go back to school? [John had been away ill with mumps.]

J. 2. Last week-end. We just had three, two to-day and one yesterday and I am afraid I missed the whole week before that.

T. 2. How do you feel you did?

J. 3. I think I did quite well in two of them, the English Language and Geography, but I don't think I did very well in French. I am rather anxious just to see what the marks are, to see what they are like. The exams themselves weren't too bad, really, not as hard as I expected them to be.

T. 3. It is not only a case of going back to school and the exams, but also of coming back here and how difficult it is going to be here.

J. 4. Yes, in a way. My father really wanted me to come up last Friday, but I had to skip that. We were rather worried really about the strike, you know, whether it would come off and – [The reference is to a threatened railway strike.]

T. 4. Here the most important point is, your father would have liked you to come, but what about you?

J. 5. I wanted to come as well. He said: if you feel all right by then. I am still a bit shaky in my legs, you see and I thought, well, do you good to get out and – I really wanted to come up because – then – we could – start again before this strike, if it had come off, of course, and been able to arrange an alternative as far as possible. (pause)

T. 5. I think it is most important for us to see that it is your father's wishes you put first, not your own.

J. 6. Yes, he did suggest it first.

T. 6. Perhaps you, left to yourself, would not have worn down so quickly.

J. 7. I don't know about that, really. I thought that it would be just as good – you know, at the beginning of the week, like that and stopping at home – and I don't know what my mother thought, really, because she had to make a meal in the evening and it would have rather messed her about a bit as well as she would try and keep something for me.

T. 7. And the times and coming here rather messes you up, particularly with regard to meals, which was something you commented on the last time you were here.

J. 8. Yes, it is really a bit awkward at home, but at school, it is o.k., you have a meal anyway.

T. 8. So it is father's wishes that mess people about, you and your mother.

J. 9. Well, sometimes they do, sometimes they don't and we all have that kind – we all have wishes sometimes, when they cause some bother. (pause)

T. 9. You have something in mind?

J. 10. No, I haven't really, but – it is always there. (very long pause) I mean, like that – going home for convalescence really messed my father and mother up a bit.

T. 10. Well, yes, can you tell me about it?

J. 11. Well, it caused a bit of bother, it caused some bother, of course, there is another one to cook for and to clean up after.

T. 11. You are not quite sure how welcome you are or how much you cause bother.

J. 12. Well, I don't know, I think I am welcome, I do my fair share –

T. 12. But the picture you give me is a picture of yourself a little anxious and worried, you are going home, are you going to be welcome, are you going to cause bother? You can get round the bother by doing your fair share.

J. 13. I want to go home.

T. 13. I get an impression of a picture of insecurity about it. Am I wanted? And perhaps this refers to us here too, how much are you a bother here, how much are you working here, how much do I want to have you or do I say: oh, yes, another patient!

J. 14. I suppose you could look at it like that, but I would think it would be rather unlike me.

T. 14. What you have been telling me about home, that you are really not quite sure how much of a bother you are and perhaps also because you are coming for help here, how much it is a sign that you are a bother, that you are a worry.

J. 15. I don't really like to ask for help at school either, really, try to puzzle it out on my own quite often and I suppose I act upon it as well, trial and error sometimes, but this is different –

T. 15. And perhaps correspond with a wish to get help. You said there are some wishes that cause trouble or disturbances, perhaps one of your wishes, you feel, that causes disturbances, is a wish to be at home, a wish to be helped, a wish not to be sent away, not be left to sort it all out by yourself, but I think an active wish to be at home, to be helped, to be in people's company, not to be left alone; with something also inside you, that you have got to be grown up, you have got to stand on your own feet, you have got to do things yourself. (pause)

J. 16. Yes, at school it is so small you know everybody, really pretty well, and – you are never completely alone at school at any time. You are always in a group.

T. 16. Except when doing exams or doing difficult problems.

J. 17. Yes, in a way, yes. I was thinking generally. I hadn't thought –

T. 17. And perhaps when you did the exams, when you did the French you felt, how does one do this, how does one put it into French, what does this mean?

J. 18. Yes, in a way I suppose I did. I did not really enjoy it, probably because I have not been doing very well, really.

T. 18. Or is it that you don't do very well, when a strong feeling comes up of being all alone, of being lost, there being nobody around. There may be people, even in the sense, externally, but it seems that they are not really perhaps with you, in touch with you.

J. 19. I mean, not doing well at French, there are quite a few people that don't do particularly well as well and they are not in a group as well. (pause) I don't think anybody really – in our form – I don't know, they just seem to – I don't think anybody really enjoys it, but – it's just that. You can look at all my exams like that, except English Language, but – Sometimes you find the odd person who really enjoys a particular subject and gets on very well at it, but very few in our school, really, enjoy French and take it up afterwards, very few. (long pause)

T. 19. So that this is a matter in which you feel less lonely.

J. 20. Yes.

T. 20. But my impression is that loneliness has a great deal to do with mother and father and although the school may give you a lot of activities and a lot of things to do, you feel that there is a loneliness about it, not being with mother and father.

J. 21. Well, I enjoy going home, but after a long holiday, I am quite glad to go back to school, because honestly there is nothing to do at home, very little to do. It is rather boring, especially for four weeks, and when you go back to school, even though you are in a routine, you have plenty to do, plenty of sport.

T. 21. Plenty of activities to keep you there. As it is at home, as you said, there is nothing to do; there is also a sense of emptiness and deadness.

J. 22. If I was at school and we haven't so much to do, there would be a comparison with being at home and then, I suppose, everybody would be a lot more, including myself. (pause) [The transcription of J.22 is obscure.]

T. 22. So although home is a place to be wished for, a place where you wish to be at and where you say it will be nice to be home and it will be nice to have a convalescence, we have seen, that before you had the mumps, there was a very strong wish about to retire to the San for a couple of days to recover your strength. Perhaps there was a very strong wish therefore also to get home and recover your strength, recuperate, then a feeling of disappointment, when you get there. Something that it seems you wish for, but are perhaps disappointed when you get there; doesn't live up to your expectations. (pause)

J. 23. Yes, at times I feel like – leaving off work for a couple of days, I suppose everybody does.

T. 23. The disappointment was I thought, very important, the disappointment to have a couple of days laid up, it was a week or so wasn't it?

J. 24. Yes, it was.

T. 24. You have a week laid up and then the disappointment, nothing to do, glad to get back to the activities and bustle.

J. 25. Yes, it was rather, I mean, – for the first few days I had plenty to do, I hadn't got to get up early, took it easy, did some work in the afternoon and then watched television or something like that in the evening, and that passed the day away quite easily, but towards the end of the week, I started getting up a bit earlier and I couldn't have a ride on my bicycle because it was still at school, or I would have gone out, and done some shopping, but just sticking around, there was not much to do.

Let us take note, in passing, of some preliminaries. The transcribing was not carefully checked, and therefore we must not place undue weight on the actual words of the record. Apart from this, we can accept the record as a reliable one – *as far as it goes*. But it does not go very far, since, except for the spoken words, it leaves out virtually everything else. The rate of speech, the intonation, and all such features are missing. We can appreciate how serious these omissions are when one compares a transcript with the actual tape of the session transcribed, and this defect is likely to be important when we ask, for example, 'did John accept a certain interpretation or not?'

If this record is shown to the man on the Clapham omnibus, he is likely to find it very surprising. For though he would admit that he is very uncertain about what actually happens in psychoanalysis, and so does not know what to expect, this record of Session 5 is very different from what he expected it to look like. And, of course, this record looks very different from Freud's report of the material in the case of L., and from all such case reports by analysts. If we make the not unreasonable supposition that this record gives us a good glimpse of what contemporary analysts actually do, then the record brings out at a glance how very far Freud's report on L. is from the reality of the psychoanalytic situation at the present time, and hence how misleading it is. In so far as the man on the omnibus has been relying on Freud's and other case reports for his picture of what happens in analysis, it is quite understandable that this picture should diverge from the reality, and that he should be surprised when confronted by Session 5.

If an analyst complains that this taped record does not represent 'standard', or 'orthodox', or 'good' psychoanalytic practice, the immediate question he has to answer is: 'How does he know? On what does he base his complaint?' Have a representative sample of analysts allowed their sessions to be recorded and examined? Have they cooperated with scientific investigators so as to arrive at established norms of standard and non-standard psychoanalytic practice – by reference to which they can then assess the analyst's practice in Session 5? The answer seems to be: 'No, there appear to be no such records and norms available for comparison'.[9] Of course, it may be tempting for the working analyst to complain that 'The record of Session 5 is quite different from what *I* do – it is not me!' And the analyst may be right. But unless he has had his own work recorded and independently examined, he would be well advised not to stress his complaint that Session 5 is very different from what his own records would look like, *if* they were made. For his role as a participant in the dyad of analysis may serve to mislead him greatly about the character of his own work as an analyst.

What does the argument from truth criteria look like when we try to apply the criteria to the actual record of Session 5? Does the argument look better or worse?

Consider Acceptance. The boy John says 'Yes' a number of times, and produces some other responses that could perhaps be construed as those of acceptance. But when we try to categorise all these responses, it is evident that we cannot do so with much assurance. Thus, there are a number of instances where John's 'Yes', or other immediate response, does *not* seem to mean acceptance, because it goes along with reservations about the interpretation; or because it seems to have some other function. These instances are: J.4, J.6, J.7, J.12, J.14, J.17, J.18, J.21, (?)J.22. There are three other instances where the Acceptance function of the response seems uncertain – namely, J.8, J.9 and J.23. In contrast, John's 'Yes' does seem to be that of Acceptance in J.20 and J.25. (The 'Yes' of J.24 is not relevant, since it is in answer to a question of fact from the analyst). In J.15 and J.21 John seems to accept without saying 'Yes'.

But this piece of categorising of John's responses has been done by one judge, namely, the author. Another judge may categorise John's responses here rather differently. The chief reason, no doubt, for these possible differences and uncertainty is that John's 'Yes's' and his immediate responses of apparent acceptance can play various roles, and it is far from certain from the record just what role is being played in any given instance. John's responses, therefore, are themselves open to different interpretations. Thus, a 'Yes' may be a full-blooded acceptance, but it may also be a stalling device, or a fobbing-off move, concealing all sorts of reservations, or a preliminary to an expressed reservation. What is more, we have to remember that John was a very polite, ultra-obedient, schoolmaster-dominated, 'Yes-Sirring' adolescent. Hence, to a remark coming from an imposing adult psychiatrist, like Turquet, John will be disposed to say 'Yes' from sheer force of habit. Obviously, a 'Yes' cannot be judged in isolation. But, if we have to judge it in its context, how is this context to be characterised so that we can then formulate a reliable criterion of Acceptance in general terms? Similar difficulties arise about any immediate response sequence in which the patient appears to 'accept' the previous interpretation.

What about the Movement criterion? Can this be applied to our extract from Session 5? It is unclear what we are to say here. For the criterion is so vague that it is uncertain whether we are justified in pointing to *any* sequence of responses by J. as an instance of 'Movement'. Perhaps the best, or indeed the only, candidate is the sequel to T.20, that is, J.21 to J.25. But now the question is: 'To *what* interpretation precisely is John moving here? What interpretation, therefore, is he perhaps confirming?' We cannot say T.20, because the analyst goes on at once in T.21 to emphasise the emptiness of home, and in T.22 he offers a new interpretation altogether, namely, that John wishes to be home and yet feels disappointed when he is there.

Suppose we alter our stand and say that Movement is shown to the interpretation in T.22 by John's responses in J.23, 24 and 25. And let us suppose that it would be generally agreed that this is a case of Movement. Now let us remember Turquet's Kleino-Freudian theory or orientation, with its connected views and expectations about John. When we look at the analyst's behaviour in Session 5, it is clear that this orientation is being fed into the analytic situation and this is obvious in T.22, 23 and 24. But John's movement in J.23 to 25 will not help to support the analyst's Kleino-Freudian interpretation in T.22, *unless* we can categorise J.23 to 25 as an instance of *restricted* response or movement, which can be explained *only* by the Kleino-Freudian theory that the analyst is using.

Can J.23 to 25 *only* be explained in this way? Common sense is likely to protest that John's responses here are typical of schoolboys at boarding school in this country. When they are sent home in term time because of illness (or some similar reason), they are apt to be bored stiff and disappointed very quickly, and to long to return to school – and all for very obvious reasons. What is more, as we shall see (Chapter 6), it is indeed quite possible to offer a plausible, alternative explanation of John's responses in J.23 to 25 – by means of a psychodynamic theory which is *not* Kleino-Freudian in character. So the (supposed) Movement in J.23 to 25 cannot be said to confirm the interpretation in T.22.

In the light of this examination of Session 5, what does the argument from truth criteria look like? The argument looked rather weak *before* we applied it to the verbal record of an actual case. Now that we have done so, the argument looks weaker still. It is very difficult to apply these criteria so as to produce a clinical assessment, about which we can have the degree of confidence that is normally required of such assessments. Still less can we apply these criteria with the confidence required to enable us to claim with reasonable assurance that we have 'tested' and 'confirmed' an interpretation, and thereby shown that it is true.

Of course, we are restricted to the verbal record of John's case. We may think that everything would be much easier if we had the full oral and preferably video-taped record. And we may be right to think this. But the scientific investigation which is required to show that we are right does not seem to have been done. In the absence of such investigation one can but voice some commonsensical doubts. When one listens to some tapes of John it is tempting to say that, though the addition of the actual speech-sounds sometimes makes matters easier, on other occasions it makes it more difficult to arrive at a confident judgement about John's conduct. Hence, on these occasions it is more difficult to be confident about what truth criteria, if any, his conduct has satisfied. It is possible that much the same may be true if we had the video-tape in front of us – with all the massive, non-verbal information that this is likely to contain. So the addition of oral and visual information about John may not do much to help the argument from truth criteria. Again, this is a matter for objective empirical investigation.

It is important that, if and when an analyst applies a truth criterion to an interpretation, he should be able to do so with the confidence appropriate to, and normally demanded of, a good clinical assessment. For he has to convince the sceptical outsider that he is justified in asserting that an interpretation, p, is true, in virtue of the (alleged) fact that it satisfies some truth criterion. But if analysts cannot apply the criteria in ways which are reliable and produce a consensus, then they run into the objection that the criteria are not truth-determiners, but are merely aids the analyst uses to help him present his own personal view of his patient. We outsiders are at the mercy of the analyst's own individual whims and judgement; and case reports built upon them are obviously *not* a good foundation for the generalisations and theories about human nature outlined in Chapter 2. Our examination of truth criteria shows that it is far from certain that they can be applied in a way which is reliable and productive of consensus.[10]

We have now examined the argument from truth criteria, and the upshot can be expressed quite shortly. It is doubtful whether the argument is good enough to enable us to establish the truth of any interpretation whatever. It follows, therefore, that the argument is not good enough to establish the truth of the interpretations that go to form the main and essential part of the narrative an analyst constructs about a patient. This means, for example, that Freud cannot use L.'s (alleged) acceptance of interpretations, or any (alleged) movement by him, to establish the truth of Freud's narrative about L., including his account of L.'s early history and development. So the argument from truth criteria fails to give an analyst good grounds to believe that a narrative of his is substantially true or a good approximation to the truth.

IV

What has gone wrong with this whole argument? Why is it so weak?

For many years analysts were too shunned intellectually, and, at the same time, too self-confident to be bothered by the epistemological problem: *how* does Freud, or any other analyst, *know* that an interpretation is true? When at last they came round to this problem, they did so when they were under the impact and influence of Natural Science as *the* paradigm of rational inquiry (cf. Chapter 3). In consequence, they assumed that, in order to justify an interpretation they had to treat it like a hypothesis in science, and to confirm or disconfirm it by subjecting it to testing. A standard way of testing a hypothesis in science is to derive observable consequences from it, and to discover whether these hold or not. So, it was assumed, the appropriate way of testing an interpretation is to test the consequences of using it. The responses of the patient, therefore, provide the means of testing the interpretation and thereby establishing it as true or false.

This assumption is a mistake. A remark offered in the analytic situation (even though it looks *grammatically* like a hypothesis) works very differently from a hypothesis in science. This should be clear from our discussion in the last two sections; and we do not need to spell out here the differences between interpretation and hypothesis. It is these differences that are chiefly responsible for the failure of the argument from truth criteria. It is no good trying to treat an interpretation like a hypothesis when it is so unlike one.[11]

But working analysts are very unlikely to be upset by our negative conclusion about the argument from truth criteria. The reason is that in general they do not in practice rely on this argument. Nor have they ever done so in any important way at any stage in the history of the subject. Historically, psychoanalytic theory and the other psychodynamic theories did not grow up by basing themselves on the argument from truth criteria. This suggests, in turn, that if we try to justify an interpretation and a narrative by means of this argument, we are in danger of misrepresenting the actual practice of analysts. We are in danger of artificialising and intellectualising the way in which an analyst handles and thinks about his patient. In actual fact he does not arrive at his own view about the patient (that is to say, the narrative he would spin if asked) by the use of truth criteria. Furthermore, he tends not to use this argument from truth criteria to show that his view is true, because the demand that he justify his story about a patient is not apt to arise in practice.

As we have noted already, analysts accept *in theory* that, in order to show that a narrative is true, it is not sufficient to show that it gives us intelligibility and understanding. But *in practice* analysts are very apt to forget about this fundamental consideration. They tend to take it for granted that, if they have spun an intelligible narrative about an analysand, they have good and even sufficient reason to believe that it is also a true account. But when an analyst is forced to try to justify this account, he may *then* resort to the use of truth criteria. He may then be able to convince himself, or a sympathetic colleague, by looking up his notes on the case, or by consulting his memory about it, and applying the criteria to the material so revealed. But, in the light of our previous examination of the argument from truth criteria, it is obvious that he is likely to have great difficulty in satisfying a critical colleague or the sceptical outsider that his view is true, in part or in whole.

But what is the argument really getting at? Though the working analyst is unlikely to be upset when shown that the argument will not work, he is also very likely to insist that the so-called truth criteria *do* point to features of the analytic process and situation, features which are genuine and important. And here the analyst seems to be quite right. There is no doubt that the features picked out by the truth criteria are authentic, and can be very obvious and striking indeed. When the analyst sees a patient for the first time he brings with him his theoretical orientation. In the course of the first session or two, he is likely to form a tentative, barely articulated, outline sketch or picture of the patient and his problem. Freud's account of L. makes it clear that he did so with L. If the patient has already been filtered through psychiatric and psychological interviews (as John was), then the analyst is likely to have seen an account of the patient's problem written by his interviewers, and will bring with him to the very first session an outline sketch or picture of the patient and his problem – as Turquet seems to have done. This outline sketch or picture represents the way in which the analyst is disposed to apply to the patient his general orientation at the beginning or very early stages of the analysis. In the subsequent course of the analytic work, the analyst fills out his initial picture of the patient. He enlarges it and fills in gaps so as to arrive in time at a fairly complete account of the patient – one which he could write out in explicit narrative form, if asked – an account which enables him to order and explain much or most of the patient's problem, in terms, typically, of the theoretical orientation with which he began.

In his efforts to arrive at such an account, he makes use of features of the analytic process that the so-called truth criteria have picked out. He uses these features as cues to help him to maintain the dyadic interaction of analysis, to help him to develop transference and so on; and thereby to help him in the task of fitting his general theory to the patient. When, therefore, Turquet picks on some response of John as a cue for acceptance (say) of some interpretation, he will then follow up this interpretation, or be ready to do so. These cues therefore guide him all along in how to fit his Kleino-Freudian orientation to John.

But is he justified as a general rule in using these cues as guides to his theory fitting, and to his account and narrative construction about John? Are these cues generally trustworthy? Or may they not mislead him into building a narrative about John that is largely fiction? Suppose for the present that we ignore the analyst's answer to this question (see Chapter 6), and resort to common sense. When we get what looks like acceptance from Smith in ordinary life, or when a remark or question of ours seems to produce 'quite a reaction' in Smith, we take it for granted that we have grounds for believing that our remark about Smith may be true, or uncomfortably near the truth. Of course, we have seen that the analytic situation is very different from the ones we meet in ordinary life, and it may be different in the respects which are relevant to the very question we are dealing with now (see Chapter 6). Nevertheless, common sense does give us *some* grounds for believing that, when John or L. responds to the analyst in the way Smith responds to us in ordinary life, what the analyst says *may* be true or pointing towards the truth. So at the very least, we have some reason to believe that the cues the analyst uses to build and fit his theory are *also* pointers to the truth about the patient. Now because the theory is fitted, and the narrative about the analysand is constructed in the light of these cues, we have some reason to believe that the interpretations, which are connected with these cues, may be true; and that a narrative, which is built round such interpretations, and which makes the material intelligible, is *not* just a nice coherent fairy story. The narrative may also be an approximation to the truth about the patient.

Therefore, the argument from truth criteria does do something to help us to build a bridge from the clouds of speculative story-spinning down to the solid earth of truth. It is a weak bridge, and, as we shall see shortly (Chapter 6), it is even weaker than it looks at present. But it is better than nothing.

When a historian spins a coherent story, about some historical character, a story in which he tries to make the character intelligible and so understandable, he does not usually have to worry much about the truth of the story. For in spinning it, he relies on concepts and generalisations of common sense, which we all take for granted as valid and true; and also on the established concepts and generalisations of science, where these are relevant. The historian has good grounds, therefore, to take it for granted that a coherent narrative, which relies on such concepts and generalisations, is also true or a good approximation to the truth. Hence, he does not have to worry much about the bridge from intelligibility and understanding to truth.

The analyst is in no such fortunate position. He cannot rely on any generally accepted and established body of concepts and generalisations. Indeed, the validity of his concepts and the truth of his generalisations are the very topics under examination. Therefore, he is right to be concerned about the bridge from narrative and intelligibility to truth. In recent decades this very proper concern has taken the form of a hunt for truth criteria. It is clear from our discussion that this hunt is misguided, and the analyst would be well advised to give it up. He will not succeed in this way in building the strong bridge he needs to move from intelligibility and understanding to truth.

In a nutshell, then, our conclusion so far is this. The argument from truth criteria does a little to relieve the analyst's concern over the truth of narratives about L., John, and the rest of the flock of analysands. But it is far too weak to do much to make the sceptical outsider happy with the narratives which Freud and others have given us about their flock.

6 The validity of psychoanalytic method

Analysts are unlikely to be much disturbed by the acids of scepticism we have been pouring on their theory and practice. Their chief reaction is likely to be one of mild boredom. The reason for this response is of fundamental importance.

I

We have noted that the analyst draws a distinction between the intelligibility of a narrative and its truth; and he is concerned about building a bridge from the former to the latter. But he is also liable to be in serious conflict about the distinction and the bridge-building. For there is another side of himself which leaves him bored with the distinction, and ready to ignore it in practice. An important source of these counter-attitudes and impulses lies in the fact that, when an analyst gets to work on an analysand, he brings with him a certain presupposition, namely, that the method of analysis he uses is a valid procedure – that it does enable him, with care and patience and time, to discover the truth about the analysand. Hence, it is really quite unnecessary to look round for reasons to justify the truth of the considered narrative which he gives of the analysand. The hunt for truth criteria, for example, is really a needless exercise. Because the method is valid in his view, he just *knows* that his narrative is true, and hence he is not really bothered about the bridge from its intelligibility to its truth. When an analyst is challenged to support his presupposition that his method is valid, he is liable to look blank, to splutter, and to start groping around for reasons. This response suggests (as he should be the first to agree) that he had not really thought about the presupposition, and that his acceptance of it is founded, at least in part, on non-rational considerations.

What are the non-rational considerations that make him claim to *know* that he can and does typically uncover the truth about the analysand?

Common sense suggests some tenpative and partial answers. We have to remember that the analyst has been an analysand himself at some time in his past. In the course of his own analysis, he arrived at a large battery of 'insights' about himself. He came to see himself, to reconstruct his own personal history, and to see his relations with his parents, and so on, in ways that to him were fresh and usually surprising. He arrived at the new 'insights' through hard and sometimes painful work; for analysis is a somewhat trying experience, in which the analysand is typically a bit under the weather. The upshot was that he won through to what he, his analyst, and the training institute all believe to be 'self-knowledge'. This belief is, typically, central to his whole training and education as an analyst, along with the concomitant belief that the acquisition of such self-knowledge is a necessary and key condition for the personal change involved in therapeutic improvement. So, as a practising analyst, he uses his professional training and skills to help others to acquire insights about themselves, and a similar sort of self-knowledge. Moreover, he uses his own self-knowledge in the psychoanalytic situation to guide himself throughout his work – and especially in helping him to notice and to control his own feelings and attitudes towards a patient.

The practising analyst, therefore, is personally and professionally committed to the presupposition that psychoanalysis is an authentic experience – that it is a valid method of personal discovery. But *now* we are asking him to question this presupposition. This means that we are asking him to question his own putative self-knowledge, to admit the possibility that he may have a view of himself and his past which is mistaken – that he may be deluded in part, or even in large measure, about himself and his past. We are also asking him to question the foundations of his professional practice. For if the acquisition of insight and self-knowledge is said to be a necessary condition for the improvement of the patient, and yet analysis may not really yield insight and self-knowledge, then the whole rationale of his professional treatment seems to be destroyed. Clearly, all this is far too much to ask an analyst to contemplate.

II

It is obviously a matter for further inquiry to determine whether the analyst's presupposition really does rest on the non-rational considerations which common sense suggests. However, it may also be the case that, quite apart from such considerations, if any, which are at work, there are some *rational* ones which are sufficiently strong to justify us, analysts and all, in believing the presupposition. Can we find such rational considerations?

It is very natural and reasonable for an analyst to draw attention to the insights that the analysand achieves, and to the parallel insights of the analyst about the analysand; and to argue that these represent the truth, or part of the truth, about the analysand. For the achievement of these insights by both parties is a very striking and convincing experience. No one who has conducted an analytic dyad, or run a group analysis, or who has had personal or group analysis will deny the experience of insight and its impressive nature. Now in ordinary life we would all agree that such an experience of insight was a good reason, at the very least, for believing that the person concerned had come to understand something true about himself, which he had not appreciated before. Of course, the analytic situation may differ in the relevant respects from ordinary life (Chapter 5). But until we have reason to believe that the analytic situation *does* differ in relevant respects from that of ordinary life, we seem to have good grounds to go on believing that the insights achieved in analysis are as veridical as those of ordinary life.

Furthermore, analysts argue, if a patient is to improve as a result of his analysis, he can only do so in virtue of the insights he has acquired during his analysis into his problem and personality. In other words, it is a necessary condition of his improvement that he should come to see 'the truth' about himself and his problem. Analysts claim that, at least, some of their patients do show improvement as a result of their analysis. Hence psychoanalysis discovers the truth about some people, and in these cases, at least, it is a valid method of discovery.

In discussing the correctness of an interpretation, the distinguished psychoanalyst Erik Erikson has said that 'the proof' of an interpretation 'lies in the way in which the communication between therapist and patient "keeps moving", leading to new and surprising insights and to the patient's greater assumption of responsibility for himself'.[1] Here Erikson is arguing, in effect, that it is not possible for an interpretation to assist movement, and yet be false or widely off the mark. That is to say, if an interpretation does assist movement and lead to insights, and so on, then this fact is *sufficient* to show that it is true or an approximation to the truth.

How weighty are these reasons?

III

Is the achievement of insight in analysis by the analysand *sufficient* to establish the truth or correctness of the insight?

The answer seems to be a firm 'no'. Though common sense gives some support to the contention that analytic insight is self-validating, it is a weak prop, because common sense *also* lends support to the *opposite* contention. Thus, we are all too familiar in ordinary life with people coming 'to realise' things about themselves that their relatives and friends would not accept as true. How often, for example, on the death of a loved spouse do we not hear of the surviving partner starting to blame himself or herself for past neglect, and the like, of the deceased? – an insight that relatives and friends all too frequently do not accept. Moreover, in recent years certain psychological studies have suggested that common sense can be seriously misleading here.

The general design of these studies has been as follows. Groups of people, or subjects, were given a personality test; and their answers individually examined and assessed. The psychologists also prepared a description of some *hypothetical* person, which was made up of a number of statements. These statements were very carefully chosen so that they could reasonably be said to apply to anyone. For example: (i) You have a great need for other people to like and admire you; (ii) While you have some personality weaknesses, you are generally able to compensate for them; (iii) Your sexual adjustment has presented problems for you; (iv) At times you have serious doubts as to whether you have made the right decision or done the right thing. The subjects were then each separately given two reports on themselves – one being the *genuine* account based on the personality test; and the other a *bogus* account, which was the prepared description of the hypothetical person and made up of the selected statements, of which (i) to (iv) above are examples. This latter bogus account was identical, obviously, for every subject. The general finding has been that a subject accepts the statements of the bogus account as containing good and revealing insights about himself. He accepts them as being just as accurate as, or even more accurate than, the statements of the genuine account: he accepts these whether they are offered by prestigious or non-prestigious investigators, and whether they are personally complimentary or uncomplimentary.[2]

But, of course, a sophisticated analyst would not require any psychological investigation to make him hesitate about accepting the simple-minded claim that psychoanalytic insight is self-validating. For he will recall that some of Freud's very early patients apparently achieved the insight that their difficulties took their rise, in part, from sexual seduction in childhood by an adult. But later on, as is well known, Freud decided that these seductions had not actually occurred, but were fantasies of the patients. This means, presumably, that the analytic insights achieved by the analyst at the time (namely Freud) and by the early patients were false. And this raises the whole problem of what analysts are to say about interpretations, and connected insights, which flow from earlier and (on current orthodoxy) defective versions of psychoanalytic theory. These interpretations are known as 'incomplete' or 'inexact' ones in the analytic literature; and it is accepted that they are not correct. Yet the analyst and the patient apparently achieved the usual analytic insights by means of them. To date, analysts do not seem to have dealt with this problem to their general satisfaction.[3]

IV

Is the achievement of psychoanalytic insight *necessary* in order to bring about the (alleged) improvement in patients?

We have to accept the fact that there is no agreement at present on what brings about changes and (alleged) improvements in patients generally. In so far as there is an emerging consensus, it seems to be that analytic or psychodynamic insight is *not* a necessary condition. This negative evidence is to be found in the work of those who use what is loosely known as 'Behaviour Therapy'. This therapy can take various forms – such as Desensitisation, Aversion Therapy, the application of techniques derived from Operant Conditioning. There is considerable controversy at present about the extent to which these methods of treatment do successfully *exclude* the interpersonal factors and intra-psychic processes that psychoanalysis and psychotherapy use, and whether they can therefore be sharply distinguished from analysis and psychotherapy. Nevertheless, the work of the Behaviour Therapies has done enough, to say the least, to make it very difficult to maintain that psychoanalytic or psychodynamic insight is a necessary condition of any improvement.[4]

But let us consider the (alleged) improvement which follows on the use of psychoanalysis itself. Are analytic insights necessary to bring about *this* improvement? Doubts arise at once because of the fact that *all* psychodynamic therapists claim that patients of theirs change in a fruitful way, and show improvement. Moreover, objective inquiry has so far failed to show that the patients of analysts do better in general than patients who are given other forms of psychotherapy.[5] These facts strongly suggest that the (alleged) improvement in patients treated by a psychoanalyst is not due in any way to the *specific* psychoanalytic insights these patients acquire; but to something *general*, or *common*, to the use of all psychodynamic methods of treatment. One of the things that is general or common to them is the acquisition of insights by the patient. If we assume that this acquisition is a necessary causal condition for improvement, it seems to follow that it is the acquisition of insight *per se* that is the causal factor here, and *not* the acquisition of insights *à la*

Freud, or Jung, or some other psychodynamic psychologist. Roughly speaking, as long as the patient acquires *some* insights, then this necessary condition of improvement is satisfied. It does not matter what the intellectual content is of the insights that happen to be acquired.

So the acquisition of specifically *psychoanalytic* insights does *not* seem to be a necessary condition for the (alleged) improvement, which analytic method brings about in patients. These doubts have an important consequence. If the acquisition by the patient of some specific psychoanalytic insights *were* a necessary condition for (alleged) improvement, then we would have *a* reason for claiming that the content of these insights represented the truth about the patient. But because this acquisition is not, apparently, a necessary condition for improvement, it follows that the mere fact the patient accepts certain insights as a great personal revelation – that he comes thereby to see himself with conviction in a certain light – does nothing in itself to show that the insights and conviction are true of himself.

V

These criticisms are likely to produce a degree of apoplexy in most analysts. Some psychodynamic workers may be ready to agree that the achievement of an insight *per se* is *not* sufficient to establish its correctness or truth; and that the achievement of some *specific* set of insights, psychoanalytic or Jungian or some other, may not be necessary to bring about the (alleged) improvement. However, an analyst will still want to maintain that, if some interpretations and related insights do help to bring about what would be accepted *as fruitful change* in the patient (if, that is, they do help to transform the patient in the desired direction), then this fact *is* sufficient to establish that the interpretations, and related insights, are true or approximations to the truth.[6] So the achievement of insight *per se* is unimportant. What is important is whether this goes along with fruitful change. If it does, then this fact is sufficient to establish that the insight and related interpretations have uncovered and discovered the truth about the patient.

Is this fact sufficient? The orthodox picture of what happens in analysis is that the analyst and situation merely help the patient to bring to the surface what he could not face before. The sources of what is produced in the analysis lie inside the patient; what the analyst does is to allow, and to help, this inner material to see the light in ways that will be of therapeutic value. It is argued that this orthodox account – when fully elaborated – can explain what happens in analysis; and no other account can do so. Hence it follows that, if an insight and related interpretations go along with fruitful change, then the insight and interpretations do represent true discoveries about the patient.

If this orthodox view of what happens in analysis were true, then this consequence would be established. But its truth is very doubtful indeed. There seems to be a consensus among psychologists that the process of psychotherapy and analysis is very complex indeed, and that we do not yet know the whole story about it by a very long chalk. On the other hand, we do know enough to say that the orthodox psychoanalytic picture of it is just simple-minded and will not do; and that all sorts of other conditions, not noted in this picture, also contribute to what happens in analysis. Some of these conditions are logically connected with our problem about the validity of the method.

(*a*) There is a respectable body of theoretical work in psychology which suggests that the analyst's talk or speech *in itself* may serve to increase the probability of the patient responding in certain ways. That is to say, the talk or speech serves as 'a reinforcer' – to use the language of the industry.[7] There is also some experimental work which suggests that this is in fact the case. Thus, it has been found that the use of mild affirmatory words (for example, 'good', 'fine'), and also interpretations of the psychoanalytic type, can be used to alter and control certain verbal behaviour in some psychotic patients. Another study tested, and confirmed, the hypothesis that 'even when the content of an interpretation is apparently unrelated to the subject's statements', verbal behaviour may still be modified, in that the frequency with which subjects responded in a certain way may be increased, even when the interpretations had no psychoanalytic or dynamic connection with what the subject had said, but were presented quite randomly.[8]

Of course, these very small studies were done on highly selected classes of patient responses, and in an experimental situation known as 'verbal conditioning'. The events they study are obviously very different from what happens in psychotherapy and psychoanalysis. But these, and other, small studies *are* enough to make one hesitate about the orthodox view of the psychoanalytic process. What is more, the differences between these conditioning situations and psychoanalysis may go the *wrong* way for the orthodox view of the psychoanalytic situation. The differences may be such as to make it likely that patients are far *more* open in analysis than they are in the conditioning experiments to verbal conditioning, and to the control and direction of their personality in quite fundamental ways.

(*b*) There are some weighty reasons to believe that this is indeed the case – that people are much more open to such influence in analysis than has been generally realised. One of these reasons resides in a very striking aspect of therapeutic work in medicine in general.

It is well known that patients may get better even when given treatment, for example a drug, which, unknown to the patient, is of no real help at all. This is known as the 'placebo effect'. It is very pervasive and important in a variety of ways in general medicine. With the development in psychiatry in the 1950s of pharmacological methods, it became crucial to take account of the placebo effect in psychological medicine; and it has now been very extensively investigated.

The present outcome of this investigation, in respect of analysis and psychotherapy, is still very incomplete and uncertain. This is wholly understandable in view of the fact that the effect is a complex, and obviously very subtle, psychological affair. However, we do seem to know enough to be reasonably sure about two matters. (i) The placebo effect appears to play an important part in analytically oriented psychotherapy; and in the (alleged) improvement of patients. (ii) Psychologists have discovered some of the conditions that contribute to the effect, and to the way it operates. These conditions centre round the therapist and his relations with the patient. Thus, it has been found that if the therapist likes the patient, or exhibits interest in him, or believes in his own method of treatment, or is interested in the results obtained by it, then the placebo effect is likely to be found. From this the suggestion has emerged that, if the therapist is young and trying out a new method about which he is enthusiastic – whether it be jogging or primal screaming or some other latest fashion – then he is likely to get a strong placebo effect and better (alleged) results.

This effect can be explained, in part, by the further findings that the therapist does communicate his own attitudes and interests quite unwittingly and in very subtle ways to the patient, ways which are not open to casual observation. It is also worth noting that the placebo effect does not appear to be connected with differences of personality, though it is positively connected with the expectations people have on starting therapy, and possibly also with the hopes they entertain about it. Two students of the subject conclude their review of the role of placebo in psychotherapy and psychoanalysis in the following way. 'Many psycho-analysts believe that analytic treatment is differentiated from other therapies because it has specific, non-placebo, and non-suggestive effects. This review suggests the contrary position that it may have extensive, potent, and subtle placebo effects on patients for whom the treatment is appropriate.'[9]

The logical consequence of the placebo effect is clear. If an interpretation and insight (or a cluster of them) is followed by fruitful change in the patient, this fact is far from sufficient to show that the interpretation and the insight are true or getting at the truth. If the analyst himself is convinced that the change is the consequence of the interpretation and the insight, he may just be deluded. For the fruitful change in the patient may be the outcome, in part or in large measure, of something that is *not* specific to his particular theoretical orientation and interpretations, or even specific to psychoanalysis in general; but to something that is *common to* psychotherapy in general and perhaps also to all methods of healing whatsoever. The fruitful change in the patient may be a placebo effect – the outcome, in part or in large measure, of placebo conditions.

It is not at all surprising that analysts may be inclined utterly to reject this view, and to remain firmly convinced that fruitful change in the patient is the specific outcome of their own treatment and consequential insights in their patients. For similar convictions have been held by healers throughout the history of medicine right up to the present day, and they are essential to the practice of the quack and the charlatan.

(*c*) It should be obvious from Freud's report on L., and from John's Session 5 (Chapter 5) that psychoanalytic situations are close encounters of a very peculiar kind. It is necessary to notice some additional features they exhibit in order to appreciate just how peculiar they are. In recent decades psychologists and others have drawn attention to these additional features, and to the great transforming influence they seem to exert on the analysand.

Let us look again at the behaviour of Turquet in relation to John, especially as shown in Session 5 (Chapter 5) and in Session 2 below (page 104L ff.).

Turquet requires John – like all other patients in analysis – to accept and abide by the rule that he should say whatever comes to mind no matter how unpleasant the material may be. This is the well-known rule of free association. Turquet also exercises his professional skills in accordance with (what can be described as) certain norms or rules, which are those characteristic of the tradition of psychoanalysis in this country, in which Turquet was trained. Accordingly, he only meets John in the analytic situation, not outside it. Here he behaves in such a way that John is not in a position to determine what Turquet's attitude is on any of the issues John raises, and is therefore unable to put Turquet firmly in any one role in respect of these issues. If John were to ask a direct question, Turquet would not answer it. So John can never tell whether Turquet is for or against him, accepts or does not accept his view of school or parents, and so on. In short, Turquet behaves so as to be for John an indeterminate or anonymous figure, to use the jargon of the industry. But in order to achieve indeterminateness, he has to behave in a way that disables John from challenging him rationally. So he does not let himself be drawn into any argument or discussion. If John does contradict any interpretation he offers, he does not answer back. There is no way, therefore, in which John can rationally challenge Turquet; and this makes the discourse of the analytic session, in an important way, a non-rational one. Because Turquet does not allow himself to be faulted, he becomes a person who, for John, is infallible.

It is very plausible to argue that it is these two rules – of indeterminateness and non-contradiction – that, in particular, make the close encounters of analysis so very peculiar. For when these are combined with the basic rule of free association imposed on the patient, they serve jointly to create a personal situation with very special features. It soon becomes an uncertain or ambiguous one for the patient. He does not know what is going on, whether he is producing the sort of thing that will help or not, what the analyst thinks of him, and whether he is progressing or otherwise. So the situation is anxiety arousing. Accordingly, he starts hunting for clues to try to reduce the anxiety and ambiguity of the situation. But he is given no direct help in finding these clues. Consequently he develops a perceptual hunger for guidance. At the same time he is perpetually being encouraged, or (as it may seem to him) goaded, by the analyst into bringing up material connected with his difficulties, his anxieties, feelings of shame and guilt, and so on. All this breeds frustration, and consequential regression and depression. Because of all this, also, he soon becomes emotionally involved with the analyst. He develops what is known as 'transference', both negative and positive. He becomes emotionally dependent on the analyst; he plays out his fantasies in respect of the latter, and these come up in the analysis; he needs the analyst's love, but as always is quite uncertain whether he has got it, and what the analyst's attitudes to him really are.

The consequences are likely to be very striking. The patient is made very confused about himself, about his real feelings and attitudes and about how he should be changing, if he is to change for the better. All this renders him unstable in respect of himself, and hence very suggestible.[10]

Now let us look at the other side of Turquet's activity. In the permissive atmosphere of the analytic situation, he is continually disturbing and goading John, as we have seen, into speaking about his worries and fears of all sorts. Yet the dire results, which John may fear will result from speaking about them, do not take place; and his anxieties are thereby lessened. In this way Turquet rewards him for speaking up, and so involves John with himself and helps to maintain the analysis in being. Moreover, he flatters and comforts John by the mere fact that he listens to and takes an interest in this adolescent's troubles (the first time anyone had ever done so for John). However, Turquet selects certain recurrent features of John's conduct for mild punishment or non-rewarding treatment – for example John's silences or his wish to retreat, or a willingness to embrace an inconsistent view of himself and his situation. Turquet hands out these non-rewarding measures in his comments on the silences, in pointing to the inconsistencies, and so on. But, concurrently, he also selects certain themes that John brings up, and comments on them in ways which serve to reward John for bringing them up. This encourages him to go on speaking about them and facing up to themes of this sort. What is more, when Turquet comments in these ways on all John's conduct in the analysis, he is presenting John in his interpretations (see Chapter 5) with views about himself – about how the origins of his troubles and how his present difficulties can be regarded. But Turquet does not present these views directly – the rule of indeterminateness, for one thing, prevents this. He presents them indirectly, as hints, in his interpretations. If John objects to these interpretations, Turquet does not argue with him. Because the analytic situation is ambiguous, he starts to catch on to the clues contained in the interpretations in his effort to reduce the ambiguity and uncertainty of the situation. Because, after a time, he becomes confused and sugges-tible, he is very ready to pick up these clues. By doing this unwittingly, and by accepting the alternative view of himself contained in the interpretations Turquet has offered him, John's confusion and anxieties both in the analysis and about himself outside are considerably reduced. Acceptance, therefore, of this alternative point of view brings consider-able rewards. And this process of emotional re-learning and cognitive reorganisation occurs without John being aware of the subtle clues on which it depends, and how it all comes about.

We have now presented a sketch of certain psychological features of the analytic situation, which have been emphasised in recent years. For ease of reference let us adopt a neutral label and call these the 'K features'. Most students would probably agree that we still lack direct confirmation of the presence and operation in analysis of the K features we have just sketched. But there has been some discussion of their operation; and the upshot has been to suggest that the K features are authentic and are probably potent sources of personal change.[11]

It is also worth noting that the account of the analytic situation which emerges when we look at it through psychological spectacles is congruent with some suggestions that are to be found in the psycho-analytic tradition itself. In the early years of analysis, it may have been natural to believe that what the analyst did essentially was just to set and maintain a stage in which the patient could reveal and find out about himself. But then it became clear that it was difficult to distinguish between fantasy and reality in the patient's recollections of his past, and hence difficult to reconstruct the past with confidence. It also became clear that resistance from the patient was a very prominent feature in the analysis; and that this had to be worked through. The undermining doubt then crept in among analysts that, perhaps, they were only ready to agree that a patient had worked through his resistances and transference successfully, when he had come to see himself as the analyst sees him. This suggested that, in helping him to work through, the analyst was exerting considerable influence on him – sufficient, indeed, to bring him round to the analyst's own view of himself. It is no wonder, then, that Freud could write as follows towards the end of his life: 'Quite often we do not succeed in bringing the patient to recollect what has been repressed. Instead of that, if the analysis is carried out correctly, we produce in him an assured conviction of the truth of the construction which achieves the same therapeutic result as a recaptured memory.'[12] What really matters, what is essential, Freud is saying, is *not* the truth or correctness of the construction (or interpretative narrative); but whether the patient develops 'an assured conviction' of its truth; and this is something that the analyst 'produces in him'. Analysts and everyone else may all believe that the past of the patient has an important causal role in bringing about his present condition. But, according to Freud himself, analysis is quite often not strong enough to discover the truth about the past of the patient and its actual contribution to his present condition. However, it is clear that, even in making this very concession, Freud is still clinging to the basic presupposition we are examining. For he is claiming that in *some* cases at least, psychoanalysis *is* strong enough to discover the truth about the patient's past, and is therefore a valid method of discovery in these instances. Unfortunately, Freud does not tell us adequately, if at all, how to distinguish the valid from the invalid instances – how to tell when analysis is strong enough to discover the truth about the past, and when it is not.

We have now examined some standard and very familiar reasons in support of the analyst's presupposition that analysis is a valid method of discovery. The conclusion of our discussion – in Sections II to V – can be stated in a sentence. The reasons are weak, and quite insufficient to justify us accepting the presupposition as true.

VI

Let us try to bring this whole problem down to earth a little by looking again at John, so as better to appreciate how the analyst's influence actually worked on him. Because we are interested in the discovery claims of analysis, we must concentrate on the role of Turquet's theoretical orientation in the analytic situation. We have noted how an analyst's orientation provides him with a perspective, which is necessary in practice to enable him to order and 'to understand' what happens in the analytic situation (Chapter 4). We have also noted that Turquet has a Kleino-Freudian orientation (Chapter 5), and we have seen something of the way in which he feeds this orientation into the situation in Session 5 (Chapter 5). Let us now take a further look at the way in which he uses his theoretical stand to order, control and direct the interaction in the analytic situation.

Freud is reported to have said jokingly – in considering how to show that analysis was therapeutically effective – 'that the best control is to treat the same person twice – once with analysis and once without, and then compare results'.[13] What we need here is something that, like Freud's suggestion, is also impossible to obtain, namely a control experiment. We need to have John go at the same time to a therapist with an orientation other than Turquet's, and then to arrange that these two, concurrent treatments, have no mutual effects. We could then study the role of the two orientations in the two parallel treatments and records. But in the absence of this (impossible) experiment, we can do something analogous to it, which is of some help. We can run what is known as a *Gedankenexperiment*, that is, an imaginary or thought experiment.

Let us imagine that John had gone to a therapist who performs according to the rules or norms that Turquet uses, but who brings to, and puts into, the situation a different type of theory. We can then construct a *hypothetical* session that John had with this analyst. The material we obtain can then be viewed as *like* the sort of material that we *would* have obtained if John actually had gone to this analyst.

What analyst or therapist shall we choose? Let us pick on the late Dr. Karen Horney (see Chapter 2) – largely because she would have been very happy to treat John, and choosing her does not prejudice issues in any way. We can summarise the relevant parts of her orientation in the Adlerian tradition as follows.[14]

The basic neurotic conflict has its source in the person's 'loss of capacity to wish for anything wholeheartedly, because his very wishes are divided, that is, go in opposite directions'. He has acquired fundamentally contradictory attitudes towards other people. Looked at psychogenetically, these attitudes stem from the 'basic anxiety' of the child – the child's feeling of 'being isolated and helpless in a potentially hostile world'. To meet the disturbing world, the child develops 'ad hoc strategies' and 'lasting character trends'. When we take a panoramic view of the main directions in which the child can move, it is evident that he can move *towards* people, *against* them or *away* from them. In moving towards them he accepts his own helplessness, and in spite of fears tries to win their affection and lean on them. In moving against them he accepts the hostility around him and determines to fight it, consciously or unconsciously. In moving away from people, 'he wants neither to belong nor to fight but keeps apart' in a world of his own. Any one of these moves is the predominant one he makes; and he cannot make any of them wholeheartedly. If his early experiences have been too powerful, then no new later experiences will be able to break through his rigidity – which does not leave him open to any new experience. But if his early experiences have been not too prohibitive of spontaneous growth, then later experiences, particularly in adolescence, can have a moulding influence.

There are various ways in which a person can try to deal with his neurotic difficulties. One of them is by the creation of an 'idealised image' – an image of what he believes himself to be, or of what at the time he feels he can or ought to be. He then has to deal with and bridge the gap between his real self and the idealised image. One of the ways he does this is by 'externalisation' – the tendency to experience internal processes as if they occurred outside oneself, and, as a rule to hold these external factors responsible for one's difficulties. These unresolved conflicts – Horney points out – have all sorts of consequences, which involve a general impoverishment of personality. With a person who, for example, moves predominantly and rigidly away from people, there will be an impoverishment of affect, his creative abilities will be inhibited, he becomes panic-stricken if he can no longer safeguard his emotional distance from others, and so on.

Now let us return to John. In Session 1, Turquet and he merely discussed arrangements for the analysis. The real work began in Session 2. Let us imagine that John also went, *per impossibile*, to Horney for Session 2. Given John's presenting symptoms, Horney is already disposed at this early stage to see in John someone who has dealt with his basic conflict predominantly by moving away from people. This contrasts with Turquet, whose orientation disposed him at this stage to see in John someone who had suffered the trauma of parental desertion, and who was weighed down by father and an overpowering conscience (Chapter 5, page 77). Accordingly, Horney is ready to pick on and develop items in John's performance somewhat different from those that Turquet made use of.

We can now construct John's imaginary Session 2 with Horney. We present a part of the two Sessions in parallel – the actual one with

Turquet on the left-hand column (with a few corrections of some very minor and obvious errors of transcription), and the hypothetical one on the right. The explanatory comments from the author are in the square brackets.

Second Interview with John (Dr. Turquet)

T. 1. I think you will be most comfortable here. Now I think there is only one rule here, that is to try and tell me whatever it is you might be thinking or feeling or imagining, however difficult it may be and try and tell me about it. (Long pause). I had your letter and it seems the times are all right. Was the journey all right? [In the first sentence, T. is obviously pointing to the couch. In the second sentence, he gives John 'the basic rule' of analysis for the patient.]

J. 1. I had to hurry a bit, otherwise it was all right.
T. 2. You would let me know, if you want to alter the times?

J. 2. Yes. (pause). Hm, generally, I suppose, being in the blue form in the junior school put me back a bit.
T. 3. Being in a –?
J. 3. In a blue form, you know, a B.3 and I suppose I have got the attitude that I wasn't any good at work that –
T. 4. Getting into a blue form, B.3, how did it come about?

J. 4. Well I joined the school and –
T. 5. When was this?
J. 5. In 19 –. [the date has been omitted.] When I went into the first form, I found it quite hard going and at the next year I was put up, but told that generally it was a bit of a doubtful decision. Anyway, I came back to the first form again, had a year there and when I

Extract from hypothetical Session Two: John and Dr. Karen Horney

[From H.1 to J.6 the session is identical with Turquet's. With H.7, it begins to diverge. For, unlike Turquet, Horney takes up the very first theme that John introduced – following the Adlerian view that this is important.]

was supposed to go to the next form, they started the two stream idea and I was put into the lower stream.

T. 6. So it really all happened in your first year at school, when you were nine?

J. 6. Yes.

T. 7. What do you feel about going to this school?

H. 7. Hm, hm. You were saying that being put in a B form put you back a bit and gave you – how did you put it? – the attitude that you weren't any good at work. Is that right?

J. 7. Yes (pause).

H. 8. Tell me more about this attitude of yours. How do you feel it put you back a bit?

J. 8. Well, it didn't make me keen about the work. I felt – you know – that I could not do anything. Some of the other chaps I knew – they weren't all that bright really. But they were in the A stream, and I wasn't. It was a bit – well, a bit discouraging.

H. 9. Are you trying to tell me that being put into the B stream – the blue form – made you feel very depressed?

J. 9. Yes.

H. 10. And that this put you back seriously – in a way from which you don't feel you have ever recovered, that you don't feel you have ever got over this early handicap?

J. 10. Yes, something like that. One feels pretty hopeless really in that sort of situation. I mean, one goes to a new school and one thinks one's no end of a great chap. Of course, this is a bit silly and one expects to be taken down a few pegs, and put in one's place in a new school, as a new boy. But to be put into the blue form – well it's serious really.

H. 11. You seem to me to be saying that being put into the B form was *so* serious for you that this is *why* you are behind now in your work – in your work for O levels; that being put into the B form explains why you now find your school work heavy going.

J. 11. I suppose so. I do sometimes have the idea that this is why I am behind.

H. 12. You think, do you, that being put into the B form is enough to explain why things are difficult for you now? (pause)

J. 12. I don't know really –

H. 13. Well, you give me the impression that you are rather using the fact that you were put into the B form originally as a comforting excuse to explain your present backwardness – your present inability to cope. It's so easy, is it not, to put the blame on to something in the past over which one had no control oneself? It seems to me that you are doing something rather like this here. And so encouraging yourself to overlook what you can do about your problem at the present time (long pause) [Here H. is using her concept of externalisation, and so is injecting some theory.]

J. 7. Well, it was the first year at boarding school and I wasn't very keen, but after the first term or so I started to enjoy it, I didn't mind so much, but going there and having a big difference between my parents and myself over the distance away, hm. –

T. 8. By difference you mean long –

J. 8. Yes, you see, the Far East, that didn't help matters, really.

T. 9. You mean that your parents then went abroad, is that it?

J. 9. No, they – my father was abroad already and I went into the boarding school and my mother then went out to my father and they were both in the Far East while my sister was at the University. (pause)

T. 10. And something about the present situation here with me, which reminds you of going to Boarding School, starting something new there, as you are starting something new here.

J. 13. Well, I don't know really. I don't know what to say to that. I suppose going to the new school was a bit of a thing all round.

H. 14. In what way? How did you feel about going to this new school? [The session now returns to Turquet's at T.7.]

J. 14. Well, it was the first year at boarding school, and I wasn't very keen, but after the first term or so I started to enjoy it, I didn't mind so much, but going there and having a big difference between my parents and myself over the distance away, hm . . .

H. 15. By big difference you mean long –

J. 15. Yes, you see, the Far East, that didn't help matters, really.

H. 16. You mean that your parents then went abroad, is that it?

J. 16. No, they – my father was abroad already and I went into the boarding school and my mother then went out to my father and they were both in the Far East while my sister was at the University. (pause)

H. 17. How many brothers and sisters have you? [Here it diverges again from T. because of her orientation. She asks about John's siblings because position in the family is important in the Adlerian tradition, and she wishes to explore John's relations with people, how easily and closely he relates to them.]

J. 17. Two sisters, no brothers.

H. 18. Are they *both* older than you?

J. 18. Yes, they are 27 and 30 now.

H. 19. So you weren't very keen to go to boarding school, and you were upset by the fact that your mother soon afterwards left you to join your father. Is that it?

J. 19. I don't think it was my mother going that affected me so much. It was just having two in one go. My mother went abroad and I went to school – in a space of a month or so. Shook me up quite a bit, I think.
(pause)

H. 20. You found it alarming and frightening to become a boarder at this school?

J. 20. Yes.

H. 21. In what way? What was frightening about it?

J. 21. Well, when you're a boarder, you've got to mix in with everyone else, whether you want to or not. I just used to like messing about with my things on my own. And just be independent, doing things in my own way, when I wanted to do them. When you're a boarder, you've got to meet all sorts of types all the day long – and be pleasant to everyone all the time, and keep the rules. It's a bit of a sweat – until you get used to it.

H. 22. So what frightened you about boarding school was chiefly the fact that you had to mix with other boys very closely all the day long – you were forced to enter into close personal relations with them – whereas, before you went to school, you were very much a little boy who preferred to play by himself. You give me the picture of a solitary boy who was without close playmates – and who was then thrown into the close contacts of a bear garden at boarding school. And who was very upset by it. [H. has now reached the point where she can offer for the first time the important interpretation that John is a solitary.]

J. 22. Yes, my mother sometimes used to say: what about asking someone round to play with you? Why don't you go to play with the boy next door? But I was never very keen, not really. (pause)

H. 23. And how did you feel about your mother urging you to play with other boys?

J. 23. I don't know really. I just took it as it came. Mothers will be mothers, they will fuss. Quite unnecessary, really. I suppose she thought that because she was out such a lot, doing all sorts of things, I would be lonely without someone to play with. Quite silly really. (pause) If she had been around, at home more, it would not have made much difference. Because – well – you can't play trains and tricycles with your mother. So it would not have made any difference really. But I give it to her – she looks after things at home very well – makes things nice for father and everyone. If I came into the house with dirty shoes, I would catch it hot from her.

H. 24. So it seems that, even before you went to boarding school, you had lost your mother – you were not very close to her. You say: it would not have made much difference if she had been around more at home. Because presumably you would not have had much more to do with her if she had been more often at hand. She was not your playmate – the person to whom you gave your confidences and on whose shoulder you could weep. Even before you went to boarding school, you had moved away from her emotionally into isolation. Then, notice, you also said 'you couldn't ask your mother to play trains and tricycles with you'. And you said this with a touch of contempt and a slight sneer in your voice. This leads me to suspect that, concealed behind your tone of contempt and slight sneer, is a deep-seated, strongly felt wish that she *should* play with you – that you *should* move towards her, in some way you know not what. And that your loneliness at the time concealed a heartfelt wish for closer relations with her – to know her better, to be able to share your thoughts and wishes with her, and so on. (Pause) [A key in-terpretation for H. – that John had moved away, and yet that he wished to do the opposite. By now H. is hard at work putting her theory into the analytic situation – as intensively, perhaps, as T. was doing at this point.]

J. 24. Well, I don't know. I suppose I – well, some of the chaps at school seem to know their parents less than I do. No good at all some of those parents. (pause) But, yes, I suppose it would be nice to know one's mother like one knows a friend. (pause)

H. 25. You said earlier on that what shook you up was the *joint* occurrence – your mother going off to the East and you going to Boarding school. Do you remember?

J. 25. Yes.

H. 26. You feel that you could have taken either occurrence separately, but not the two together?

J. 26. Yes – one by itself would not have been too bad.

H. 27. But why did you feel that it was the two together that was so upsetting? I mean – if you had already lost touch with your mother, lost her emotionally, why was it so upsetting to lose her physically – for her to go away to the East – when you became a boarder?

J. 27. I don't know . . . I haven't thought of it. I suppose it's just, er, nice to know one's parents are close by. One is not going to be a cry baby and run to them. But it's something to know they are just there.

H. 28. The impression you give me of yourself at this time is that of a lonely little boy who had lost touch with and moved away from his mother; but who had at the same time a deep-seated wish to move towards her, to make genuine contact with her. This seems to me to have been an essential part of your difficulty at the time. Mother then vanishes from the scene. This destroys your hope of regaining touch with her, of moving towards her. From now on there is no hope of finding the motherly bosom on which to weep. And at the very same time, you are packed off to boarding school – thereby forcing you to move out of your isolation into some sort of personal relationship with strangers, other boys and masters. So you become depressed and frightened. [Offering a fuller interpretation of his problem, in terms of H's orientation.]

J. 28. Yes. Being forced – all on your own – to live with a number of other chaps. It's a bit shaking. One's got to get to know so many people, and got to learn what's what, the rules, and all that. It's a bind.

H. 29. And becoming a boarder, for the first time, is rather like coming here. [Here the session returns substantially to Session 2 at T.10 and sequel.]

J. 29. Yes, it is in a way.
H. 30. In what way?
J. 30. I don't know – a new experience, really.
H. 31. But a disturbing experience, really.
J. 31. Yes it is.
H. 32. What do you find disturbing about it?
J. 32. Well, (pause) well, suppose being interviewed is

J. 10. Yes, it does, it does in a way.
T. 11. In what way?
J. 11. I don't know, a new experience, really.
T. 12. But a disturbing experience, really.
J. 12. Yes, it is.
T. 13. What do you find disturbing about it?
J. 13. Well, (pause), well, suppose being interviewed is

quite a trial. At the same time — I don't know. It is just the general atmosphere we are in. It — it is rather peculiar.

T. 14. What you feel is peculiar about the atmosphere? (pause)

J. 14. I don't know, really.

T. 15. In what way is it connected and it seems it might be with mother leaving you, like a loss of protection. [Putting his theory into the situation by offering the mother desertion theme to John.]

J. 15. I don't think that this affected me so much. It was just having two in one go. My mother went abroad and I went in a space of a month or so, shook me up quite a bit, I think. (pause)

T. 16. You were not quite sure what you were let in for.

J. 16. Yes, quite, and it is the same here, I suppose.

T. 17. You are not sure what you are letting yourself in for.

J. 17. Yes.

T. 18. You were rushed to get here, the strangeness, and it is also connected with father, just as going to school is connected with father being in the Far East. In a way coming here is connected with father.

J. 18. Well, yes, it was his idea. Actually he said what do you think about it and I said, yes, well, perhaps it is quite a good idea and that was that and it was fixed or just about and I don't suppose he wanted to say,

quite a trial. At the same time . . . I don't know. It is just the general atmosphere we are in. It . . . it is rather peculiar.

H. 33. What do you feel is peculiar about the atmosphere?

J. 33. I don't think I know really.

H. 34. Perhaps it is connected with the fact that here you have to move towards me, and enter for the first time into a new personal relationship with me. [Diverging again from Session 2 along predictable lines.]

J. 34. Yes, this — this is a bit of a shake up.

H. 35. You find it frightening, you aren't sure what you are let in for?

J. 35. Yes, something like that.

H. 36. You have spoken of your mother. But where does your father come into all this — into the arrangements to come here for instance?

[J.36 up to the penultimate intervention by H. are omitted.]

right, I won't be seeing you again, he rather asked me first and encouraged me to go, so that it feels as if I say I like to go.

T. 19. It seems as if almost you said it with some spirit, wanting to be agreeable to him, –

J. 19. Yes it would be.

T. 20. Falling in with his wishes.

J. 20. Yes, in one respect, but if it was going to help, it would be my wish as well, you see, as well as my father's.

T. 21. On the other hand you may be hinting at some problem, that you find it difficult to say no to him.

J. 21. Well, I don't like to say no, but –

T. 22. As if you were saying: I like to be a good boy. [In T.18, T. brings the father into the picture, in accordance with his theoretical expectations. In T.19 – T.22, T. is suggesting that John may have sub-ordinated his own wishes to his father.]

J. 22. Not like that. If it would help me as well, (in-audible) my father's mind.

T. 23. But the implication is also that here, at this moment, you may not be saying all that is on your mind, the same as you didn't say all that was on your mind to your father about coming here or about his leaving you at Boarding School, when he went to the Far East.

J. 23. I certainly let him know what I was feeling then.

T. 24. But I wonder whether here you are letting me know all your feelings or whether you are really here saying: well, I must be good, I must do as I am told, it is for my best, but is this really what you feel or not? Are there other feelings about? (pause)

J. 24. I wouldn't say there are. (pause)

T. 25. And yet you remain very silent. (long pause) Although you may have gone so far about what you say about boarding schools (inaudible) to let me know what you feel about things now, what you think about this one.

J. 25. I was just thinking about rugger at school –

T. 26. Can you tell me about this?

J. 26. Well, the mock exams are in three weeks, it is going to be quite an exam, really they always try to make it harder than what the real thing is and I am not too happy, really.

T. 27. What frightens you?

J. 27. Well, in a way, but I don't think it gets that bad, I seem to be frightened about – (pause), it is something you have to face, really.

T. 28. But also something that involves discovering and learning, what it is that you have remembered, what it is that you have got inside you, how well you can cope or how badly you can cope. Just as here involves very much finding out what is going on inside you, what is it that is preventing you from being in the

Fifth form as you might be. Here, too, is in some ways an examination, an examination, in which you and I work together to see, what is going on inside you, to examine what is going on inside you. [Offering part of his own view, suggested by his Kleino-Freudian stance, of the nature and origin of John's difficulties at school.]

J. 28. Yes, it is the same idea, you can compare them both fairly closely.

T. 29. And here, too, – What will come out, what will be discovered? How good, how bad are you? You wish to be good, but the fear is there, you have got bad things inside you, difficulties, inabilities, feelings of being frightened. What was it the parents thought about rugger?

[J.29 to T.41 are omitted]

J. 41. Well, being in this blue form puts me back a bit, I suppose, gave me the impression well, this is no good and just hopeless and then generally deteriorates it. (pause).

T. 42. It makes you feel really defeated.

J. 42. Yes, in a way, yes it has and it gives me a guilty conscience, really, when I think being in such a good school, quite a lot of money being spent, that you ought to work hard (pause).

T. 43. Then you know that here you are being seen under the National Health Service.

J. 43. No, I didn't know that at all. Still I didn't realise how. I thought my father was paying for this as well.

T. 44. This would have dismayed you or added to the sense of guilty conscience.

J. 44. Yes, it would in a way.

T. 45. And this is being done under the National Health Service, in that way it is not costing your father anything. (pause) It seems very much that you felt inside you that you had a father, who was saying: look what is put in front of you, look what is being spent on you, look, how you are wasting it. As if saying: look at all the good things that are offered to you, the good school, the good treatment, good home, whatever it may be. What use are you making of it? I don't know whether in fact he says these things, but it seems as if inside you you felt he was saying them.

J. 45. Well, he does not say them, but I get, I just get a guilty conscience.

T. 46. Well, what do you feel the guilty conscience is saying?

J. 46. Well, what you said, really.

T. 47. Then put it into words.

J. 47. Well, the good school – you know – the good aspect, the large grounds, a school you would not get anywhere else without paying a lot more and having a very comfortable home, really, only some people have nowadays.

T. 48. And what are you making of it all? But this is what conscience says, but I wonder what you yourself feel, whether you don't feel somewhat in opposition to this conscience? Whether you don't feel the good school was because there he was away in the Far East and wanted mother. [T. has been picking on John's conscience, and is suggesting that it may be a focus of conflict for him. cf. T.52.]

J. 48. (Pause) No, well, I know my parents looked for a school and the one I am at now was suggested to them. They had a look round and liked it very much and that was how it was settled.

T. 49. But that you were not consulted.

J. 49. Well, I knew I was going there about, oh, a good six months beforehand and, anyway, you have got to advance from the Junior school to an – an – exam school, where you do the G.C.E.

T. 50. What would have happened, if your parents had not gone to the Far East?

J. 50. I think I would have still gone to the same school, but I don't know whether I would have gone as a boarder or not. (pause) Maybe I would, but being a boarder and having parents living within five miles away or so, doesn't sound so bad, really, than having parents living 5,000 miles away.

T. 51. At present they live 5,000 miles away?

J. 51. Not now, but before when I first went to the school, now they live only 12 miles away near –.

T. 52. But what strikes me very much at the moment is the extent to which you are aware of what conscience says. It seems that conscience is very much modelled on father, it is conscience and father that are talking to you, but much less aware of what you, yourself, are saying to yourself. It seems as if you yourself were saying: I must accept, I must admire, must admire my father for his intellectual abilities his games, my uncles, for their games. I must accept what is being done for me, but I wonder whether this is what, in a way, you yourself do feel? Whether there is not another part of you, which might be feeling rather different? It may well be that this part is having difficulties in expressing itself, just as earlier on today, you were so very silent, as if there was difficulty in expressing your feelings. We knew that you wanted to be good, you wanted to be the good boy, the good patient and therefore, in a sense, we can't be that, but perhaps you were silent because there were other feelings there and I wonder whether the 'you' that wants to express other feelings, perhaps that would not make you into such a good boy, has difficulty in expressing these feelings. And we do not hear enough about this 'you', we hear about what the conscience says, but not what you say, except that you would like to be successful against your father. (long pause) [T. is applying to John the standard psychoanalytic view that the obsessional patient is a person crushed by an overpowering Super-Ego. So he suggests to John that he is father dominated, and yet that he may have other very different feelings about the whole matter. Cf. Freud's view of Lorenz in Chapter 4.]

J. 52. I suppose that is true, yes.

T. 53. But there is a you which has difficulties in expressing itself.

J. 53. Yes, I often find it difficult to express myself.

T. 54. You can express what conscience says, that works quite easily.

J. 54. Yes, I suppose it does.

T. 55. But the 'you' that doesn't want to be always good has difficulties in expressing itself.

J. 55. Yes. (long pause).

T. 56. That has difficulties at this moment to express itself, you are again silent.

J. 56. Yes.

T. 57. What would it like to say? (long pause)

J. 57. Hm, in a way I suppose, it is coming up here, but on the other hand, hm, it's all for my own good. It takes up an awful lot of time, time you can't replace that easily.

T. 58. What you want to say about going to boarding school, that it is an awful bind, great shame to be sent away from home in this sort of way.

J. 58. Yes, but –

T. 59. There must have been, I think, quite strong feelings about being sent to boarding school, especially strong feelings. It seems they made learning for you difficult.

J. 59. Yes that was, at first I thought like that, but –

T. 60. And then you got a bit discouraged.

J. 60. Yes.

T. 61. So the feelings again came up, the feelings of loneliness, of having lost mother, being left in this boarding school while they were 5,000 miles away. It must have felt a long, long way away, impossible to get at, to get in touch with and that this perhaps made it difficult for you to learn.

J. 61. Yes, I always have it on my mind.

T. 62. Perhaps you think a great deal about them.

J. 62. Being practically isolated.

T. 63. You could get in touch with them, really.

J. 63. Yes, I do feel like that.

T. 64. So that part of our work here would be to help you to get back in touch with work, with the things you want to get at. My suggestion is that you wanted to get at your parents, you wanted to get in touch with them, but then they were so very far away, that you

[H. concludes perhaps as follows:]

H. So part of our work here will be to help you to release your feelings, to learn to be genuinely spontaneous, to relax your excessive self-control, and to make you less afraid of making mistakes. In this way we will help you to express yourself more freely and spon-

couldn't, felt that you couldn't. It seems that emotionally you couldn't, my impression is that emotionally you felt that they were even further away than perhaps in reality they were. And that this feeling that they were so far away was a feeling of anger, because you said it was a bind to come here, a feeling of anger of having to come here. A feeling of anger, that they have gone away. To what extent did these feelings prevent you from learning? Or interfere with your learning? It is part of our work here, our work, yours and mine, is to help to bring you back into touch, what you want to learn, what you want to know. Well, yes time is up. [In T.61 and T.64, T. offers John a brief view, based on T.'s Kleino-Freudian orientation, of John's problem and its origin.]

J. 64. (inaudible) I see you tomorrow then, at 5.30.

taneously than you do at present. So that when you are faced with an examination paper, you can express spontaneously on paper and put down what you do really know, something which at present you find very difficult to do. [H. ends in the same sort of way that T. did (T.64), hinting at her explanation of John's difficulties, and at the work that they would, therefore, have to do together in therapy.]

VII

Now this imaginary experiment undoubtedly exudes the warning smell of parody and artificiality. Nevertheless, its point remains: it helps us to free our imaginations and, along with Turquet's Session 2, to draw our attention to some further important features of the analytic situation and 'the material' it produces.

When the man on the omnibus is shown Session 2, or Session 5 (Chapter 5), he may feel like saying, *inter alia*, that John is 'under great pressure' from the analyst. It now seems reasonable to assert that the pressures on John are very great indeed, and that the man on the omnibus has a much stronger case than he realises. The analyst is in a position of great influence over John, largely in virtue of the fact that John is caught up in a situation which encourages verbal reinforcement and learning, which satisfies the placebo conditions, and which works in accordance with the K features. As we have seen, these properties seem to serve as potent agents of change in the direction the analyst, Turquet, is aiming at. When one compares Turquet's Session 2 with Horney's Session 2, it seems reasonable to offer a similar description of the influence that Horney would have exerted on John.

We noted (Chapter 5) that John's responses do not establish the truth of any narrative about himself, but do offer Turquet clues as to how to fit his Kleino-Freudian orientation to John. In doing this, common sense suggests, the clues do give us some reason to believe that they are pointers to the truth; and, hence, that the connected narrative about John may also be an approximation to the truth, and so lend support to the whole Kleino-Freudian orientation, which Turquet uses. But this commonsensical account has to be revised in the light of the way we have seen that Turquet's influence works on John. Turquet starts by giving John his own theoretical orientation and early views about him from the very outset (in Session 2). He does the same thing in Session 5 (Chapter 5); and, in the author's judgement, it is characteristic of his analytic practice throughout the course of the recorded sessions. Because he does this in a situation which appears to function in accordance with the verbal reinforcement and placebo conditions, and the K features (which make for suggestibility and personal change), it follows that what John will do is to give back response clues to Turquet which are progressively influenced by the orientation that Turquet has been giving him. These clues will then guide Turquet in his further theory-fitting and narrative-building. In other words, Turquet *will get back from John* a flux of items which will fit in with his own orientation, and which in turn will help and encourage him to continue to apply it, and to build a related explanatory narrative about John. In the course of all this, John will come to accept the account of himself – about his past and present – that Turquet has been offering him.

Observe, however, that our imaginary experiment suggests that the *same* would be true if John had gone to Horney instead. She would also have obtained from him a flux of items that would have fitted in with her theoretical stand, and helped her to go on applying it and constructing a related explanatory story about John and his difficulties. If she had ignored the limitations of the argument from truth criteria (see Chapter 5), she could have pointed to sequences in her Session 2, which 'confirmed' *her* interpretations about John, just as satisfactorily as sequences in Turquet's Session 2 could be said to have 'confirmed' *his* interpretations. (See the immediate sequels to H.22, 24 and 28.)

The consequence of this is obvious. It means that psychoanalytic method is a tool which gives the analyst some power to obtain support or confirmation for his own theory. It is to some extent a *self-confirmatory procedure*. Now this is a consequence which embodies a complex hypothesis about analytic method; and this has not yet been directly investigated. The support for it is indirect, and is to be found, primarily, in the work about the K features, and the placebo and reinforcement conditions, to which we have already referred. This support is far from conclusive; and it leaves us quite uncertain about the *extent* of the self-confirmatory power that analytic method puts into the hands of the analyst. We do not have a good idea of the conditions that vary and control its strength.

Of course, one thing is clear about this power: it is not unlimited. The analyst cannot do whatever he chooses with the patient. For example, if he tries to treat the anxiety shown by a fifty year old in a crisis of middle age as if it were like the anxiety of a young person, such as Joe or Sue, then very probably the analyst will not get far. He will fail to bring about much therapeutically beneficial change in the patient; the latter may fail to become involved in the therapy, lose heart and bring the analysis to an early end. In short, to suppose that the analyst's power here is unlimited is to overlook that he is dealing with a person, usually a patient, who brings his own unique contribution to the analytic situation, and over whom this situation gives the analyst only a limited influence. In this respect analysis contrasts with what has been called the pathology of psychotherapy, namely, brainwashing. Here the operator's power is very great indeed, and sufficient to make the subject say that black is white, and to accept a totally alien view of himself and the world. The psychological differences between brainwashing and psychoanalysis (as distinct from the moral and socio-political) lie in the fact that with the former the person is a prisoner and cannot escape the operator; and the degree of stress applied is enormous, amounting to torture, and is very far removed from the benign stresses and anxieties of analysis. Nevertheless, even when we allow for these large differences, the fact still remains that there are sufficiently striking psychological similarities between brainwashing and analysis to make the psychological analogy between them a sobering one. Again, analysts do themselves and their subject no good by taking defensive flight away from this unpleasant bit of reality.[15]

Our examination of analytic method has some further implications at this point. One of the puzzling features of the psychodynamic scene, outlined in Chapter 2, is the very existence of different psychodynamic traditions. If the method used by members of these various traditions is one that makes genuine or valid discoveries, how is it that the method seems to generate different and incompatible theories, and is unable, apparently, to settle these mutual differences? What is the explanation of these puzzling facts? Here, again, we have an empirical question, which has not yet been adequately explored and to which no satisfactory answer is forthcoming. It has been suggested, for example, that part of the explanation lies in the fact that the different traditions arose because their practitioners sampled different sorts of patients in different cultures. Freud found himself dealing largely with young persons in sexually disturbed Vienna; Jung with older patients in a different society; and a post-Adlerian like Horney with Americans, very different from the patients in Germany with whom she started her professional life. It is still unclear how sound this suggestion is. But, if it is sound, it seems to have a very awkward consequence, namely, that the theories sketched in Chapter 2 are not universally true. It seems to make psychoanalytic theory true only of a certain class of people, Jungian theory of another class, and so on.

Our imaginary experiment suggests a further partial explanation for the existence of different psychodynamic traditions, namely, that the method of analysis just has the self-confirmatory power we have indicated. When we look at Horney's imaginary Session 2 with John, it is not too difficult to imagine how Horney could have obtained, over the next seventy sessions or so, a record which would have left her assured that *she* had discovered the truth, in part, about John, just as the actual record left Turquet assured that *he* had done so. When, therefore, an analyst puts his theoretical orientation into the analytic situation, he gets back items from the analysand which it is natural for him to regard as supporting his orientation. This suggestion not only helps to explain why analysts do not often present us with interpretations that their material has *disconfirmed*, as well as those it has confirmed (see Chapter 5). It also helps to explain why analytic method is not strong enough to resolve the differences between psychodynamic traditions. Indeed, far from being strong enough for this purpose, it obviously seems conducive to the breeding of differences. Naturally so, for the method assists in obtaining responses from the analysand that support any psychodynamic type of orientation that the analyst chooses idiosyncratically to put into the situation. So the hypothesis helps to explain the existence of different psychodynamic traditions, as well as the schismatic tendency which has been endemic for so long in the psychodynamic world.

VIII

The hypothesis we have been considering – that analytic method is at tool with some self-confirmatory power – has two further logical consequences of great importance.

The enormous virtue of scientific method is that it is self-corrective, and in ways that go to produce a consensus. It follows from the limited, self-confirmatory power of analytic method that it is not a self-corrective procedure in the same way that science is, or in the way that we expect self-correction to work in any rational inquiry. On the other hand, it will be obvious from our examination of L. and of John that there are some close relations between the theoretical orientations used and the flux of items produced by the patient in analysis (cf. below Chapter 7). Since these relations do not appear to allow for self-correction in a straightforward way, it follows that whatever powers of self-correction analytic method does possess, they must be seriously limited at best.

When an analyst takes for granted the validity of his method – that analytic experience is authentic in character – he *ipso facto* also takes it for granted that the facts of human nature are there awaiting discovery, and the method just helps to uncover them. But it follows from the hypothesis of self-confirmation that this assumption is false. It is not true that the method *just* uncovers the facts. For the analyst uses the analytic situation to transform or change the patient, and in such a way that he does fit the theoretical orientation of the analyst, and so gives back items that support this orientation. Turquet changes John so as to make him respond in a way that fits the Kleino-Freudian orientation; as our imaginary experiment shows us plainly, Horney would change him in a way that would make him fit *her* theoretical position. In other words, it is not merely that the analyst views the patient through the spectacles of a certain theoretical perspective (see Chapter 4). It is *also* the case that, by using these spectacles in analysis, the analyst changes the patient so as to fit in with his perspective, and so support it. This means that the method helps to *manufacture* the alleged facts; it does not merely 'discover' or 'uncover' them. It means that, when the analyst presents 'the material' (Chapter 4) of a case, this material is infected with artefacts – which is the inevitable result of the very process of interaction that constitutes the use of psychoanalytic method. We saw earlier (Chapter 5) that what an analysis offers us as 'the material' of a case is dependent on the perspective he uses. It is 'P-dependent', for short. We see now that this material is also dependent to some extent on the method employed. It is 'M-dependent' as well.

The M-dependence of analysis seems to have frightened analysts, so much so that they have virtually tabooed the whole topic, in their attempt to fly from this unpleasant bit of reality. Admittedly, it is a logically awkward consequence for them. It weakens the support that the case material lends to the theory. It weakens still further the analogy they like to stress between their work and that of, say, an archaeologist or historian. Psychoanalysis now seems to be like a method of digging which by its very nature confused the layers of earth and remains, and in such a way that the archaeologist is always uncertain of the extent and character of the confusion. But it is well known that the archaeologist does not use this sort of method. Thus, when doubts were raised about the account Sir Arthur Evans had given of the placing of the tablets at Knossos, students could examine the notebooks of Evans, and his assistant, to try to determine whether he had been in error or not. The doubts raised there do not appear to be intrinsic to the methods of archaeology. Though, naturally, reasonable differences of opinion are possible, it also seems possible in principle to remove the confusions and to settle the question.[16] But analysts are numbed by the dread that to admit that their material is M-dependent in *any* way at all is to make their work *quite* different from that of the archaeologist; it is to destroy *all* support which the case material can lend to the theory, and hence to concede defeat. This dread is unrealistic. After all, there are other disciplines which are also faced by problems arising from M-dependence. For example, in psychology itself it has been found that experimental work is liable to influence the subject so as *to produce* behaviour which confirms the hypothesis in which the experimenter is interested.[17] What M-dependence does, therefore, is to raise further empirical questions about the analytic method. How extensive is this M-dependence? Is it especially connected with the working through of resistances and the transference? Can we allow for it, and make corrections for it? In view of our present ignorance on these matters, pessimistic and optimistic answers are both quite reasonable. There is no need yet for analysts to commit professional hara-kiri.[18]

In this Chapter we have looked at the presupposition of analysts that their method really does enable them to discover the truth about human nature. We have found good reasons to be sceptical of this presupposition. Consequently, we cannot obtain much support for the truth of a narrative about an analysand by appealing to it. The bridge from the intelligibility of a narrative to its truth remains weak, and may now appear even weaker than it did before we started to examine the validity of analytic method.

7 The support from the case material: reconsidered

In the last few chapters we have emphasised what the case material does *not* achieve. But what *does* it achieve? What, if anything, does it do – with all its defects – to support the plausible and exciting-sounding stories we outlined about Joe and Sue (Chapter 2), and about patients such as L. and John? We can try to answer these questions by bringing the case material closer to the stories and theory presented in Chapter 2, and to the narratives about L. and John.

I

Let us recall that what comes to us as case material is unreliable – being an unavoidably defective report by the analyst himself. It does not enable us to establish that any narrative, which it encourages us to construct about a patient, is true. The material is perspective-dependent; and it is self-confirmatory and therefore method-dependent to some degree, and hence artefact-infected. Nevertheless, in spite of these defects, it became clear in the course of our sceptical onslaught on analytic method that the case material did lend *some* support to the psychoanalytic narrative which was spun about a patient, and hence to psychoanalytic theory itself. For the narrative offers an account of the patient, and the material, which makes them intelligible. In so doing it satisfies a necessary condition for its truth. The more difficult it is to provide an alternative, non-psychoanalytic account of the patient's difficulties and the material, the stronger the narrative becomes, and the weightier the support provided for analytic theory. In his reactions to the analyst, the patient regularly offers responses, which we would regard, in ordinary life, as pointers to the truth about himself. In addition, the experience of analysis contains many occasions which, in ordinary life, we would count as authentic – as providing in themselves good evidence for the truth of the insights and understanding achieved.

But this discussion has concentrated on the single, individual patient. What about the collective experience of the analytic profession?

It is orthodox to claim that Freud, and his colleagues, helped to discover that there was a certain type of human disorder, namely the neurotic, recognisably distinct from other types; and that psycho-analysis contributed, therefore, to the development of psychiatry by helping to 'establish' the neuroses as a distinct clinical category (Chapter 1). This achievement has sometimes been highlighted in a well known thesis: what Freud helped to discover was that there are certain disorders, namely the neurotic, in which 'symptoms can have a meaning for the patient'.

Unfortunately, this orthodox and widely accepted claim is vague and misleading, and will not do. If we claim that the neuroses constitute a certain type of disorder, how are we to distinguish this type? There is no generally accepted set of characteristics which pick it out. If we resort to the characteristics suggested by analysts (Chapter 2), then, in effect, we use their own theory of psychopathology or abnormal functioning – a theory which presents an account of what is wrong with the internal psychic system and functioning of the person in neurotic difficulties. But this account is very far from being generally accepted as established (cf. below Chapter 8).

In recent years the orthodox claim has run into further and worse trouble. Psychiatrists and others have undertaken careful clinical ratings and objective and statistical studies of the relevant clinical material. Though the results seem far from conclusive, it is clear that some of the results suggest that neurotic disorders do not constitute 'a type' at all, but lie at one pole or end of a continuum or dimension of differences, with psychotic disorders at the other end. It is not easy to see how we can save the orthodox analytic claim by fitting it to a dimensional account of the neuroses. Since no acceptable way has been found of drawing the line between these two poles, the suggestion has gained currency that the two concepts of neurotic and psychotic should be discarded as useless for theoretical purposes.[1]

Nor is it any good trying to save the claim by maintaining that Freud discovered that 'symptoms can have a meaning in certain disorders'. For this merely amounts to maintaining that, on the strength of case material, which is far from watertight (Chapters 4 and 6), Freud has given us reason for believing that regulative principles 2 and 3 (Chapter 2, Section VII) have application to certain sorts of conduct. This somewhat insecure assertion leaves 'the type' of disorder we are dealing with as vague and uncertain as before.

Still, though the orthodox claim will not do, what does remain – in spite of all the criticism – is that Freud, and others, in the early stage of the history, produced material which helped to persuade contemporary psychiatrists that it *could only be ordered by supposing that* it was the manifestation of a certain distinct type of disorder, namely, the neurotic. This was the reason which led psychiatrists to give to the neuroses a particular accepted and large place in their classification of human disorders. And this is a very important fact in the history of recent psychiatry. What it meant to the subject can be seen at once by looking at, say, Kraepelin's work at the turn of the century, and then comparing it with a later, post-psychoanalytic text in psychiatry.[2]

Moreover, even the most sceptical of contemporaries will still grant that the distinction between neurotic and psychotic disorders is important when it comes to decisions about treatment. This suggests that the distinction is pointing to something very authentic, no matter how we characterise the distinction and describe the differences between these two 'types' of disorders. Since the current classificatory scheme in psychiatry is largely devoid of any adequate foundation – in neurophysiology, biochemistry, and so on – it follows that some current distinctions may turn out to be of fundamental importance. If, for example, Freud's High Level theory is filled out and supported in the future (Chapter 8), then the account analytic theory offers of the distinction (Chapter 2) may turn out to be of great scientific value.

II

It can be argued that the material analysts *collectively* produce supports psychoanalytic theory in a way which resembles, in important respects, the way case material plays a supporting role in much of clinical medicine.

Consider, for example, the work in clinical psychiatry on psychotic depression in the course of this century. If one may boil down some of this history into a nutshell, what happened was this. Psychiatrists accumulated a large and growing amount of clinical experience and related case material. The literature contained reports of cases and runs of cases exhibiting certain features of the condition, and bringing out this or that aspect of the problem. In the course of this work psychiatrists came to distinguish psychotic depression from schizophrenic states; to distinguish between endogenous and reactive depression; to relate symptomatic differences to age differences; to trace the detailed symptomatology of the condition, and so on. This accumulation of material, and discussion about it, led on to the gradual emergence today of a well-filled out, though still incomplete, picture, or view, containing certain internal disagreements about the whole condition. This view picks on certain clinical features for emphasis, offers certain regularities about the condition, and draws attention to the problems it produces. When the medical student goes on his ward rounds, this clinical picture is one of the things he has to learn to recognise – along with the wide spectrum of clinical 'types' the picture embraces. If pressed, a psychiatrist would probably be ready to agree that the case material does, in general, support the current picture of psychotic depression; and that, inadequate though it is, it is nevertheless pointing in the right direction. For it fits or covers much of the material and represents a convenient way of ordering the latter; and it can be used for clinical prediction and prognostication. The material also brings out where the current picture runs into trouble, and that it is difficult at present to think of an alternative way of looking at the whole condition and of ordering the material, which could do the job any better.[3]

In the course of the last seventy years, the argument goes on, psychoanalysts and psychodynamically oriented psychiatrists have accumulated a large amount of case material which stands to analytic theory in a somewhat similar way. This large accumulation of case material exhibits a conglomerate of patterns of human reactivity. Analytic theory reduces this conglomerate to some degree of order by finding in it a variety of regularities and of recurring features of human functioning. The fact that the theory reduces the case material to a considerable degree of order gives us a reason for saying that the collective material analysts produce goes to support the theory. It suggests that the theory may be true, or pointing in the same direction of the truth.

Is is no good the sceptic at this point rejecting the theory on the ground that the concepts it uses to do the ordering cannot be operationally defined. The fact that this is so, and that its concepts are empirically indeterminate in consequence, does *not* mean that the concepts are empirically empty. They are clinically based, and can be elucidated by the clinical means used to teach them (Chapter 4). Moreover, if we do reject analytic theory on this ground, then we would also have to reject much of clinical psychiatry. Thus, the current picture of psychotic depression makes use of concepts such as mood disorder, endogenous and reactive, lack of judgement; and these are not, and probably cannot be, operationally defined either. Nor is it any good the sceptic rejecting analytic theory on the ground that some of the important regularities it finds in human functioning are only vague tendencies. For when we start to explore a new field of phenomena, regularities of this type may be the best we can achieve to begin with; and it may be much better to have *some* regularities at our disposal rather than none at all. Again, moreover, if we reject analytic theory on the ground that it contains tendency regularities, we would also have to reject, for example, the current picture of psychotic depression in psychiatry. For tendency regularities are prominent in this picture too. Thus, we are told, for instance, that depressives tend in their body build to be pyknic or thick set; they are apt to suffer from a lack of judgement about themselves and their situation; they may have delusional ideas; and elevation or depression of mood alternates typically with intervals in which the patient returns to normal. Indeed, statements of tendency regularities are a familiar feature of the whole psychiatric scene.

Nor can the sceptic reject analytic theory on the fashionable ground that no predictions can be obtained from it. The regularities in human functioning, which the collective experience of analysts has found, and which are embodied in the theory, *do* license predictions, even when the regularities are no more than vague tendencies (Chapter 3). And in actual fact, of course, clinical workers in psychiatry and clinical psychology – whether they are analytically oriented or not – are constantly making predictions about patients. It is commonplace to hear from them remarks such as 'I think Mrs. Smith's depression is so serious that she is liable to commit suicide if we let her go home'; and 'John [Turquet's patient] will probably be able to manage some A-level exams next year'. No doubt, inferences and predictions in this field will seldom take the standard forms to be found in science. The prediction usually does not follow deductively from any universal law-like generalisation. Nor does it usually follow from a statistical generalisation, and hence it does not state what the probability is of the patient committing suicide, or of doing satisfactorily next year in examinations. It is the case, rather, that predictive inferences in the psychiatric and analytic fields take, typically, one of the following two, legitimate forms (cf. Chapter 3).

A. (i) Depressive patients with such and such serious features are liable to commit suicide.
    (ii) Mrs. Smith is a depressive with these serious features.
  Therefore,
    (iii) Mrs. Smith is liable to commit suicide.

B. (i) The same as A (i).
    (ii) The same as A (ii).
  Therefore, we have some reason to assert that
    (iii) Mrs. Smith will commit suicide.

Clinical psychiatrists and analysts make predictions of these two types, in particular; and it is these inferences, largely, that serve to justify the clouds of anticipations and expectations, within which psychiatrists and analysts breathe and grope their way in handling their patients.

III

But if we claim that the case material supports analytic theory, then we are claiming that the theory is open to the influence of empirical fact. How does this influence work? It seems clear that the case material does not, and cannot, work by confirming or falsifying hypotheses and related parts of the theory, as is done in the natural sciences (cf. Chapter 3). The relation between them is not anything like as tight as this. Moreover, we have to remember that the case material is also infected by various defects – more especially by the self-confirmatory defect – so that the material is partly artefactual in character. These defects are more serious than those attached to the case material of the non-analytic psychiatrist working on, say, depression. Hence, the support the latter's material provides for *his* theoretical stand is more straightforward, easier to understand and stronger than the support which the analyst's material provides for his. How then does this material influence and help to keep analytic theory under rational control? Does it really do so at all?

These questions plunge us into a region of some darkness – of unexplored and confusing territory. Thus, Freud has told us, in speaking of the sexual seductions of children by adults, that 'he was at last obliged to recognise that these scenes of seduction had never taken place'.[4] But he tells us little, if anything, about the *clinical* considerations that led him to change his mind.[5] When Jung discusses the disagreement between Freud and Adler, he argues that 'this difference can hardly be anything else but a difference of temperament, a contrast between two types of human mentality'.[6] If Jung is correct, then it follows logically that rational considerations do not contribute to this difference between Freud and Adler; and hence that the clinical material is logically irrelevant. Again, we are told by a distinguished British analyst, Glover, that some analysts were rapidly able to discover birth traumas in their patients after Rank had offered his theory, and before this was 'officially exploded'. But Glover does not tell us how Rank was officially and rationally exploded in orthodox analytic circles.[7] Our worry is increased when we see that, elsewhere, Glover also comments adversely on the 'distorting biases fostered by the very conditions of analytic life'[8] – biases that allow the new views by an analyst 'of established prestige and seniority' to have his view 'canonised with the sanctimonious phrase "as so and so has shown" '.[9] In contrast, Ernest Jones, Freud's biographer, appears to have the naive, simple-minded view that clinical material functions for the analyst just like that of observational material for the naturalist in the field. If a view is put forward in analytic work, then it is simply a matter of having it confirmed or disconfirmed by further observation in analysis.[10]

It is undoubtedly the case that the material from patients bears some logical relations to analytic and psychodynamic theories. But it also seems to be the case that the discourse and practice of 'analytic life' have not yet been adequately examined with a view to uncovering the ways in which theory is logically related to the clinical or case material. Accordingly, all we can do here is to offer some tentative and superficial suggestions about the rational considerations of a clinico-factual kind that make the analyst strengthen his views or change them. How logically does the input from the patient work to this end?

Let us consider the situation that is, perhaps, characteristic of the sort of thing that happens in the practice of analysis.

When an analyst is confronted by a patient who appears to him to fit the concepts and generalisations of the accepted theory at the time, which he is using, then he will probably be in no difficulty. The contribution from the patient will go to constitute another case, which supports the accepted, and his own, theoretical stand. But suppose he takes on a patient who presents him with a contribution which he finds a little difficult to bring within his own and the accepted analytic theory. There seems to him to be something a bit anomalous about the patient, so that he has some difficulty in building up an orthodox analytic narrative about him or her.

What does the analyst do in this situation? He may choose to ignore, or to try to explain away, or in some way to depreciate the anomaly he experiences. On the other hand, he may choose to face up to the felt anomaly or incongruity. His inclination to face up to it will be strengthened, no doubt, if several of his patients produce the same felt anomaly, or if a colleague expresses similar discomfort. A point may then be reached when he can put up with the increasing discomfort no longer; and he acknowledges to himself that there is something 'wrong' with the accepted theory. He may then branch out and describe these patients in a new way, which involves a modification of the accepted view, but which accommodates the anomaly and so removes his discomfort, and which satisfies him intellectually. He then presents his views in a paper or two in some of the analytic journals. His modification of the accepted view may strike a chord, it may 'ring bells', for other analysts who had felt a similar anomaly, but who had not yet got to the point of admitting to themselves that there was something 'wrong' with the accepted view of these patients. These other analysts may then take up the new formulation, appreciate its theoretical advantages, and produce supporting papers or comments at meetings and conferences. The new formulation may, or may not, 'catch on' widely in the analytic community, nationally or internationally; but at least it will then be 'on the map' as a respectable formulation, which all analysts have to take note of, even if they do not accept it themselves.

Consider an example of this sort of change. For many years the accepted or classical view of depression was based closely on Freud's view in his essay on *Mourning and Melancholia*. On this view, when a person was depressed, what had happened was that his relations with a loved object had been undermined and the loved object lost. The person's Ego then identified with the lost object, which meant that the Ego was diminished, and the person suffered a loss of self-esteem. The unconscious reproaches directed towards the lost loved one are turned against the person's own self; and this may develop into self-hatred and self-destructive and aggressive tendencies. On this classical view, therefore, the self-reproaches of the depressed person or patient were seen as an attack on the person's own self, as identified with the lost objects.

However, the analyst Bibring[11] came to experience anomaly in respect of the classical account – an anomaly which he acknowledged and tried to deal with by modifying the account. According to Bibring, what happens basically in depression is that the Ego is shocked by something – actual, imaginary or symbolic – into an awareness that it is helpless to realise its aspirations. This results in a partial or complete loss of self-esteem, with a more or less intensive and extensive inhibition of function; and under some conditions aggression is then secondarily directed against the self (as in the cases described by the classical view above). Bibring claims that his account covers 'the core of normal, neurotic and probably also psychotic depression'. And, what is important for us, on this view the self-reproaches of (say) the neurotic depressive are not necessarily seen as an attack, or aggression, against the self; but as revealing a loss of self-esteem.

Now this departure by Bibring from the classical story was accepted as respectable, and to a number of analysts it proved a helpful modification of the earlier classical position. But it was not universally accepted. For example, Kleinians did not accept it, and would not consider doing so. For on their view adult depression involves a reactivation of the stage of infantile depression. This means that the adult feels menaced and persecuted. So the self-reproaches of the depressive are seen as, in part, a manifestation of persecutory impulses directed against the self. They would not be seen by Kleinians as evidence, in the first instance, of a loss of self-esteem.[12]

Well, then, if this is characteristic of the sort of way in which the contribution from the patient helps to change analytic theory, what exactly is going on? Can we say anything further about it which is helpful? Some analysts and others may be tempted to use the language

Thomas S. Kuhn has developed for the description of change in science, and to say that what happens here is that the accepted paradigm ran into an anomaly. Analysts put up with this for a time, until it became unacceptable, and then a new formulation and paradigm took the place of the old.[13]

The temptation to talk and think Kuhn-wise has to be resisted. A Bibring-type of situation is very different indeed from that of paradigmatic change, which Kuhn has described for science. When a new paradigm emerges in science, it is, by definition, generally accepted by the scientific community in place of the old. This is not what necessarily happens in the Bibring-type situation. Moreover, the anomaly in science is open to public observation and corroboration. The anomaly that Bibring reported is to be found in his case material, which is not open to public observation and corroboration. Though Bibring reacts to the contribution from the patient as anomalous, other analysts may not do so, and they cannot be faulted rationally for not following in his footsteps. It is open to them to argue, for example, that Bibring, and those who think like him, are misreading the patients' contributions, and are taking a narrow and non-developmental view of the whole matter.

Still, there is *something* to be said for comparing the Bibring type of situation with paradigmatic change in science. It draws our attention to the fact that the development of science appears to contain two interweaving strands: the psycho-social and the rational. For a paradigm to be replaced by a new one, certain members of the scientific community must react to felt incongruity or anomaly; and the new formulation they suggest for dealing with the anomaly must be generally accepted in the scientific community. But all this is only possible in virtue of the fact that the members of the community are controlled by canons of rationality sufficiently binding or strong to ensure a general consensus.

The history and development of psychoanalysis also appears to contain these same two interweaving strands – the psycho-social and the rational. The chief difference seems to be that in the analytic community their relative weights are very unlike what they are in the scientific. In particular, the rational is much weaker – a weakness which shows itself in various ways (see Section IV below). But the fact that the rational strand is relatively weak must not mislead us into supposing that it does not exist at all. At present, however, we do not know much about the ways in which the two strands interweave and interrelate in the analytic community. What we need – to remove our ignorance – is for students, armed with the noses of social anthropologists and the ears of philosophical logicians, to live with the analytic community, to explore the logic of their working discourse, and so to display the interweaving of the two strands for all the world to see.

IV

The Bibring example is only *one* sort of way in which rational considerations of a clinico-factual kind bear on analytic theory. There are other ways in which they do so.

(*a*) Analysts may take on patients of a familiar type, but who present features which it is generally agreed had not been previously noted, and which constitute good reasons for amending the theory. An example of this seems to be the case material that made Freud and others extend their view of the obsessional to allow for the anal-sadistic side of his make up and problem.[14]

(*b*) Analysts, like scientific workers, are eager 'to do research' and 'to make a contribution' – especially if they are still young and enthusiastic. If one of them is confronted by what seems to him to be novel input from a patient, or develops a hunch that some aspect of personal functioning and dynamics has been overlooked or misrepresented in the accepted theory, then he is likely to emphasise the novelty, and to feed his own hunch into the analysis. He is then likely (Chapter 6) to get back input from the patient which he, and his colleagues, will regard as support for a new point of view about this aspect of human functioning. Though this new case material which he presents is infected by the self-confirmatory artefact, nevertheless the patient does make a contribution to the material; and this does therefore supply *some* reason to support the modified and new point of view that the analyst has suggested. But without further and usually unobtainable information, we do not know how strong this reason really is.

This defect of analytic method is, of course, one of the reasons why it is difficult to make up one's mind about any particular instance of the Bibring-type of situation. The more the method is artefact-producing, the more influential is the psycho-social strand in the whole situation, and the less influential is the rational. It is this defect of the method, perhaps, that also helps to account for the facts mentioned by Glover about the influence of Rank. After the publication of Rank's work, a number of analysts were influenced, perhaps, by his work in ways that led them to generate material (cf. Chapter 6) which supported the theory about the trauma of birth. Then they came to hear about Rank's strange activities and sad history; and to appreciate also the theoretical difficulties in his theory. In consequence, they ceased to be influenced by him in their work, and in turn ceased to affect their own patients and case material in ways which made this support Rank's theory.

In recent decades, however, the sort of situation in which the enthusiastic analyst makes a quite 'novel' contribution has become less frequent and important. The reason is that analytic method – and its cognates – have long reached the stage of sharply diminishing returns. By now the method seems to have explored most of the territory that it is able to cover, and there is not much still left to be uncovered. Consequently, the young and enthusiastic analyst is unlikely to find much new turning up, which will give him a ground for revising accepted theory. It is this feature of analytic method which contributes, no doubt, to the impression of intellectual fatigue and decay which, in general, the psychoanalytic journals present to the world.

(c) But, of course, when an analyst first employs some new form of psychoanalytic *method*, he is likely to obtain novel input from patients. Thus, Klein argued that the free play of young children was functionally equivalent to the free verbal association of adults, and could be interpreted psychoanalytically. Accordingly, she proceeded to analyse young children, and she and her co-workers obtained a great deal of new material in this way. This provided a ground for a considerable revision of analytic theory. But this ground was far from conclusive, partly because her extension of analytic method raised serious doubts about its validity (for example, the suggestibility of small children is notorious).

Klein's modification of analytic method, like any other, points to a very serious limitation in analytic theory and practice. When analysts are confronted by some 'novel finding' – some new case material – they are quite unclear whether to say that in this instance (i) the analyst reporting the finding has misapplied psychoanalytic method, and therefore the theory does *not* need to be amended to accommodate the alleged 'new material'; or (ii) the analyst has applied the method correctly, and therefore the theory *has* to be amended to allow for the 'new case material'. So when an analyst 'imposes' the accepted theory on the 'novel' input, is he doing the right or the wrong thing? When some new analytic ideas are 'exploded', does this simply represent the political victory inside the analytic community of one analytic tradition? Or is it much more and other than this? The fact that analysts are quite unclear on this fundamental matter leaves us all uncertain about the weight to be attached to novel material, as a ground for the revision of analytic theory.

(d) The input from patients may remain much the same, but the analyst comes to see it in a new way. He develops the view that it can be better organised and explained by modifying the theory. This is what

Freud seems to have done on several occasions – for example, and notably, in his emphasis on Narcissism, his development of the Structural story, and his revision of the Instinct theory.

But an analyst cannot modify the theory in any way that his freely floating fancy takes him. On the contrary, he is subject to some severe constraints. His modification of the analytic position must be such as to contribute to building a 'better' theory – just as it would have to do in any other field of rational inquiry. Then his modification has to fall within the bounds set by the regulative principles common to all psychodynamic theories; and it has to be congruent with the state and drift of contemporary science. The latter constraint is obviously vaguer and more flexible than the former. Nevertheless, its influence on the thinking of analysts is very great; and helps to determine their attitude to Freud's original story, conceived as this was in a scientific climate very different from the one we are in today.

Still, it seems fairly clear that the rational considerations which refer to the case material alone are not anything like strong enough to settle these theoretical debates among analysts. So it is not by reference to further case material that an orthodox Ego-Freudian will be able to convince a Kleinian, or a traditional Freudian, that he is right and they are wrong. Indeed, it is not clear that there are *any* rational means of doing so which are available at the present time. But, of course, this does not mean that there are *no* rational considerations available in terms of which the competing theories can be discussed and assessed (Chapter 10); or that no rational grounds will *ever* be found which are strong enough to settle these theoretical differences (Chapter 8).

We have now looked at some tentative suggestions about the ways in which the empirical facts of the patient's conduct are logically related to analytic theory – ways that show how the facts and case material do lend some support to the theory, and ways that also show how the theory is open to influence and control by them. The facts are obtained in ways that make the corresponding case material seriously defective; and the ways they influence and control the theory are not anything like as tight as we should wish. Nevertheless, the ways in which the facts are related to the theory do serve to bring out how the theory is *not* a closed story like a pre-scientific myth (Chapter 3), but a theory that is open to development and modification in the light of rational considerations about it.

V

So the case material, in spite of its defects, does lend some support to analytic theory. But the latter is a complex affair, with Low and High

Level parts and accompanying regulative principles. Does the large accumulation of case material – with its conglomerate of patterns of human functioning – support *all* parts and sides of analytic theory equally well? Or does it support *some* better than others?

There is no simple and easy answer to this question. What does seem clear, however, is that the conglomerate of regularities and features contained in the case material does little to support the high level generalisations with their theoretical concepts. The reason is obvious. Turquet and his colleagues may have collected much case material about adolescent under-achievers with obsessional difficulties like John. The regularities displayed by family upbringing and learning experience in these cases may be glaringly obvious to the clinical eye. But they do little to constrain us in our choice of higher level concepts and generalisations to explain them. It is open to an analyst to explain them in terms of mental machinery powered by certain instincts, containing certain mental elements charged in certain ways and kept out of consciousness by repression, and so on and on (as per Chapter 2). But it is also open to a Kleino-Freudian to explain these regularities by means of unconscious fantasies and part and lost objects, etc. And it is open to Karen Horney to adopt yet a different explanation. Because the case material does little to constrain us here, it obviously also does little to support the high level generalisations and concepts of analytic theory.

What support does the case material offer to the low level generalisations? An instance of case material consists of a narrative containing, in essential part, reports of the patient's difficulties, his personal history and his (apparent) psychodynamics. These case reports, let us remember, collectively present a mass of recurring patterns of human functioning, and the low level generalisations and concepts of analytic theory are attempts to extract some degree of order and regularity from this mass of material. So the low level generalisations and concepts are, to a large extent, just a way of summing up and describing the regularities that the case material appears to have uncovered. These generalisations and concepts are 'close to' the case material, and it may be difficult to think of other ways of extracting and stating the regularities contained in it. Naturally, therefore, the material lends considerable support to these generalisations and concepts.

Consider a tiny sample – from those about obsessional patients. The material lends support to generalisations such as the following:

Compulsion neurotics are generally and obviously concerned about conflicts between aggressiveness and submissiveness, cruelty and gentleness, dirtiness and cleanliness, disorder and order.

It is constantly found in such patients that they have overt or concealed tendencies towards cruelty, or reaction formations against them.[15]

These patients are in fundamental conflict between hating the parental figures and fear of giving way to this hatred.

These patients have a very severe over-developed conscience, which is used to punish the person into developing a very great degree of scrupulousness and sense of guilt.[16]

These generalisations are illustrated in the case material of the patients L. and John (Chapters 4, 5 and 6). The case material from depressives, like our hypothetical patient Joe (Chapter 2), illustrates related generalisations; and the same is true of the mass of other standard cases reported by analysts.

Unfortunately, there is not much point in merely listing further examples of such generalisations here. For unless we also go on to offer some information about the case material on which the generalisations are based, the examples we offer are likely to sound quite unfounded and even absurd. Nor can we even run out, or point to, a list of these generalisations. For there is no agreed store or textbook containing them, because analysts do not all agree on what exactly comes out of the case material, and how precisely to formulate what it has revealed. This is quite understandable, because, naturally, there are different ways of extracting and formulating regularities from the case material – just as there are in clinical medicine. The only way for the student to find out about the general regularities, which the case material of analysis does illustrate and support, is for him to get as close to the material as he can, and to familiarise himself with it (cf. Chapter 4, II).

Is the support from the case material equally good for the low level generalisations from *all* sections of analytic theory? Or is it stronger for those from (say) the theory of Pathology than it is from the theory of Development and the Mechanisms of Defence? These questions raise difficult matters of assessment, and the answers seem quite uncertain. An orthodox psychoanalyst – such as Fenichel – would claim, no doubt, that the case support *is* equally good right across the board. Other analysts within the Freudian tradition would be more cautious. They would probably agree, for example, that the support is not good for generalisations about biologically fixed stages of libidinal development, about the genital character of the Oedipal period, and about adult neurotic difficulties always representing a revival of the child's early sexual difficulties (Chapter 2). They would probably suggest that these generalisations of the theory were premature, having been based on too narrow a range of patients. On the other hand, they would agree, probably, that the case material does lend good support to generalisations and concepts (a) which emphasise the links between the patient's relations as a child to the parents and his later adult personality and difficulties; and (b) which emphasise the role of the Mechanisms of Defence, and their connections with patterns of psychological make up. But we cannot say with much confidence what *comparative* support the case material gives to the various parts of analytic theory. There is no established consensus on this question.

However, when we concentrate on the generalisations and concepts to which – on a fairly wide consensus – the case material *does* lend good support, we seem forced to recognise something else about them, which is of considerable moment. It does seem to be the case that they *are* pointing to something pervasive and important about human functioning. It is difficult to avoid the impression that, in these generalisations, analysts are trying to formulate something very genuine about human nature, something authentic, which an adequate psychology of the future will have to incorporate in some way and form. And this is a feature of the psychoanalytic achievement that any short exposition of the theory (as in Chapter 2) is apt to make us overlook, and which the man on the Clapham omnibus is also likely to miss.

VI

We have been concentrating on psychoanalytic theory, and the support – with all its limitations – that the case material lends to it. But what of the *other* psychodynamic theories – some of which were mentioned in Chapter 2? Does the case material of these psychodynamic therapists lend support to their theories? If so, what are the implications of this fact for psychoanalytic theory?

It is clear that what is sauce for the goose of Freud is sauce for the ganders of Jung, Adler, and the rest. It is only a matter of industry to show that the case material of these other workers stands to *their* theories in the same sort of logical relation as the case material of analysts stands to analytic theory. Of course, this fact would be of little importance if the other theories and analytic theory were *merely* different ways of speaking about the input from patients, or about the case material which all workers report. For then it would follow that any one theory could be mapped into every other (that is, they would all be mutually isomorphic). They would all, therefore, be saying *the same thing*; and the differences between them would only be locutional in character. Now, though *some* of the differences between these theories are, no doubt, of this locutional sort, it is quite clear that the *major* differences are ones of substance. These theories are mutually inconsistent at critical places, and cannot be mapped into one another. Freud's theory of development is not Adler's; Jung's view of the Libido and the Unconscious is not Freud's; Klein's view of infantile development is not Freud's; and so on. Therefore it *does* matter that the case material of these other workers bears to their theories the *same sort* of logical relation that it bears to psychoanalytic theory. It means that the most the case material does for these other theories is to lend to them the same sort and degree of suggestive support it lends to psychoanalytic theory. It is difficult to find any good ground which would justify us in saying that, whereas the case material psychoanalysts obtain does suggestively support psychoanalytic theory, the case material which other psychodynamic workers obtain (for example, Jungians) does not support their theories of human functioning equally well.

But what is the relation between the different theories, and between them and the realities of human nature? Can we say anything about all this? Though the method used by psychodynamic workers is not strong enough to settle the conflicts between these different theories, though the case material of psychoanalysts does not enable us to determine what is *really* the truth about the development and make-up of, for example, Joe and Sue (Chapter 2), does the material allow us to say anything?

It seems to allow us to say one thing at least. In the last Chapter we offered a partial explanation for the production of the different collections of case material, with their related theories. This partial explanation plus our analysis in this Chapter do jointly hint at a further, and quite fundamental, relation between the theories in the whole field of psychodynamics.

It seems reasonable to suppose that these different theories are jointly pointing towards some more fundamental psychological reality, which lies behind the various doctrines and the use of analytic method in all its variations. A psychodynamic therapist is armed with his own doctrine, and variety of analytic method, and deals primarily, perhaps, with certain types of patients. In interacting with his patients, he produces a certain sort of case material, which supports a certain theory to account for the material. Another psychodynamic therapist differently armed and so on, gets back from his patients a somewhat different sort of case material, which supports another theory. This all suggests that *no one* theory embodies the reasonably complete and definitive truth about the case material. This has to be found, presumably, in an account of human functioning that is *generic* to all current psychoanalytic and dynamic doctrines, and which may or may not itself be psychodynamic in character. If we possessed this generic story, and if we had reasonably definitive knowledge about the way in which analytic method worked, then we could explain the emergence of different types of case material, and not just speculate about it (as we did in Chapter 6). We could then exhibit the truth that each doctrine contains. We could then go on to fit together these different doctrines inside a more embracing and fundamental account about human functioning, and thereby exhibit the respective contributions that each makes to the truth about human nature.

But, of course, we do not possess this generic story at the present time, and so we cannot safely describe the fundamental reality about human personality that may be lying behind the various theories. If we are to move along the road towards such a generic or fundamental account, there is one thing we will need to know. We will need to know how to discount, or allow for, the very serious limitations of analytic method and the case material, which we have described above (Chapters 4 to 6). We will have to know how to make good the unreliability of the method, how to transcend its perspectival limitation, and its artefactual infections, and so on. We cannot discount these limitations at the present time, because we lack the knowledge about human interaction which would permit us to tell with reasonable confidence what analytic method really does, and does not, discover about the analysand. Of course, we can find hints in the corpus of scientific knowledge about personality and about personal interaction – hints about the directions to look for the fundamental or generic account we require. But psychologists would generally agree that these hints may not all be reliable, and do not constitute the corpus of knowledge which we need.

In Chapter 2 we saw that these different analytic and psychodynamic doctrines also have something in common. They all go along with the use of certain Regulative principles, namely, psychic determinism, the importance of purposive and unconscious functioning, and the importance of early experience. Our supposition – that these different doctrines, psychoanalytic and dynamic, are pointing jointly to some underlying psychological reality – is further supported by the fact that the case material of all workers also goes to support the Regulative principles they employ, with one qualification.

The qualification concerns the principle of psychic determinism. Analysts usually state this as: 'No item in mental life, etc. is accidental, but is the outcome of antecedents', or in some similar way. This formulation is vague; it appears to amount to the well-known and quite general principle of determinism; and on this formulation it is not clear how the case material is supposed to support the principle. In practice, however, analysts seem to use the principle in a *narrower* sense, where it amounts to the regulation that analysts and psychodynamic therapists should always be on the look out for the hidden motive or wish, or what not, 'behind' and determining every (apparently) random or psychologically accidental mental item, piece of behaviour, and so on. But in this sense the principle seems to become just an aspect of two other Regulative principles – those which direct the analyst's attention to the purposive and unconscious character of human functioning (numbers Two and Three, Chapter 2).

With this one qualification, we can say that the case material of the various psychodynamic traditions does seem to lend support to the regulative principles. Admittedly, when a psychodynamic therapist puts them to work, he does so in the context of analytic and psychodynamic methods. The former is defective (Chapters 4, 5 and 6); and in so far as the methods of all traditions resemble the analytic, they will have similar defects. Still, even allowing for these defects, we are forced to recognise that the themes picked out by the principles are recurrent and prominent features of the material. If we attempt to unify the latter within the compass of a single description, we can hardly avoid giving a conspicuous place to these themes in our description of it. This can be glimpsed by looking at the material of L., and at the extracts from the records of John. So the total impact of the material does strongly suggest that the principles are important and valuable rules to follow.

What, then, in a nutshell does the case material achieve? We have explained that it is defective as evidence. This means that whatever support we may claim it lends to psychoanalytic theory, High or Low, and to the Regulative principles, this support is very limited and far from conclusive. However, in spite of its defects, the material does seem to point to a large core of something authentic about human nature – about patterns of connection between past and present, of ways we deal with our difficulties, and of psychological make up with related motives and functioning. The concepts and generalisations of analytic theory, in their Low Level role, are an attempt to order this core of apparent authenticity. Hence, the case material suggests that the Low Level theory of analysis is pointing in some degree to the truth. Along with other psychodynamic theories and related material, it also seems to be pointing to some further, more generic or fundamental psychological truth about human nature, by reference to which we may be able to unify the theories of the various dynamic traditions, and delineate the truth they may each really contain. So the case material of the analyst has this suggestive force.

We may be inclined to think that this is a very small mouse to emerge from the mountain of case material that has been collected and discussed. But whether it is a mouse, or some much larger animal depends on its importance. And this raises other and further issues. Analysts, on the other hand, may want to reject this conclusion as too mean or deflationary in character. But they would do well to reflect that it is hardly a surprising conclusion. It flows naturally from the defects of their theories and method; and it is, perhaps, a conclusion which is, or is close to, the view about the analytic material that a sceptical and sympathetic psychiatrist would be ready to accept.

8   The support from scientific inquiry

I

We have now seen that the case material of analysis only provides poor support to the low level generalisations of the theory; that the validity of psychoanalysis as a method of discovery is very uncertain; and that the case material provides poor support for the interpretative remarks offered to the analysand – remarks around which the analyst develops his explanatory narrative. But are the case material and the reactions of the analysand the *only* sources of support for psychoanalytic theory? Is it not possible that, if we were to investigate analytic generalisations of the Low Level type, and the suggestions in the High Level theory, by methods that are independent of analytic material, we might obtain evidence that could be said to support them, or to go against them – to confirm or disconfirm them? We have also seen that, when an interpretation *p* is offered John in S.2 or S.5, or elsewhere, *p* does not function as a hypothesis; and the reactions of John to *p* cannot be safely construed as a confirmation or disconfirmation of *p* (Chapter 5). But if Turquet were to utter *p* *outside* the analytic situation, in, say, a case conference about John, it is clear that, in *this* context, *p* could and very probably would function as a hypothesis. Is it not possible for us to find support, or lack of it, for *p* in ways that are independent of the analytic situation and material?

The answer is: yes, it is possible to find evidence which bears on the truth or adequacy of analytic theory, and which is independent of the case material and analytic method. Indeed, the fact is that ever since the 1920s attempts have been under way to obtain just such evidence. Most of these are to be found in the inquiries made by psychologists using methods generally accepted as scientific. Some attempts have also been made to obtain evidence from communities other than the Westernised ones, which have supplied the case material on which analytic theory has been almost wholly constructed.[1]

In the early 1930s, a psychologist by the name of Rosenzweig did some experimental work, which he claimed was about the concept of repression. He sent an account of this work to Freud, who replied as follows.[2]

My dear Sir,

I have examined your experimental studies for the verification of the psychoanalytic assertions with interest. I cannot put much value on these confirmations because the wealth of reliable observations on which these assertions rest make them independent of experimental verification. Still, it can do no harm.

Sincerely yours,
Freud.

Now it is generally accepted today that Rosenzweig was mistaken in claiming that his experimental work studied the analytic concept of repression. But Freud did not dismiss Rosenzweig's work for *this* reason. He dismissed it by saying he could not put much value on it, 'because the wealth of reliable observations on which these [psychoanalytic] assertions rest make them independent of experimental verification'. In saying this Freud was wholly mistaken. 'Reliable observations' are the one thing on which psychoanalytic assertions or generalisations *cannot* be said to rest (cf. Chapters 4 and 6). Of course, it was all too natural for him to claim that analysts were already fully warranted in making these psychoanalytic assertions – without having to wait for experimental inquiry to establish them. But it is most unwise for others to follow Freud's example here and speak as he did. For in reality the generalisations of analysis are so vague, and of such uncertain weight and status, that we are well advised to seek all the evidence we can to clarify their standing. It is very necessary, therefore, that we consider the large body of non-clinical inquiry, which has accumulated since the 1920s, into the worth of psychoanalytic generalisations. It is also necessary to bear in mind the state of play in the sciences in fields that bear on analysis.

All this is no easy task. Since the relevant scientific studies run into the hundreds, the most that can be done is to offer a quasi-judicial assessment of the state of the evidence from science – illustrated by some examples of the studies that have been made. Being an assessment, it is naturally a personal one, and leaves much room for discussion and difference of opinion. In its structure it will follow closely the order of the exposition which was given of the theory in Chapter 2.

II

Is the mind of the infant Joe (or Sue) powered by two fundamental or basic instincts – Death and Eros?

The notion of the Death instinct runs into two immediate objections. To say that an organism has an instinct is to say (it can be argued) that the organism has a capacity, or power, to react in certain ways that contribute to the survival of the organism or the species. But since the goal of the Death instinct is the cessation of all excitation in the death of the individual, it is not aimed at helping the individual to survive, and it appears to have no relevance to the survival of the human species. Hence, the very dichotomy between the Death and the Life instincts seems to be incoherent. Moreover, it is unclear what a psychobiologist could logically do to confirm or disconfirm the claim that we are driven by the Death instinct. Therefore, it is doubtful if this claim is really what it purports to be, namely, a claim about fact.[3]

What is even more serious, this whole theory of instinct has been overtaken by the development of science. It is evident that the theory embodies a late nineteenth- and early twentieth-century view of this matter – a view according to which it is useful to draw the distinction between what is innate and what is acquired or learned. Today it would be widely accepted that this view is simple-minded and will not do. The organism and its world are in continuous interaction of such a sort that it is unhelpful and misleading to try to impose upon the organism any simple distinction between the innate and the acquired.[4]

But suppose we waive this objection and adopt a current fashion by restating the Death instinct to mean merely an impulse to destroy and to be aggressive. At once we face another objection. Analytic theory now leaves it quite unclear what is to count as the manifestation of an instinct. Suppose we try to fill out the theory at this point by adopting as criteria of the instinctive some suggestions which flow from certain scientific discussions in recent years, and which we will formulate roughly. Suppose we adopt the following as a guide. For an instance of behaviour to be a manifestation of an instinct, it must: (1) exhibit a recognisable pattern which is the same for all members of the human species; (2) appear at certain stages or periods in the development of the human organism, in spite of wide differences in environmental conditions; (3) happen after the presentation of a certain recognisable pattern of input or stimuli – a pattern which appears 'to release' the behaviour.[5] It is difficult to discover *any* pattern of behaviour of a destructive or aggressive type, which can be said to satisfy these criteria of the instinctive. Human suicide, human warfare, or the self-destructive stupidity of Afrikaans–speaking whites in South Africa satisfies none of the criteria listed. Each of these examples is, prima facie, the outcome of an extraordinarily complex interaction of conditions which are only partially understood, and to which, no doubt, the original biological equipment and powers of the human organism make a contribution. To explain these phenomena as manifestations of the destructive or aggressive instinct would be to say something very vague and explain nothing.

Much more plausible candidates for aggression and destructiveness, and ones which analysts do emphasise, are the biting, slapping and 'rage' behaviour of the infant after a few months at the breast. However, it is quite clear that not *all* infants exhibit this behaviour. But even if we concentrate on those that do, we have no evidence that, at this stage, the infant can form any intentions at all. Hence it cannot intend its biting, hitting and 'rage' to be destructive or aggressive. This behaviour is, at most, a piece of animal-like behaviour which serves other purposes. For example, biting to ease its gums made tender by developing teeth, arm-thrashing to explore its immediate world and exercise its growing muscles, 'rage' when it is upset by its feeding regime. So, even if these behaviours by the infant were to satisfy the three criteria listed, this fact would be insufficient to show that they are manifestations of some one identifiable inner power or force. Of course, infants are purposively behaving organisms, and so exhibit a variety of tendencies in the course of which they strive to do or to achieve this or that. But to describe these tendencies as in themselves manifestations of an aggressive instinct is utterly misleading, for reasons which should now be clear.[6]

However it is open to neuropsychologists to discover that we do possess some cortical or sub-cortical centre, which, when suitably stimulated by implanted electrodes, or when damped down by pharmacological agents, will interrupt or stop all destructive and aggressive behaviour. But such a discovery would only establish that the normal functioning of this centre appears to be necessary for this very varied and highly flexible type of behaviour. If we were to discover that the infant's so-called destructive and aggressive behaviours were dependent on some brain-centre, this discovery would be quite compatible with the *further* discovery that such behaviours in the *adult* are largely and critically dependent on the experience of frustration and the acquisition of cortical connections, which then potentiate our wide variety of destructive and aggressive manifestations.

So the claim that little Joe (or Sue) is powered by a destructive and aggressive instinct is a feeble one. The available scientific evidence fails to establish this claim with reasonable assurance. It is worth noting, in passing, that the psychoanalytic world in general never accepted the Death instinct. The widely accepted analytic stance on the latter is, perhaps, close to Freud's early view, namely that this conduct is the result of interfering with the child's libidinal impulses anally or Oedipally. The chief Freudian group which has accepted Freud's later view is the Kleinian.[7]

What of the instinct of self-preservation? It is clear that the infant is built so as to preserve its integrity as an organism with the aid of a variety of homeostatic devices, and it is predisposed to learn defensive behaviours to deal with a variety of noxious stimuli. But these self-preservative behaviours are different from one another, thereby failing to satisfy criterion (1) (page 150); and a variety of different neurochemical mechanisms are responsible for them. No doubt it may be helpful for some purposes to classify them all together as reactions that are inbuilt and preservative in function, but this description does not explain them. Moreover, to go on to describe them as 'instinctive' is to suggest, in this context, that they are all the manifestations of one identifiable type of machinery and energy source. We have no good reason to believe that this is the case.[8]

It is important to note, however, that, in the course of the last few decades, students of animal behaviour seem to have uncovered certain patterns of behaviour, which satisfy the natural criteria for an instinct which we have suggested, and which are of importance for analytic theory and practice. These make up what is known as Attachment behaviour. The infant monkey, for example, exhibits recognisable patterns of Attachment behaviour to the mother or mother surrogate; and these patterns clearly satisfy the suggested criteria. Thus, for example, the infant will cling fiercely to the mother, or to a surrogate mother consisting of a cloth-covered wire frame; and if the mother is herself incapable of mothering, and punishes the infant when it approaches her, the infant will go on trying to attach itself. Moreover, it has also been found that, when the female infant is inadequately mothered and the Attachment behaviour of the infant suffers interference, she in turn, when she becomes an adult mother, will reject the Attachment approaches of her own infant. It seems clear that this Attachment behaviour is of survival value both to the individual monkey and also to the species.[9]

Is there anything similar at work in little Joe and Sue? If there is, then the mother is not only, or even primarily, the supplier of oral gratifications, and analytic theory needs to be supplemented and corrected. The position at present is inconclusive. There is no evidence of a hard-headed, experimental sort – because of the moral objections to such work on humans. The evidence is to be found in observational studies of mothers and of infants in families and in institutions. This evidence is suggestive, and coupled with the obvious analogy between human and primate behaviours, the upshot is impressive. It may well be that the human neonate releases bonding behaviour from the mother; and that she in turn serves, at the sensitive times in the development of the infant, to release pre-programmed Attachment behaviours from the infant. But, suggestive and attractive though this story may be, it has not yet been reasonably established.[10]

III

What, now of the (alleged) sexual instinct which, according to analytic theory, plays such a large part in the development and life of Joe and Sue? Here we move into muddied waters.

We have to ask at the start: is it the case that Joe (and Sue) exhibit activity which at first focuses on the body zone of the mouth, next on the anus (and sphincters) and then on the penis (or clitoris)? There is some evidence to suggest that this, or something very like it, is indeed the case. Some years ago careful naturalistic observation of children over the early years revealed that there was such a progression of activity – though Sue's genital interest did not reveal itself as specifically clitoral in direction.[11] But does this activity reveal itself in recognisable patterns which are impervious to environmental variations and which are triggered by releasing stimuli? It is very doubtful. Still, let us pass this difficulty; and let us suppose that further more careful observation will show that this activity by the infant is a manifestation of instinctive behaviour on the criteria we are using.

Is analytic theory right to claim that it is a manifestation of the *sexual* instinct? Well, obviously it is not *only* the manifestation of this instinct, and analytic theory does not make this claim. What the theory claims is that this activity is *also* the manifestation of the sexual instinct. Thus, the infant is driven by self-preservative impulses to suck at the breast. But in doing so the infant is *also* driven by his sexual instinct to obtain erotic pleasure from sucking. He is driven in the same way to obtain erotic pleasure in defecating and urinating, and in playing with his (her) genitals.

There is some scientific evidence to support part of this claim. Studies have been made into the relations between the feeding times of infants, the amounts of thumb-sucking, and weaning dates. These relations have been found to be complex; but it is reasonable to claim that the overall upshot has been to support the analytic thesis that infants not only suck for nourishment, but also for oral pleasure.[12] However, there is no such support for anal eroticism, since no such studies have been done – perhaps for obvious social reasons. Though studies have been made of the incidence of infantile masturbation, no attempts seem to have been made to separate out the (supposedly) pleasurable aspect of this activity from *other* aspects. That there *are* others is strongly supported by the old discovery that the incidence of masturbation is greater among little boys than little girls.[13] The boy's penis is far more open and sensitive to exploration, friction and so on, than the little girl's clitoris, which suggests that the activity of the phallic period may also be the manifestation of bodily curiosity and exploration, and a reaction to stimulation from clothing, full bladders, and the like.

But let us suppose that the small child *is* also driven to obtain bodily pleasures from its (so-called) 'erotogenic zones'. Why is this activity the manifestation of the 'sexual' instinct? Why should we describe the organic sensations it obtains as 'erotic', and the zones as 'erotogenic'? Freud's supporting argument is based on a behavioural analogy between adult sexual activity and the behaviour of the child; and on the claim that, when the adult develops some sexual perversion this is causally connected with interference (typically, excessive inhibition or indulgence) and fixation at the corresponding stage of infantile sexuality.[14] This argument is very weak, and probably not congruent with the current drift and emphasis of scientific inquiry.

When little Joe has an erection, this reaction, of course, looks like the erection he has when he is grown up. But it does not follow that the former is sexual in function and origin. Even if we were to grant that little Joe's difficulties at the oral stage contribute to produce his later sexual and other difficulties, this does not show that his oral activity is sexually driven. Likewise for any other infantile activity, which allegedly contributes to an adult perversion. The reason is the obvious one that the infant's early reactivity does *infantile* jobs for it. One of these is to *prepare* little Joe (and Sue) for adequate or 'normal' functioning when he (she) becomes an adult. It has been discovered, for example, that, if young male, rhesus monkeys are isolated during the normal period of youthful play, then, when they reach maturity, they have difficulty in mounting a female.[15] Similarly, there may be some evidence to show that early interference with the oral, and other interests, of the infant will damage in a variety of ways his ability as an adult to function adequately, or within normal limits. This will include his ability to function 'normally' in the sexual sphere. But all this does not require us to say that the infant's early interests and activity are sexual in character, any more than we have to say this of the young monkey's play. On the contrary, if we do say this of the human infant, we plunge into the confusing silliness of having to claim that, since any bodily feeling may be involved and open to perversion, etc., in *adult* sexuality, therefore *all* pleasant infantile bodily feelings are sexual in nature. It is understandable, but unfortunate, that Freud embraced this silliness, and so greatly extended the range of application of the word 'sexual'. This confusing extension of the word was the natural outcome of his out-of-date nineteenth-century view of instinct. But it is quite unnecessary for the purposes of analytic theory and practice. An analyst can claim all he wishes to about the connection between early experience and adult behaviour, with its difficulties, *without* having to suppose that the infant's oral and other activity is driven largely, or in part, by a sexual instinct.

This conclusion has some immediate consequences. Given the meaning of the word 'erotic',[16] it follows that we have insufficient justification for speaking of the child's 'erotogenic' zones; for describing his self-directed activity as 'auto-erotic'; or for claiming that the child has early 'libidinal' interests at all – whether self-directed or mother-directed. There *may* be a sexual instinct and libidinal energy at work in all this. But objective evidence and the drift of scientific work suggests that the phenomena can be more parsimoniously explained without them, thereby making it unnecessary for us to postulate them.

What of the next stage – the Oedipal? Are we justified in describing and explaining the activity of Joe and Sue at this period, in respect of the mother and father, as sexually driven – as the manifestation of the sexual instinct? We appear to have no more reason to do so than we have to describe their pre-Oedipal behaviour as sexual in character. So it is misleading to speak of their relevant activity and interests as sexual at this time. But let us pass this negative conclusion, about the pre-Oedipal and Oedipal periods, as being only of theoretical interest. Even if we drop the sexual ascription, it may still be the case that, during the years we are now considering, little Joe and Sue do have the feelings and exhibit the sort of conduct that analytic theory says they do. Consider Joe and all his peers. Do they always, or generally, exhibit a *genital* interest in the mother, in which they show that they wish to have sexual intercourse with her? There is no evidence of this. But does he always, or generally, exhibit a wish for bedroom and bed access to her, and reveal jealousy of the father and of the latter's interest in and access to the mother? Though it is quite commonsensical to suspect that Joe *would* exhibit this wish and jealousy, it is difficult to find any worthwhile evidence, which either supports this generalisation of analytic theory, or refutes it. Likewise, there seems to be no direct evidence to support or refute the next (alleged) steps in his Oedipal history, namely the development of his fear of castration, which he deals with by giving up his libidinal interest in his mother and absorbing the standards of the father.

An analyst would not be at all surprised or upset by the absence of direct support. For, he could say, these Oedipal wishes, attitudes and fears are all so dangerous to Joe that he cannot allow them to become overt and conscious. Hence he represses them. If therefore we are to uncover them, we can only do so by indirect means. Now this is just what psychologists and others have tried to do in recent years. Their general strategy has been to use projective tests (that is, tests such as the Rorschach ink blot test), stories by children, the analysis of dream reports, and the analysis of cross-cultural material. Let us consider some few studies, which (it has been claimed) provide good support for Joe's (alleged) Oedipal history.

Friedman found[17] that when children were asked to finish two 'Oedipal' stories, they gave more 'negative endings' to stories in which, starting from a child being initially and happily alone with the opposite sex parent, the child in the story then met the parent of the same sex. When the children were asked to make up stories about two pictures (one with a father and the other with a mother surrogate and child), boys produced stories containing more conflict themes than the girls in relation to the father figure; and the girls did the same in relation to the mother figure. We are likely to be impressed by this study when we read its details. However, it is open to the doubt that, in the community in the United States from which the children studied were drawn, it is only to be expected, for example, that boys should have more conflictful attitudes to their fathers and girls to their mothers; should be more attached to parents of the opposite sex at the ages chosen; and should produce stories which 'fit in with' analytic theory. All this is to be expected. For the children have already been subjected to much 'sex-typing' by the great pressures of American society.[18] It is plausible to suppose that similar pressures were at work in all the Western societies which supplied Freud, and his colleagues, with their clinical material. Hence, it is difficult to see how Friedman's method can separate out the contribution of the (alleged) innately determined Oedipal stage from the contribution of the society.

Friedman also presented an 'unfinished' story about a boy finding his favourite toy, an elephant, broken; and the child is asked to say what is wrong with it. Friedman argued that, when, on analytic theory, 'castration fears' are high, namely at five and at thirteen, the stories produced would contain fewer references to 'castration' items. What he found was that the boys produced more stories with no reference to 'cutting' at five and thirteen than at other ages; and that for the girls there was no difference between the Oedipal and latency periods. Other workers in this field have tried to study castration anxiety by exposing male teenagers and adults to stimuli assumed to be sexually arousing (for example, pictures of nude women), and then exploring the possible connection with fears of death and/or castration (as represented by damage to their bodies).[19] The upshot is that such males do then exhibit greater fear of death and of bodily damage; and greater than that found in females. These results (from Friedman and others) have been regarded by some as a weighty confirmation of the castration story in analytic theory, and unpredictable on any other existing theory.[20]

But such confidence in this work is exaggerated. We would only be justified in placing much weight on these findings if it were the case that the castration story *alone* can account for the differential responses of males and females in this work. But is this so? We must remember what every mother of a large family knows, namely, that the play of little boys is more rumbustious than that of little girls; they indulge, like puppies, in much more rough and tumble than girls.[21] It is quite possible, therefore, that they are much more conscious of bodily injury, being cut and bruised, and the like, than girls; that by 'latency' they have adjusted to these fears; but at puberty they are very conscious of their genitals and uncertain of their own strength and vulnerability. Friedman's elephant story may just tap these different fears. Moreover, in Western culture pleasurable genital feelings and erections in small boys are still surrounded by much uneasiness, or even alarm, and Joe's genitals are more vulnerable than Sue's. When he comes to adolescence and adulthood, he has to protect them from very painful injury in schoolboy games, to learn to cope with, perhaps, worrying masturbatory impulses, and to appreciate that in sexual intercourse it is he who has to be active, to erect and to penetrate. It is not altogether surprising, therefore, that when sexually aroused with this background of insecurity, he should exhibit all sorts of anxieties, including fears of bodily injury. Clearly, much more work is required before we can be reasonably confident about any interpretation of the findings in this field. As matters stand, the castration story of analytic theory just looks simplistic. Anatomy may be destiny, but probably not in the single-track way which analytic theory has maintained. We should also remember, at this point, a lesson from the history of psychological investigations: any field of inquiry generally turns out to be much more complex and subtle than the picture painted by the first or early hypotheses about the field.

The castration story has also been investigated by studying the reports of dreams. For example, Hall and his co-workers found that there are more male strangers in the dreams of males than in those of females; that there are more aggressive encounters in dreams with male strangers; that male dreamers are unable in some dreams to use the penis or a penis symbol, such as a gun or spear (which is treated as symbolic of castration anxiety).[22] Now, even if we put aside any methodological doubts that can be raised about these studies, it is clear that their findings support the castration story if we accept the analytic account of dreams. But this in turn is open to serious question (see below page 164 ff.). Moreover, it is only too plain that some of the findings are open to other interpretations. Thus, it is perhaps hardly surprising that there should be more *aggressive* encounters with *male* strangers in dreams than with female ones!

Since the analytic story about Joe's development purports to be universal in character, he should develop in the same way and therefore go through the same Oedipal period, were he to grow up in Japan or in Zululand. Does he? This question has been investigated by cross-cultural studies of different types. For example, Stephens used the reports on seventy-two primitive societies by Whiting and Child.[23] He picked out what would be, on analytic theory, the antecedents of castration anxiety in the individual (such as, the severity of mastur-bation punishment, the length of the post-partum taboo on parental sexual intercourse, and the length of time the boy spends with the mother). He then noted the extent of the taboos surrounding men-struation in these societies. He argued that, on analytic theory, high castration anxiety, which was felt by the men of a society, would go to produce extensive menstrual taboos; and what he found was a high correlation between the antecedents of castration anxiety and the extent of the menstrual taboos.

Let us suppose that the statistical methods Stephens used are strong enough to establish a causal connection. It has also been shown, however, that, by similar methods, a similar conclusion and causal connection can be established – for the same societies (approximately) that Stephens used – between the social rigidity (and related masculine dominance) shown in these societies and the extent of menstrual taboos in them. This finding suggests that the ceremonies and social practices involved in the menstrual taboo, and so on, can be explained more parsimoniously in sociological terms. It suggests that there is no need to postulate hypothetical connections, of an analytic type, with infantile experience in order to explain the social practices and institutions under consideration.[24] It seems clear, moreover, that we cannot make any simple move from a generalisation of analytic theory about individuals (namely, about the connection between a boy being brought up in a certain way and his adult anxieties about menstruation) to the con-clusion that the *institutionalised* menstrual taboos in the society are the product of the child rearing practices in the society. (For how, then, do we account for the origin of the institutions? – to mention one difficulty). Stephens's argument traps one into this simple and misguided move – a move to which analytic theory, as stated in Chapter 2, does not commit us. It seems, therefore, that the best we can do for Stephens's argument is this. By establishing his correlation he suggests that the causal connections with childhood experience, stated in the Oedipal story, may have to hold generally, in order for menstrual taboos to be maintainable in any particular society. In this way his result does provide *some* very roundabout support for the Oedipal generalisation in analytic theory about individuals. Stephens's work is also instructive in that it reveals the characteristic confusion and inconclusiveness of cross-cultural studies in this whole field.[25]

Is it through fear of castration that Joe is led to develop the Super-Ego of his father? Various studies have suggested that the acquisition of conscience in men is far more complicated than analytic theory implies. In the first place, what is acquired seems to be typically an inconsistent affair – strict in certain fields, and not in others. It can be affected by the man's relations with his mother, as much as with his father. And firm moral standards seem to go along, not with punishing fathers, but with fathers who were loving and supportive. Though the picture is still unsettled, there seems to be no evidence that the acquisition of conscience is connected with fear, let alone the fear of castration.[26]

What about little Sue, and the very different history for her at this stage which the theory gives us? We have seen that it is difficult to place much weight on the different bodily (? = castration) fears of girls and boys. But what of penis envy? There are a couple of studies which have used projective tests (for example the Rorschach), and which have found that non-marrying women, with a masculine style, produce a significant amount of imagery of the 'penis envy' type.[27] Now, even granting the validity of the Rorschach test (and tests of this sort), does this work do much more than suggest that some 'masculine' women would really like to be men, and hence would like to have a penis themselves? Does it support the hypothesis that *all* women have penis envy? Only if we suppose that the most reasonable or plausible way of explaining the wish and penis envy of masculine women is by postulating that *all* little girls have penis envy during the Oedipal period, and that the 'masculine' women's wish and envy is the result of their failing satisfactorily to resolve the conflicts of the Oedipal period. But there is no evidence to support this supposition. While some little girls may develop a fascination for everything boyish, including the genitals, common sense would suggest that this could be produced by certain sorts of interpersonal relations in the family, plus the girl's experience of sex roles in her society. The postulate of universal penis envy would seem to be quite gratuitous. Furthermore, there is some evidence which suggests that, far from having penis envy, Sue is unlikely to regard her own body as defective, and is probably happier with it than Joe is with his.[28]

Nor does there appear to be any evidence that Sue transfers her susceptibility to genital stimulation from clitoris to vagina as she comes to maturity. Nor does the evidence allow us to assert with confidence, if it allows us to assert at all, that Sue's Super-Ego differs from Joe's in not being as strong or clear cut as his.[29] So the evidence as a whole seems to go against the well-known view of female sexuality contained in analytic theory.

What is the overall upshot of the evidence on the Oedipus complex? Some studies seem to go against the story; many have little weight either way, for one reason or another; some do support the story (as we have seen), but the support is apt to be weak, partly because their findings are open to other interpretations or explanations. In so far as these other interpretations come from commonsensical psychology, they are *ad hoc* in nature. But it may not be difficult to think up some other theory of personal development, which emphasises the motive of cognitive mastery, and which is strong enough to cover both the developmental ground which analytic theory does, and a good deal more besides (but cf. Chapter 10, III).

Still, be all this as it may, when we gaze through the surface of the appearance presented by these scientific studies and trends, it does look as if the 'pre-Oedipal' and 'Oedipal' stories may be pointing to something authentic and important in the development of the child. They seem to be pointing to the importance at different periods of several things. (*a*) the child's bodily needs, its reactions to its own bodily feelings, and its interest in the bodies of the adults and siblings around it; (*b*) the child's needs for human attachment and affection; (*c*) the interpersonal relations with the first adults around it – relations which are involved in satisfying these needs of the child; (*d*) the imaginings of the child and the attitudes it develops about all this at the time; (*e*) the fundamental dispositions, and so on, which it acquires as a result, by about six years of age, towards itself and to the adults and others about it. But if all this is what the 'pre-Oedipal' and 'Oedipal' accounts are really pointing to, then two things seem evident. It is doubtful whether we know enough at present to be able to formulate precisely just what they are really and correctly pointing to; and it is clear that they are also pointing at the same time in directions that are quite mistaken. Hence, taken as a whole, these accounts are very inadequate and confusing.

What of the next (alleged) stage of psycho-sexual development – the latency period? If we accept as good evidence the presence of sex play and games, and the like, between the age of six (or seven) and puberty, then there is ample evidence from a number of primitive societies that children of this age do indulge in sex play. There is good reason to believe that the same is true of children in Western societies; but because this play is socially unacceptable in these societies, it is concealed from adults, and, naturally, has not yet been scientifically investigated. So the evidence from sex play disconfirms the latency generalisation.[30] If we do not accept sex play as good evidence, then it is unclear what would constitute such evidence, pro or con.

Is the libido of little Joe and Sue bisexual in nature? Let us exclude the minority of new born infants who have some sexual abnormality of a biological character (for example hermaphroditism); and let us suppose that little Joe and Sue belong to the vast majority who are sexually normal. It seems to be the case that all these children do possess the biological equipment which allows them to respond 'erotically' to a very wide range of stimuli, and hence which allows them – *given* the appropriate experience, whatever this may be – to develop heterosexual or homosexual interests, or both. But nothing biological has yet been found which *specifically* disposes little Joe, more strongly than little Sam, to develop both interests, or homosexual interests alone. Likewise for little Sue and Ann. This null finding conflicts with Freud's belief that the strength of a person's psychological tendency to homosexuality is partly determined by the strength of a specific biological disposition. What seems to matter is the sort of learning and social pressures that the individual undergoes on the road to adulthood. In Western societies, indeed in most societies, this experience usually makes him and her heterosexual. No doubt, conditions of extreme need and external stimulation could be so arranged for heterosexual adults such that most of them would be induced to exhibit homosexual behaviour. But this is not to say that most or all heterosexual adults also have homosexual tendencies in ordinary life, and are therefore bisexual in nature.[31]

What of the concept in analytic theory of normal adult sexuality? Is it valid? If we have to discard the nineteenth-century view of instinct which influenced Freud, then we cannot speak of normal sexuality as being a synthesis of component instincts. We have to say, instead, that, for example, it is the product of much maturation and learning, and their interaction. But what of the claim that for Joe, or Sue, to function normally, they have to fuse the affective and sensuous currents in their sexuality – currents which then direct them to copulate with one person of the opposite sex? Now, though there is support from the clinical field for this concept of normality, there appears to be none from scientific inquiry. This is not surprising. The whole concept of the normal working of any single psychological function – such as thinking, or memory, or the control of mood, or judgement – is a very difficult one, which plagues the clinical psychiatrist, and which besets his attempt to handle the concept of mental illness itself.[32] Scientific inquiry has not yet been able to get to grips with the much more complex business of normal sexual functioning. In view of this, analysts would be well advised to remember the inconclusive nature of clinical evidence, and the great diversity of human sexual activity. This may save them from categorising, for example, the bisexual or polygamous impulses of Joe (or Sue) as necessarily 'abnormal', and save them from supposing that Joe (or Sue) will 'really only be happy' when they satisfy, or come to satisfy, the analytic criteria of 'normal' sexuality.

Since scientific support is pretty weak for the other (supposed) basic instinct of destructiveness, it is not surprising that there is no scientific support at present for the postulated interaction between sexuality and aggression. In particular, there seems to be nothing to support the generalisation that little Joes (and Sues) always or mostly or generally go through an anal-sadistic phase. There seems to be nothing to support the generalisation that children invariably or generally come to view the sexual intercourse of their parents as a violent and sadistic matter. This applies both to children in Western cultures, and to children in the wide variety of so-called 'primitive' cultures, where familiarity with adult sexual intercourse is accepted. Of course, this negative picture is quite compatible with the claim that *some* children go through a stage that is recognisably anal-sadistic, and so fit the analytic story. But there is no scientific evidence that all or most do so.

IV

What, now, about the development into adulthood of the person whose Ego has been able to deal fairly satisfactorily with the demands made upon it (see Chapter 2, Section II)?

It is evident that here analytic theory is spinning in part a high level account, with which scientific inquiry cannot get to grips in a straightforward way at present (Chapter 3). Some few psychologists, however, have tried to extract something which is open to investigation from the story about Psychic Structure. But they have not been very successful. Thus, work on the development of moral notions in the child, by Piaget and others, has been criticised as being irrelevant to the concept of the Super-Ego.[33] The part of the High Level theory on which psychologists have concentrated is the Mechanisms of Defence. But though they have done a considerable amount of work on the mechanisms, they have not produced much of interest. For example, the work on regression has not been good enough to enable them to say anything secure about the key concept of fixation. The work on identification leaves a confused picture, largely because of the uncertain relation between this concept and others such as modelling, imitation and observational learning.[34] Psychologists seem to have produced work of interest on only two of the Mechanisms of Defence – repression and displacement.

Consider a couple of examples on repression. Results were obtained, in a small but careful study by Levinger and Clark, which lend some support to the hypothesis that emotional factors can determine forgetting.[35] It was found, for example, that words regarded as emotional by the subjects evoked greater forgetting of associations than those regarded as neutral. This study is interesting and suggestive. But one cannot claim that it 'provides irrefutable evidence for the Freudian concept of repression'.[36] For the High Level theory, in which this concept functions, merely suggests that the forgetting of associations of emotional words may serve as an indicator of repression. The positive result of this experiment provides support for the hypothesis that the forgetting described is indeed an indication that repression is responsible for it; and this finding is well worth having. But it will take *very* much more than this result to make the concept of repression, and the related High Level theory logically compulsory on us.

Then, the results obtained by Dixon, and others, on perceptual defence are impressive.[37] Dixon used an apparatus which allowed him to present stereoscopically two spots of light – one brighter than the other – to the left eye of the subject and stimulus words, subliminally presented, to the right eye. The apparatus enabled the subject to control the brightness of the two spots, and he was instructed to work it continuously so that he could 'just see the brighter of the two spots but never the dimmer one'. It was found that when emotionally disturbing words (whore and penis) were presented subliminally to the right eye, the visual threshold went up and the subject had to increase the brightness of the spot shown to the left eye. This experimental work got round the difficulties raised to the previous studies, stemming from Bruner and Postman (Chapter 3); and, if it is firmly replicated, it suggests very strongly that some internal control machinery is at work of the sort described by the theory of repression.

About displacement. Some years ago Dollard et al. produced experimentally with humans, who were under conditions of frustration, an effect which it is reasonable to describe as one of displacement.[38] Neal Miller obtained a tightly controlled result with rats, which was uncannily analogous to human displacement.[39] Since then animal ethologists seem to have used a similar concept in speaking of the 'redirection activities' of animals.[40] But very little has been done in recent years on the conditions that produce apparent displacement in humans.

Though analytic theory makes interesting play with the concepts of sublimation and projection, it is doubtful whether anything secure emerges from the little work which has been done on these notions. So the analytic theories of art and religion – in so far as they rely on these two concepts – lack scientific confirmation or disconfirmation at present.

The overall results of the large amount of scientific work on the Mechanisms of Defence are disappointing. This is not surprising, perhaps, in view of the vagueness that characterises this part of the theory and the complexity of its high level features (cf. Chapter 3). It is difficult to generalise about the conditions under which people do regress, project, displace, and so on and difficult to pin down the internal ways in which the mechanisms work. Hence it is difficult to know what we have to do to support or upset any generalisation here, or to come usefully to grips with the high level aspects of the theory.

What about dreams and symbolism? Does the scientific work on these topics make good some of the shortcomings of the work on the Mechanisms of Defence? Well, does this work do much to support or upset the thesis that Sue's dreams as an adult are for the most part the disguised revelations of repressed wishes? The short answer is clear: there is no investigation which specifically supports or upsets this thesis. For no such work has been able to 'get at' a repressed (and therefore unconscious) wish in an independent way, infer observable consequences from it, and so go on to show that the manifest content of a dream is (or is not) a causal outcome of the wish. *A fortiori*, there is no such work which shows that an item in the manifest content does (or does not) symbolise an unconscious wish. But there is a considerable amount of work which could be said to count both against the thesis and also in favour of it.

There are considerations which point to the conclusion that all manner of items are revealed in Sue's dreams, not only repressed wishes; that the sharp distinction drawn by the theory between manifest and latent content will not do, since the former does sometimes convey information about Sue, and therefore it is not only a disguise; that (as work in the sleep laboratories has suggested) Sue's dreams seem to have a (probably) important but undiscovered biological source, because of their close connection with our regular periods of light sleep; that her dreams, therefore, do not only have a defensive role, in which they give expression to Sue's unconscious, but that they are part of her whole, complex fantasy life.[41]

But there are also considerations which point the other way. Even if Sue's dream does not always, or only, give expression to some unconscious item or items, it seems clear that the manifest content does bear a close connection with antecedent or concurrent experience, which is involving or disturbing. Thus, for example, newly paralysed persons, pregnant women, menstruating women, the hungry or the thirsty, those engaged in disturbing psychotherapy – such people all have dreams which reflect their condition. Persons who are psychologically more disturbed produce dreams that are more bizarre, vivid and 'dreamlike'. If subjects in a sleep laboratory are prevented from dreaming (by interfering with their dreaming time, as indicated by their rapid eye movements), then it does seem that they are upset.[42] This suggests that dreams, like fantasy, do have a function in relieving tension. Moreover, the work with projective tests (doubtful instruments though these may be) suggests that the reports of subjects regularly contain 'symbolic' material. Therefore, to the extent that there is an analogy between this material and the manifest content of dreams, to that extent is it likely that items in this content play a symbolic role also.

The upshot, then, of scientific work is to make it clear that the theory of dreams and dream symbolism in analytic theory just will not do. Even if it does contain part of the truth, it certainly does not contain the whole of it. Complex though the theory may be, it is still far too simple-minded to be satisfactory. It is a good example of early and premature theorising.

Analytic theory goes on to tell us something else about the normal development of Joe and Sue: certain early experiences may help to make them oral or anal characters in adulthood.

The oral character centres round traits such as dependence, of being attitudinally either very pessimistic or very optimistic, of being passively receptive. In spite of the vagueness of this concept of the oral character, it seems that scientific studies do give us *some* reason to believe that a cluster of 'oral' traits can be isolated. These are studies which use, for example, carefully constructed questionnaires, the results of which are then subjected to a statistical procedure known as 'factor analysis'. But it is doubtful whether it has been shown that the oral character is causally connected with early oral experience. Thus, different breast-feeding and nurturing experiences have not been shown to bear a causal relation to the adult oral character.[43] As for the anal character, it seems that scientific studies give us good ground to believe that the trio of orderliness, parsimony and obstinacy can be found to go together. But, again, nothing has been found to show that the anal experience of the child (in, for example, its toilet training) is causally connected with the adult trio of 'anal' traits. What does seem to have been found, however, is that there is a correlation between 'anal' traits in the adult and in the adult's mother; and this may point to other causal connections, which are at present undiscovered.[44]

But until the causal origins of these trait clusters, oral and anal, are reasonably established, it is potentially misleading for psychologists to go along with analytic theory, and to describe them as 'oral' and 'anal'. This is especially true of the so-called 'anal' cluster, since this may be better described as an aspect of obsessionality – a very well-known trait some people exhibit, but which has no special connection with analytic theory.

V

How about the psychoanalytic account of *abnormal* development – of how Joe and Sue develop neurotic or other pathological conditions? Our attention has already been drawn (Chapter 7, Section I) to the fundamental difficulties produced by the analytic concepts of neurotic and psychotic disorders. Let us now accept the defence of analytic theory offered at that place; and look at some generalisations that are either part of the analytic account of abnormality or are suggested by it.

Is it the case (see Chapter 2, pages 19–20) that a child who suffers parental loss, 'pre-Oedipally' or 'Oedipally', will be more disposed – with his (her) weakened Ego – to develop psychological difficulties and disorder later on in life? There is work to show, for example, that children who suffered early parental loss are more liable to psychological disturbance later on; and that male neurotics identify poorly with the father.[45] But though these studies are suggestive, they do not seem to be strong enough to show that the later condition is the causal outcome of loss during the 'pre-Oedipal' or 'Oedipal' periods. More generally, there seems to be nothing to date to show that adult neurotic disorders in general are critically dependent on how the child dealt with the problems of the 'Oedipal' period. There has also been some scattered work on specific neurotic disturbances, such as phobic states, and psychosomatic disturbances (for example, asthma). But the evidential upshot of this work is not impressive.[46] The general conclusion is that, to date, scientific inquiry has done little either to confirm or disconfirm the analytic theory of neurosis.

Nor has science had much to say about the analytic theory of the perversions and of the character disorders in general, or of the psychoses. What researchers have done is to concentrate on homosexuality and on paranoid schizophrenia.

The former has been investigated by the use, typically, of questionnaires, which ask adult homosexuals to report their present attitudes to their parents, and to recall how they were treated by their parents in the past. For males, it has been generally found that they have had a poor, negative relation with the father; and there is some evidence to believe that they have had a close and restrictive relation with the mother. For females, there is evidence that they have had a poor, distant and frustrating relation with the father.[47] These findings do go to support Freud's views about homosexuality. But retrospection is a doubtful tool for discovering what happened in childhood, and whether anything in childhood helped *to produce* adult homosexuality. Moreover, when we compare these findings with the richness of Freud's account of, for example, Leonardo da Vinci, an alleged homosexual, it is reasonable to conclude that the findings are very thin.[48]

Freud argued that the persecutory delusions of the paranoid schizo-phrenic were due to the patient's repressed homosexuality, which is then defensively projected to form his delusions. This view has been experimentally explored by presenting pictures of male and female figures, and determining differential fixation and response times, as well as defensive moves against the male pictures. It has been claimed that some of the findings of this work support Freud's view quite well; but there is some disagreement about the interpretation of this work.[49] It has also been argued that male paranoids, being the suspicious creatures they are, will naturally react to the male figures in the experiment as threats; and this may account for the findings without having to postulate that they are repressing their homosexuality.[50]

VI

Let us now be bold and venture to sum up our assessment of the findings of scientific inquiry.

The central generalisations from the theory of instincts – about death and aggression and self-preservation – are mistaken, because the whole concept of instinct embodied in them is a mistake. There *is* evidence to believe that the infant goes through certain early stages of bodily interest and satisfactions. But it runs counter to the state of play in science to suppose that the infant is sexually driven in going through these stages. The generalisation about the 'Oedipus' and 'castration' complexes in boys is conceptually confused, and, when clarified, of very doubtful adequacy. The parallel generalisations for girls are either unsupported or disconfirmed. But when the doubtful aspects of the 'Oedipal' story are cleared away, we seem to be left with what may be important pointers to the development of the infant in respect of its own body and its early adult figures. The generalisations about latency and bisexuality are disconfirmed. The generalisation about 'normal' human sexuality has no scientific backing at present. Nor is there any backing for an anal-sadistic stage. There is some evidence to suggest that the human being may function in the ways outlined by the mechanisms of repression and displacement. There is evidence to show that the theory of dreams and symbolism will not do, and only contains a part of the truth. There is some evidence to support the concept of the oral character, stronger evidence to support the concept of an anal one; but insufficient evidence to support the analytic story of their origins. Nor is there any evidence to support the analytic account of neurotic disorder or the perversions. There is some weak support for the analytic account of homosexuality, but the experimental work about paranoid schizophrenia is of dubious value.

VII

What light does this scientific inquiry throw on the standing of psychoanalytic theory?

Consider first the Low Level part. It is clear that scientific inquiry has uncovered evidence which *confirms* some generalisations of the theory, and thereby gives us reason to accept them as true. It has found evidence which gives us reason to believe that some generalisations *may* be true, or an approximation to the truth; that other generalisations are false; and that still others *may* be false, or pointing away from the truth. When we look at the summing up just given, we can see some, at least, of the places where it confirms and disconfirms the low level generalisations that are supported by the collective mass of case material (Chapter 7). However, scientific inquiry has failed so far to find evidence which bears in any accepted way on a large part of the Low Level theory. This failure seems to have more than one source. Contemporary scientific methods of investigation are very limited in their strength, and the Low Level theory contains generalisations which run beyond the present power of science to investigate them in an adequate way. It is also characteristic of science, especially in a new and difficult field like the psychology of personality, that its findings should be open to different interpretations. This feature of scientific work becomes more prominent when the theory investigated is a vague and loose one, like analytic theory.

It seems evident, therefore, that the total amount of light coming from scientific inquiry has not yet materially helped us to settle the standing of the Low Level part of the whole analytic theory. Hence, it does not generally give much support to the practising analyst when he produces a hypothesis about a patient. There are virtually no findings to back the (alleged) analytic aetiology of a neurotic condition. Turquet may offer a hypothesis about John's obsessionality – in which he suggests that it stems from John's early relations to a father who is felt to be overbearing, and so on. Turquet could support this hypothesis by appealing to past clinical experience; but he could not support it by appealing to generalisations, based on scientific inquiry, about obsessional conduct and its origins. Hence, scientific work does not generally and materially help the practising analyst to overcome the weakness of the hypotheses he may obtain from the interpretative remarks he makes in the course of an analysis.

Yet, small and feeble though the light is which this work throws on Low Level theory, it is also evident that the heuristic value of the theory has been, and still is, enormous. It has been one of the major sources of scientific inquiry in this whole area in recent times; and its value is still far from being exhausted – as a glance at the literature will show. Scientific inquiry has done enough already to suggest that psychologists, and others in related fields, would be most unwise to ignore the theory; and well advised to remain alert to whatever stimulus it may offer them.

VIII

Though the bearing of contemporary science on the Low Level theory of analysis is on the whole not very supportive, but somewhat inconclusive and rather negative, the bearing of science on the High Level theory is very different in nature.

We have seen that this part of the theory is logically vacuous, and hence does not generate observable consequences. Indeed, it offers us a vision which goes far beyond the bounds of the testable at the present time. Furthermore, Freud's own account of the theory makes it look like a bizarre, dualistic muddle, and this impression is compounded by the silly looking pictures he drew of 'the psychic apparatus' in his attempts to explain the theory.[51] But there is another and very different side to the matter. In recent years a number of psychologists have been interested in accounting for the behavioural data they collect, not by giving neurophysiological interpretations to them, but by means of 'formal' or 'structural' or 'conceptual' models. The hope is that these models will be congruent with what is known about the body, and will enable psychologists to derive empirical and testable consequences from them. Then, by exploring these empirical consequences, it may be possible to say, not only that a model is sufficient, but that it is also necessary in order to account for the data. That is to say, it may be possible to say that the organic system really does work in the *sort* of way that the model describes.[52] Now, as a result of this work by psychologists, we do understand rather better today the logical character of the High Level account, and model, that is contained in psychoanalytic theory. It is an early, very crude attempt at presenting a psychological model of the person as a self-regulating and directing control system. What psychologists, such as Bruner and Postman and Dixon and others, have been doing is to pick on suggestions contained in analytic theory, and the model it embodies. They have investigated these suggestions to try to discover whether we do really function in the way the theory alleges we do. As we have seen, the findings so far indicate that we do indeed function, in some degree, in ways that accord with the psychoanalytic accounts of repression and dreaming.

Of course, the analytic theory and model are very different from the good examples current in contemporary psychology. So far the empirical findings have only succeeded in giving it very little support – as our assessment in this chapter has shown. Moreover, it is very poorly stated and developed, and needs considerable restatement and development before we can begin to go on to try to obtain testable consequences from it, and thereby incorporate it into science. Thus, the concept of mental element (Chapter 2, pages 21–22) has to become, perhaps, a state of the system which has a potential to issue in a certain response by the system. 'Keeping a mental presentation unconscious and away from consciousness' has to become in part, perhaps 'Developing an inhibitory potential which is sufficient to outweigh the facilitatory potential, which would issue in a response of recognition or identification by the system.' And so on. Adequate restatement of the High Level theory is a complex and lengthy business. However, it is very difficult to find any reason why the theory cannot be restated and filled out in ways that would allow us to obtain testable consequences from it.[53] It is clear also that the theory is congruent with the current emphasis in psychobiology on the organism as a control system.[54] Further, it has been claimed that the theory, even as it stands, fits the current state and drift of neuropsychology remarkably well, and deserves more attention than has been paid to it in the past.[55] In short, it seems that in stating his High Level theory (with his schoolboy pictures), Freud did himself and analytic theory a serious injustice. He has misled many into thinking that the whole story is just rubbish. The truth is that the present state of scientific play suggests it is a story of great promise.

IX

Does scientific inquiry help us to settle the differences between analytic theory and other psychodynamic theories – in particular, those mentioned in Chapter 2?

It is tempting for psychologists to disregard Jung's theory as containing unverifiable components (for example, the collective unconscious), and as being, in general, even further removed from empirical science than analytic theory. But scrutiny of the theory suggests that it should also be possible to extract generalisations from it that are open to confirmation or disconfirmation. However, apart from Jung's ideas about personality types, this theory has not stimulated the scientific world in the way that Freud and analytic theory have done. Jung's theory has been of little heuristic value in science. In contrast with both Freud and Jung, Adler takes a stand which is theoretically somewhat thin and empty, and hence not particularly interesting to a scientific investigator. His stand, and that of others in this tradition, have also not been of much heuristic value in science. Much the same is true of the other traditions in psychodynamic psychology.

Of course, where some other tradition conflicts in some respect with what the scientific investigation of analytic theory has discovered or suggested, then this other tradition is in trouble. We then have some grounds for objecting to the latter at this point, and for favouring analytic theory. Thus, in so far as psychological inquiry supports analytic theory in suggesting that the small child's bodily feelings and pleasures (misleadingly described as 'libidinal') are generally important, to that extent are Adlerian theories disconfirmed. Again, where analytic theory or any psychodynamic theory conflicts with the whole drift of science, the theory is in trouble. This seems to be the case with the view the Kleinians offer us, since it appears to ascribe psychological powers to young children, which contemporary psychology makes quite clear that they just do not possess. What is more, it could also be argued that analytic theory, as stated in Chapter 2, clashes with the drift of science, not only in its theory of instincts, but also in the role it accords to the Ego. For in recent years cognitive and personality psychology have emphasised and explored aspects of Ego functioning which analytic theory does not recognise or emphasise sufficiently. The theoretical work of Heinz Hartmann and Anna Freud, and others, has served to fill this gap and thereby bring it more into line with the current drift of science. However, Ego-psychology seems to be primarily a way of talking, or a mode of description, from which it is difficult to extract confirmable generalisations. In consequence of this, perhaps, it has not been of much heuristic value to psychology, however stimulating it may have been to analysts themselves. Hence, if we appeal to the current drift of science, our appeal may not be strong enough to make all analysts accept the revision of analytic theory that Ego-psychology proposes.

In general, then, scientific inquiry and development, and the state of contemporary science, have not done enough to enable us to settle the mutual differences between analytic theory and its psychodynamic competitors. All that scientific work has done, at most, is to help us better to appreciate what our theoretical choices are, and to make a few steps, examples of which we have just indicated, which may take us a tiny way along the road to a settlement of the mutual differences between these theories.

But analysts in all these traditions, no matter what their theoretical differences, do seem to have something in common – namely certain Regulative principles (Chapter 2, page 25). Does scientific inquiry help to justify them?

The first is psychic determinism. All sorts of logical difficulties have been raised about the application of determinism to the life and activity of the mind – difficulties which are still the subject of considerable controversy in the philosophical world (cf. Chapter 4, Section I). But, whatever else may be the case about this Regulative principle, it is commonsensical to say that whether we ought to follow it or not depends, in part, on the success we have in following it. In other words, if, when it is applied in the psychodynamic field, it is useful in helping psychodynamic workers to arrive at causal explanations of the conduct, and so on, of their analysands, and others, then there is a good inductive reason for going on using it. We have seen that therapeutic and related work with patients and others gives us some evidence in support of the principle. But we have also just seen that scientific inquiry has not yet managed to throw much light on the causal antecedents with which psychodynamic theory is concerned, in its search for the aetiology of neurotic difficulties and the like. So scientific inquiry has not yet done much to show that psychic determinism works in the psychodynamic field.

The second principle – of goal-directedness – is uncontroversial. Scientific work in the last fifty years or so has revealed its general value and importance. But by itself it is also not particularly illuminating. For one thing, it does not tell us what goals to search for and to use for explanatory purposes. Workers in psychodynamics differ among themselves about all this (Chapter 2); and to date scientific inquiry has done little to settle what goal-directed story about humans is obligatory upon us. On the other hand, if the High Level story in analytic theory turns out to be valuable, then the general emphasis on the goal-directed nature of the human, self-controlling system will become increasingly important.

Principle Three is more troublesome. Reference to unconscious motives, and the like, can serve to make intelligible much in human life, which was previously puzzling or quite inexplicable. Indeed, it is tempting to argue that, unless we do refer to unconscious functioning, much in human life will remain unintelligible. But it is quite another question whether the explanatory narratives, which use the concept of the unconscious, and so make matters intelligible, are also *true* stories (Chapter 4). Our survey of scientific studies makes it plain that, to date, these cannot provide much or any support *for* explanatory narratives which use the concept of the unconscious. Nor do they provide much or any evidence *against* these narratives. Scientific inquiry does not seem to have reached the stage where it can do much to help us with this Regulative principle.

Principle Four is logically quite different from the rest. In stating that early experience is very potent and pre-potent over later, this principle expresses a straightforward, quite general claim about fact. This claim was formulated after the Second World War in the form of a thesis about maternal deprivation. If an infant, or young child, does not have a warm, intimate and continuous relationship with its mother, or permanent mother substitute, then as a result it will (or may) be damaged as a personality in some one or more of a variety of ways.[56] This thesis implies that the infant and child go through a 'critical' period in which it needs mothering, and which is such that, if he (she) misses it, no later experience will or may be able to reverse or undo the ill effects. But scientific inquiry has since discovered that the effects of separating child from mother depend on a variety of circumstances (for example, the temperament of the child, the sort of separation involved, and the quality of the child's new environment). Inquiry also discovered that no generalisations can be made with safety about irreversible psychological damage – especially when the subsequent environment of the child is a favourable one. The whole situation, therefore, is much more involved and untidy than previously supposed.[57] As matters stand at present, it looks as if the overall results of scientific inquiry do not confirm the principle of the potency and pre-potency of early experience. If anything, they go to suggest that, at the least, this principle is very misleading and ought to be reformulated (if possible), or discarded.

A concluding note. When one first meets psychoanalytic theory in Chapter 2, one is liable to be excited and carried away by its magnificent sweep and apparent power. Our survey of the current state of play in science deflates the excitement, and brings us back to the reality and solid earth of knowledge. This is a good thing for all of us – not least the analysts. For the latter will appreciate, perhaps, that we come back to earth bearing for them some comforting nuggets of knowledge and some reasonable promise, as well as a better idea of what we have to do to bring them more.

9 The effectiveness of psychoanalytic therapy

If the adult Joe (or Sue) is in 'mental difficulties', he (or she) will probably not care a rap about the intellectual standing of psychoanalytic theory. They will just not be interested in whether the theory is supported by scientific inquiry or not. What they will want to know is whether going to an analyst will help them to get better. Should they be analysed? Or should they have some other form of treatment? Or what?

I

Suppose Joe is in difficulties of the sort which, it would be generally agreed, are neurotic in nature (see Chapter 2). Suppose we concentrate on treatment which, it would also be generally agreed, is psychoanalytic in nature, and which is the sort of treatment that analysts in the wide Freudian tradition would be expected to practise. The first question we have to answer is this. Are we in a position to tell Joe, with reasonable assurance, that he is more likely to get better if he is analysed than if he seeks no therapeutic help at all of any special sort?

In the past this question has failed to arouse much interest among analysts. For they were apt to see psychoanalysis as a beneficial, and indeed the best, method of treating neurotic disorders; and consequently, discussion about its value was a waste of time. Analysts took this view of their therapy, because they tended to assume that it follows logically from the theory. But this traditional stance of analysts is a confusion. Suppose that analytic theory were correct and that, therefore, Joe's difficulties *are* the outcome of an unresolved Oedipal conflict, and so on. It does *not* follow from this that, if Joe is analysed, he will get better. For it is quite consistent with the theory, and the premise about the nature of Joe's difficulties, that Joe should not improve under analysis. So failure to get better does not oblige us to amend the theory (in Chapter 2), or to reject the premise about his difficulties. Far from it. The treatment may fail because it *may not work in practice* in the way the theory suggests it will. It may have effects on some or all patients that make them deteriorate. It is well known that forms of treatment in

general medicine are apt to have toxic and other undesirable consequences. We cannot claim a priori that analysis is an exception, and is
always and only beneficial.

If an analyst is to derive his traditional stance (about the effectiveness
of the treatment) from his theory, he will need, at least, the additional
premise that: 'If the patient is treated analytically, no adverse consequences will ensue, which are sufficient to outweigh the good results of
the analysis'. But it is manifestly clear that this premise embodies a large
empirical claim, and to back it the analyst will need independent
evidence about the effectiveness of his treatment. He cannot establish
this additional premise, and hence that analysis is an indicated, or the
best, method of treatment for Joe, by inference from the theory.

If we do fall into the confusion of this traditional stance, then we may
be tempted to slide into yet further confusion. We may be tempted to
argue that, if analytic treatment is shown to be ineffective, then this
falsifies the theory.[1] Of course, *if* we include the additional premise just
given above, within our *statement* of the theory, then its rebuttal would
force us to amend our statement of the theory – by dropping the premise.
But this would be a trivial matter; since the dropping of this premise
would not force us to amend the theory in any further and substantial
way.

The fact is that the relation between analytic theory and treatment is
primarily *psychological*. What the theory does is *to suggest* that a certain
type of treatment should be adopted. What confuses us here is the fact
that the theory suggests the traditional psychoanalytic stance, in virtue
of an implicit analogy that it leads us to draw with situations in general
medicine and ordinary life. Thus, we are all familiar with situations
where an event or state of affairs brings about and maintains some other
undesirable state of affairs; and where, to deal with the latter, we have to
remove the former. (For example, if a broken bone in Joe's foot is
responsible for the pain in his foot, then we deal with the pain by getting
rid of the break in the bone.) Now, on psychoanalytic theory, Joe's
difficulties were brought about and are maintained, essentially, by an
unresolved Oedipal conflict. Therefore, we are led to believe that his
difficulties can best, and only, be dealt with by removing their
maintaining causes, namely, his unresolved Oedipal problem. And this
is precisely what psychoanalytic therapy sets out to do. But, of course,
the suggestive force of this analogy may be quite misleading in this very
special field of mental disorder. We need independent evidence to show
whether the analogy really works here; and we can only get this,
presumably, by discovering whether analysis is an effective method of
treatment. After all, we must always remember that it is quite possible

for the theory (as stated in Chapter 2) to be close to the truth, and yet for the best treatment of Joe to consist in a course of sauna baths and tiddlywinks, and three cups of Lapsang tea a day.

II

Have we the evidence which establishes with reasonable assurance that Joe is more likely to get better if he is analysed, than if he seeks no therapeutic help at all of any special sort? In recent years a psychologist, H. J. Eysenck, has maintained that we do *not* have the required evidence. The argument runs as follows.[2]

From the 1920s onwards analysts have produced various clinical reports about the effectiveness of analysis. When these are examined, and the figures put together of all patients who were reported as 'cured', 'much improved' and 'improved', the figures amount to 46 per cent of the total number of 760 patients. Eysenck also put together a large number of cases of patients treated by various forms of psychotherapy, not just psychoanalysis. When the figures are brought together of those who were 'cured', 'much improved', and 'improved', they amount to 64 per cent of a total of nearly 7,400 cases. But, it is argued, we cannot infer that psychoanalysis or psychotherapy helped these patients, unless we can compare the rate or degree of success using these methods with the (possible) improvement or success rate of the people who were similarly disordered, but who did *not* have psychoanalysis, and little or no psychotherapy. Without this 'base line' (as it is called) we can make no comparisons, and therefore no judgement about the effectiveness of psychoanalysis or psychotherapy generally. Now Eysenck pointed to two sets of figures which, he claimed, gave us at least an approximation to the base line we need. The one set was from the work of Landis,[3] and was concerned with neurotic patients in the hospitals of New York State. Here the patients were given care that (we are told) was purely custodial in character. The percentage of these patients who were discharged annually, from 1925 to 1934, as improved or recovered was 70 per cent, and for the years 1917 to 1934, 72 per cent. The second set of figures was concerned with 500 patients who applied for disability claims (from an American insurance society) on account of their psychoneurotic complaints.[4] These patients were seen by their own general practitioners, but were not given any other psychotherapeutic treatment. The criteria of recovery used by the author, Denker, was such as return to work, ability to carry on well for at least five years, and no or few further complaints about difficulties. Denker then found that, after one year, 45 per cent of the patients had recovered; after two years another 27 per cent, totalling 72 per cent altogether. After five years the total went up to 90 per cent.

When we now compare all these figures, it is tempting to draw the immediate inference. If we give patients psychotherapy, or if we do not treat them with any special form of psychotherapy, we do equally well for them. Their improvement rate is about the same. If we give them psychoanalysis, they do conspicuously worse than if we give them some other specific form of psychotherapy, or do not give them any.

It is widely accepted today that this argument from Eysenck was historically important and a valuable challenge to the whole industry of psychotherapy and analysis. But it is also widely accepted today that the argument is fallacious. It simply will not do.

(*a*) The first, or Landis, figures are about hospitalised neurotics. The second, or Denker, ones are about insurance claimants. These categories of people would seem to be very different from those that psychoanalysts are typically concerned with. If we are to have a base line figure which is valid, then it must be about the *same type* of patient that the analyst tries to treat.

(*b*) As his criterion of effective or good outcome, Landis used the discharge of the patient from hospital as improved or recovered. Denker used the cessation of insurance claims. It is doubtful how far the former resembles an analyst's typical criterion of good outcome; and the latter is manifestly very dissimilar from it. But unless we use the *same criteria* of outcome to judge both the untreated and the analytically treated groups of people, we cannot place much weight on the proposed base line.

(*c*) It is clear that the people Denker is concerned with did receive psychotherapy in their interchange with their general practitioners. It appears that the Landis patients also received psychological treatment. It can be argued, therefore, that at best the Landis–Denker figures can only be used to try to arrive at a base line to assess the effectiveness of psychoanalysis against other forms of psychotherapy.

(*d*) When one looks into the details of the figures produced by the analysts, as well as of other figures available on 'spontaneous remission' or improvement, it is evident that, in order to extract overall or consolidated figures from the mass of information available, one has to make certain judgements about the information. Some assessments are unavoidable. It is clear that Eysenck, in offering us his figures, made certain assessments, which contributed to an *optimistic* figure for spontaneous remission, and a *pessimistic* figure of psychoanalytic therapy. Other students have made different assessments, which have helped to produce the converse picture – more pessimistic about spontaneous remission, and more optimistic about psychotherapy and psychoanalysis. For example, alternative figures have been suggested as low as 30 per cent for spontaneous remission, and as high as 83 per cent for patients given psychotherapy.[5] Obviously, a base line figure is not worth much if it is so dependent on the personal judgement of the investigator; and if samples of patients are liable to vary so much as to make it doubtful whether we are really justified in trying to discover a single base line rate for spontaneous remission.[6]

So the argument from Eysenck will not do. It is far too crude to work, and the base line obtained from the Landis–Denker figures is now only of historical interest. On the other hand, the argument served an admirable purpose at the time. At a stroke it served to bring up short the whole analytic and psychotherapeutic profession, and to show the profession the sort of thing that is required to justify their therapeutic work.

III

If we cannot use spontaneous remission rates to determine the effectiveness of analysis, can we devise controlled studies for this purpose? Can experiments be devised in which one group of patients is analysed, another is not, and the outcomes are then compared?

Some inquiries of this sort have been attempted. But they are few in number, and their validity and, therefore, their value have come under serious criticism in recent years. Naturally so, for the difficulties in arranging satisfactory controlled studies are formidable. The two obvious difficulties are these. First, the two groups have to be matched for the nature and degree of their personal difficulties, before being randomly distributed between the treatment and non-treatment groups. But how is this selecting and matching to be done in a way which will be generally accepted? Analysts will reject objective methods as superficial and quite inadequate; and non-analysts will be doubtful about the value of any clinical or psychodynamic type of assessment. Second, how is the life of the non-treatment group to be controlled such that no psychotherapy is given it at all? There is some evidence to suggest that even a single psychiatric interview, conducted for assessment and diagnostic purposes, can have a powerful therapeutic influence.[7] Therefore, the very attempt to set up the experiment, by assessing and distributing the patients, may upset the experiment and frustrate its purposes. What is more, how are the lives of the non-treatment group to be controlled to ensure that its members receive no day-to-day sympathy, guidance, and help from relatives and friends? In other words, how can we ensure that they receive no informal, non-professional psychotherapy in the course of the experiment? We cannot do so – without taking very special and morally unacceptable measures, which would be liable to upset the results. At best, therefore, such an experiment could only be regarded as a study of psychoanalytic therapy versus informal psychotherapy.

In addition to these unavoidable difficulties, it is obvious on reflection that an experimenter is also liable to run into a maze of practical obstacles, which will force him to relax his controls, and to depart from the strict and high-minded design with which he started. Furthermore, as we have seen, analysts take the view that analysis is the preferred treatment for certain types of patient. Consequently they hesitate to take part in experimental work, in which patients, for whom analysis is indicated on their view, are deliberately refused treatment, or given treatment which they (the analysts) regard as inferior. The fact, therefore, that the number of controlled studies are few and of doubtful value *may* be due in some degree, perhaps, to the faith or perversity or self-defensiveness of analysts and other psychotherapists. But it seems to be due largely to the fact that such studies are very difficult to arrange.

In the light of all this, it is evident that controlled studies in this field – of psychoanalysis, psychodynamic therapy and psychotherapies in general – will be pervaded and handicapped by doubts. It is understandable, therefore, that different students should arrive at different assessments of the results of the studies. Some take a pessimistic view,[8] others a more optimistic one, while agreeing that the results only support modest claims on behalf of psychotherapy in general. Thus, in one of the latest inquiries, Smith and Glass[9] examined a very large number of outcome studies of various types of therapy – behavioural as well as psychotherapeutic. They fully analysed 375 studies, which have compared any form of psychological treatment with some other, or with no treatment. Smith and Glass set out, by the use of certain statistical techniques, to determine the size of the effect reported in each study. They obtained 833 measures of effect size, and the size of the mean effect suggested that the average client who received any therapy (including psychotherapy) was better off than 75 per cent of people in the untreated control groups. When they made a more rigorous comparison between behavioural and non-behavioural therapies in fifty studies, in which the two types of therapy are directly compared, they obtained about the same average effect for both types of treatment. These results are favourable to psychotherapy, but they have to be treated with caution, if only because the average time at which the outcome was measured was very short – approximately two months for behavioural and five months for non-behavioural therapies. In any case these studies are primarily concerned with psychotherapy, to some extent with psychodynamic therapy, and not at all with psychoanalysis.

IV

These doubts and difficulties give rise to a natural question. Are there any inquiries, which may or may not try to use controls, but which are as satisfactory as we can reasonably expect in the circumstances, and which provide us with evidence about the effects of psychoanalysis versus no analysis? There do seem to be a small handful of such studies. It is well worth while looking at some examples of this rare breed.[10]

The Norwegian analyst, Schjelderup,[11] reported on the whole set of 41 psychoneurotic patients he had analysed between 1926 (when he started) and 1943 (when he was arrested by the Germans). When he started on this report in the early 1950s, he was able to renew contact with 28 of these previous patients (or 82 per cent of those who were still alive). The condition of one-time patients was rated by the patients themselves, by an outsider (in 21 out of the 28 cases), and by Schjelderup himself after a personal interview. A one-time patient's condition was rated as 'very satisfactory' if the symptoms had disappeared along with a change of personality making possible a decidedly better social adjustment. The condition was 'satisfactory' where there was a lasting and decided change in respect of symptoms and personality, but the person may still relapse temporarily under stress. Using these criteria, he rated 7 one-time patients as very satisfactory, 15 satisfactory, 2 unsatisfactory, and 4 very doubtful. The patients' own evaluations were more favourable. Schjelderup is at pains to point out that all these patients had been in neurotic difficulties for some time before the analysis began – anything from 2 to 25 years (with an average of more than 11 years); and that he was evaluating them at the distance of from 8 to 24 years after the analysis had finished. The average length of treatment was $2\frac{1}{4}$ years and the average intensity was four hours a week with vacation breaks of $2\frac{1}{2}$ to 3 months a year. Because of the longstanding character of their difficulties before analysis – without any spontaneous remission occurring during this period – Schjelderup claims that his data do support the view that the analysis did help to bring about the improvement.

In this report Schjelderup makes something explicit about his own work that many analysts feel in their bones is also true of theirs – that they, too, improve their patients, and could also show this to the world, *if* they but took the trouble and time off to do so. Consequently, Schjelderup's report brings out why it is that, when confronted by the objection from spontaneous remission, and by the demand for controls, many analysts react with a big yawn of boredom.

Orgel[12] has reported on the psychoanalysis of a group of 15 neurotic patients with peptic ulcers. Three of them either refused analytic treatment, or discontinued it after a few visits; and, when contacted 10 to 12 years later, all 3 still had the symptoms, which were then controlled by ordinary medical treatment. The remaining 12 all received analytic treatment of 'the deep variety', 5 times a week. Two of them discontinued, one after 7 months, the other after 4. They were then symptom-free, but relapsed after 2–3 years. The remaining 10 completed the analysis, which lasted on the average a little over $3\frac{1}{2}$ years. The two groups – the 5 who dropped out and the 10 who completed the analysis – were diagnostically very alike; and the symptoms appeared 4–12 and 5–15 years respectively before the analysis began. When interviewed afterwards none of the 5 was symptom-free; but all 10 in the second group were free, both at the end of treatment and at 10–22 years afterwards.

A third and somewhat different type of example comes from Cappon.[13] His sample consisted of 201 consecutive private patients between 1955 and 1960. They had had their difficulties for an average period of 15 years before treatment. The average length of treatment was 6–7 months, with (apparently) an average density of 1 to 2 sessions a week. The results were measured twice – once at the end of treatment and again at an average of 19.9 months later. They were measured in two ways: (1) the therapist's rating of marked improvement, and the patients' self-ratings of the same, and the loss of at least one symptom; and (2) the loss of all symptoms, the loss of the main or presenting symptom, and a marked change in the character of the patients' dreams. Cappon found that, on the first or less demanding measures, the percentage of patients improving with treatment was 75–76 per cent. On the stricter measures, 21 per cent of patients lost all symptoms, 40 per cent lost the main or presenting symptom, and in 51 per cent there was a marked change in their dreaming. Forms for the follow-up measure were returned by 53 per cent of patients but the sample was biased by the fact that these patients had done twice as well at the end of treatment (on Cappon's rating) as those who did not return the forms. What these results showed, however, was that about 10 per cent of patients relapsed on both the weaker and stricter ratings.

Now these patients had suffered on an average for 15 years before treatment; and they showed conspicuously greater improvement during the period of active treatment than during the inactive period in the 19.9 months following treatment. Cappon argues that these figures carry two obvious suggestions. They suggest that the improvement is the result of the treatment, and that there was no spontaneous remission – the patients got worse, not better, in the 'control' period of no treatment.

We have now looked at three examples of fairly satisfactory studies of psychoanalytic therapy. They exhibit their strengths quite easily. But they also have their weaknesses, which are not quite so obvious.

(1) In so far as these studies are based on ratings by the patients themselves and by the analysts involved, we cannot place complete confidence in them. For we do not know how reliable the ratings are. It is only to be expected that patients and analysts will tend to overrate the effectiveness of the therapy used, and we have seen that the reports of patients are indeed liable to take an optimistic view of the outcome.

(2) In so far as the treatment undergone is responsible for the improvement, it is quite uncertain how far this result is due to the influence of the *particular* analyst, rather than the method he used. Because of this, it is difficult to generalise from the work of *one* analyst to that of others, and difficult, therefore, to use these results to recommend the general use of analysis.

(3) In so far as the treatment is responsible for the improvement, this result may be due to the placebo effect, which is common to all forms of treatment.[14] This possibility is strengthened when we note that all forms of psychotherapy seem to be equally effective (see below, page 311). It is unclear how far – if at all – we can discount the placebo effect of analysis by estimating improvement a long time after the treatment has finished.

(4) In spite of appearances to the contrary, we must always remember that other factors may be cooperating during the treatment to produce the improvement – factors which, perhaps, the analysis served to release or to strengthen.

(5) Before we can generalise from these reports (or any others) to psychoanalysis in general, we must be sure (*a*) that the patients have difficulties which are *representative* of the sorts that psychoanalysis is specially concerned with; and (*b*) that they are treated by methods which are recognised to be psychoanalytic in character. It is evident that Orgel's patients suffered from psychosomatic and not psychoneurotic disorders. Of Cappon's patients, 25 per cent were diagnosed as having 'psychopathic personality (character neurosis)', 8 per cent 'psychosomatic reactions' and 8 per cent 'psychosis'. It is uncertain, therefore, how far these two groups of patients are representative ones for analysis. Schjelderup, in contrast, dealt only with neurotic conditions. But these were all chronic, not acute, and there appear to be no studies at all of patients with acute neurotic conditions.[15]

As for the methods of treatment used, it is clear that Cappon's therapy is brief and non-intensive and not 'deep', in comparison with that of Schjelderup and Orgel. It is unclear therefore how far psychoanalysts generally would be happy to accept Cappon's results as good support for the effectiveness of psychoanalysis. Their hesitation at this point is helpful. For when we question the effectiveness of analysis, we are apt to assume that it is useful to speak of analysis as being one common or uniform type of therapeutic procedure. And this may not be true. Different types or specific forms of analysis may have different results under different circumstances. The large, overall question we raised about the effectiveness of psychoanalysis *as such* may be a misleading question to consider.

V

We have now seen something of the strength and weakness of studies which have been reported about *groups* of patients treated by analysis. What about the detailed, microscopic study of an *individual* patient? Does this throw any further light on the effectiveness of analysis?

Consider again the boy John (cf. Chapter 5). What happened to him? Do we know enough to justify us in saying that the treatment he received did him any good?[16] His presenting symptoms, let us recall, were those of intellectual under-functioning. His headmaster had doubts about his capacity for sixth-form work and considered him a poor bet for a university place. He began treatment when he was nearly seventeen years old. This lasted for the next 2½ years, that is to say during the rest of his stay at school. The first 16 months of the treatment were moderately intensive, averaging nearly 3 times a week; subsequently the visits to Turquet became occasional. After a year and 5 months of treatment, John passed 7 school subjects at O-level. At the end of another year (that is, near the end of the treatment) he obtained 2 A-level passes and another O-level. After leaving school he obtained yet a third A-level with distinction, and a university place. At university he obtained a lower 2nd, which makes it clear that, though he seemed to hold his own quite well at university, he did not fulfil the intellectual promise of which he was really capable. After university he was accepted into the executive branch of a large company.

Did John get better or not? There is no need to rely on the affirmative reports of the analyst or an interviewer (B.A.F.). John was re-tested psychologically after 1 year and 8 months of treatment. The gains were marked on all sides. But if we are suspicious of all psychological testing, then we are fortunately confronted by the objective and public facts of John's scholastic record. He obtained O- and A-levels, a university place and a degree.

Can we say that the treatment was responsible – in whole or in part – for his improvement? Almost certainly we can *not* say it was wholly responsible. For, quite apart from the influence of adolescent maturation, we know that during the period of the treatment, John became a house prefect, head of house, a school prefect and captain of rugby. We should be prepared to recognise that these 'promotions' can matter enormously to an inmate in the prison of a conventional boarding school in this country. We also have good reason to believe that John actually established personal contact with one teacher, namely the History mistress, for whom he developed 'a great regard.[17]

But in almost all other respects John's life at school and during his vacations remained just what it had been before the treatment started. It seems very unlikely, therefore, that these influences could have been jointly sufficient to account for the improvement in John's condition – an improvement which enabled him to acquire 8 O-levels and 2 A-levels $2\frac{1}{2}$ years after the start of the treatment. Moreover, we do seem to have some good grounds for claiming that we can only explain John's improvement by supposing the treatment helped to produce it.

(a) His school records strongly suggest that John was already in difficulties when he arrived at boarding school at the age of nine. His problem, therefore, was one of long standing; and he appeared to be getting no better up to the time when treatment began.

(b) The only quite new factor that entered and remained in John's life during this period was the treatment.

(c) In Chapters 5 and 6 we presented some examples from the tape records of the treatment John received. When one examines these records and analyses what happened during the treatment, it is manifest that very great pressures were being brought to bear on John all the time to change in the desired direction. The description of these pressures and changes is a technical and lengthy business (cf. Chapter 6, IV). But at least it is clear to common sense that week after week John was being pressed into speech in a benign situation; he was being taught to express his own feelings and wishes, instead of bottling them up; he was helped to get all sorts of worries and troubles off his chest; and, generally speaking, to come out of his shell. No wonder, then, that he found it easier after a year or more to express himself in his school work and examinations! It would have been strange indeed if he had *not* improved. In other words, as soon as we appreciate the sort of thing that went on in John's analysis, we also appreciate what a powerful instrument of change for the better Turquet was using.

When, therefore, we consider Turquet's work with John, we cannot venture with safety to say how much it was responsible for John's improvement. But it does seem that we have good, but by no means conclusive, grounds for claiming that Turquet's work was responsible *in part* for John's improvement. How much support this gives to the psychoanalytic *explanation* of Turquet's success is quite another matter (cf. Chapter 6). Still, all this does seem to show that the report of a microscopic examination of a single patient can provide us with information about the effectiveness of analysis – information which reports about groups of patients do not provide.

VI

So far we have been examining the effects and the value of analysis in comparison with no analysis at all. Is there any evidence about the effectiveness of analysis in comparison with other forms or types of psychotherapy? A few studies have been made of this question, but the consensus seems to be that they all suffer from defects of design and method, which weaken the value of their results.[18] However, these results, such as they are, do *not* suggest that psychoanalysis is superior to other forms of psychotherapy, whether psychoanalytically oriented or not. On the contrary, they suggest that any form of psychotherapy – psychoanalytic or otherwise – is about as good as any other. This suggestion fits in with the outcome of the study of studies by Smith and Glass. As we have already mentioned (page 180) Smith and Glass conclude that 'the results of research demonstrate the beneficial effects of counselling and psychotherapy'. But their results also 'demonstrate negligible differences in the effects produced' by different types of psychotherapy.[19]

In recent years, however, psychologists and others have developed further methods of treatment, known as 'behavioural', which do not use the verbal techniques of psychotherapy. These include methods such as desensitisation therapy, operant conditioning, aversion therapy, flooding and social skills training.[20] What of the effectiveness of psychoanalysis in comparison with these methods? It seems doubtful whether it is wise to offer any short, straightforward answer at the present time about the comparative merits of psychoanalysis and any one of these other methods. For the topic is immensely complex, and is still the subject of considerable research. However, there are a few studies in which behavioural methods are compared with psychoanalysis or analytically oriented therapy. Thus, severe agoraphobics have been treated by both methods, but with little permanent improvement from either method. With groups of mixed phobic patients, behaviour therapy reduced the phobias more rapidly than dynamic psychotherapy, but the differences were no longer significant at the follow-up.[21] Still, it does look as if behavioural methods may have the advantage in dealing with relatively specific neurotic difficulties, such as specific phobias (for example, of snakes), or with particular sexual dysfunctions, like premature ejaculation or anorgasmia, when help derived from Masters and Johnson may be all, or most, that is required.[22]

If one compares analysis with one of the latest products on the market, social skills training, it is evident at once how difficult it is to make a sound comparison. For all training of patients by a therapist involves a personal interaction between the two, which is liable to generate a transference type of relation. If we cannot safeguard against this, then the results of a training in social skills may also be the outcome, in part, of one of the (alleged) key factors in analysis; and the experimental comparison is no longer sound. Moreover, social skills training, being a new method, carries with it all the hope that arises from its novelty, as well as from the enthusiasm of its practitioners. In other words, it carries with it a placebo effect, which may be more powerful than that carried today by psychoanalysis, and against which, again, it is difficult to safeguard ourselves for experimental purposes.

In view of the poor state of our knowledge in this field, it is clear that the chief desideratum is more knowledge. It is fortunate that a great deal of continuous research is going on about it. Some of this may fail, for one reason or another, to throw much light on the effectiveness of psychotherapy and analysis. But it is worth noting that interest in the scientific world is moving away from the *general* question of effectiveness to questions about what specific treatment, offered by whom, will be most effective for this specific type of disorder with this type of patient, under these particular circumstances, and why. This move safeguards us to a large extent from the danger – to which some have succumbed in the past – of using science as propaganda for or against analysis, or any other method of treatment. As such, this move is to be welcomed.

VII

We began by asking whether, if Joe is in neurotic difficulties, we are in a position to advise him to be analysed rather than not seek special therapeutic help at all. The answer is that we can tell him the following:

(a) There is reasonably good ground to believe that those who seek psychotherapeutic help improve more than those who do nothing about their troubles. But the difference is not a large one overall.

(b) We have some ground to believe that some patients with neurotic difficulties improve as the result of the analysis they receive.

(c) There is no ground to believe that such patients do better under analysis than they do under some other form of psychotherapy.

(*d*) There is some reason to think that patients with specific or delimited sorts of neurotic difficulties do better under treatment that is behavioural, rather than psychotherapeutic, in nature.

If, however, Joe were in psychotic difficulties – with schizophrenic or depressive troubles – then what we can tell him is somewhat different. There is good evidence that patients who are put on to the appropriate drug therapy (for schizophrenia and depression) and appropriate E.C.T. (for depression), along with psychiatric support, do fairly well; and there is good ground to believe that they do better than they would do if given no specific help, or if given, primarily or only, psychotherapy or analysis.[23] However, it is well known that there are persons in the analytic and therapeutic world – particularly, no doubt, the self-styled 'anti-psychiatrists' – who take moves to get round, or to disregard these considerations. There seems little doubt that, if these sorts of moves were made about some *other* topic, in which the anti-psychiatrists were not personally involved, the latter would be among the first to describe these moves as neurotically defensive in character. But the evidence cannot rationally be evaded; and hence it is generally accepted that the methods of ordinary psychiatry, and not psychoanalysis, are the preferred ones for the psychoses.[24]

VIII

If Joe is in psychological difficulties, who in actual practice *should* decide just what they are, tell him about them, and tell him also what treatment he really needs? For example, if Joe is depressed, who should decide what sort of depression it is? Certainly not Joe himself. Certainly not the untrained outsider. But even if it is manifestly clear to his family and friends that Joe is in some neurotic state, this fact does not *in itself* justify them in advising him about what course of treatment to undergo. Nor is Joe himself in a position to decide for himself. The reason is clear. Before we would be justified in advising Joe, we must obtain a great deal of information about Joe. And this is a matter for specialist examination – by, for example, a psychiatrist and a clinical psychologist. When Joe's advisers are armed with the relevant information about him, then only are they in a position to apply our public knowledge about the effectiveness of different methods of treatment to Joe's particular problem, and advise him accordingly. From this it follows that it is very imprudent for Joe to do what is so frequently done – namely, to diagnose himself and then to refer himself to someone for treatment. Unfortunately, however, there is a widespread practice among analysts which feeds into and supports Joe's imprudent behaviour. Analysts tend to take on patients who have diagnosed and referred themselves. But it is rare for analysts to have time, the detachment and skill to do the preliminary diagnostic screening and assessment themselves. The logic of the situation, therefore, makes their practice of accepting the self-referred patient very ill-advised. It is a practice which constitutes a perpetual challenge to the repute of the profession, and does the institution of analysis a serious disservice.

IX

We have spent this chapter examining the effectiveness of psycho-analysis, and discussing what advice to give Joe about treatment. But, it could be objected, are we right to make all this fuss about psychoanalytic therapy? Is all this attention justified? For when one looks at the state of knowledge and practice in the whole field of mental therapy, it seems reasonable to prophesy that analytic treatment is on the verge of being made out of date by developments in our fundamental knowledge about the neurochemical mechanisms of learning, and by the consequential emergence of new therapies – flowing in particular, perhaps, from the work of the clinical pharmacologists. Moreover, and forgetting all about the future, how often are we faced in practice today with the need to advise people whether to be psychoanalysed or not? The answer seems to be clear: very rarely indeed. The reason for this has been proclaimed from the roof-tops for many years. Psychoanalysis is not a treatment which can be given in practice to the mass of neurotic patients, because the mass of people cannot afford it. In so-called 'capitalist' countries, it is a treatment for the rich man or woman with the leisure to indulge themselves. In the so-called 'socialist' countries, it is a luxury and, presumably, *sub rosa* treatment for the wealthy bureaucrat or the high-ranking Party member who is doing well for himself and his family. Since psychoanalysis can only be effectively used to treat the economi-cally privileged few, and at a considerable cost in human resources, are we really justified in recommending that it be applied at all? Should we really bother to preserve the institution of analysis as a therapy?

We shall discuss this question in the next chapter.

10 The standing of psychoanalysis

We took note near the beginning of this inquiry that, in the first half of this century, Freud came to be generally accepted as a psychologist of genius, a Darwin of the human mind, who had made discoveries of fundamental and lasting significance; that during this period psychoanalysis revolutionised the popular view of human nature in much of the West and affected most aspects of our culture. Is this popular view justified? Is this revolution warranted?

If the account of analytic theory and practice, which we have presented in the previous chapters, is anywhere near the truth, then one thing is clear. The impact of psychoanalysis on the West cannot be justified on the ground that it contains a body of reasonably secure or established knowledge about human nature. Chapter 8 makes it only too painfully evident that analysis does not contain any such body of knowledge. In so far as the popular view assumes that it does contain such a body of knowledge, it is mistaken, and this view of the matter and Auden's 'whole climate of opinion' are riddled with delusion. If we try to justify the popular view by relying on 'Freud's great discoveries', we will fail because there are no discoveries strong enough to do the job. If we try to justify it by claiming that Freud has made us see human nature in an entirely new and fresh way, we will obviously fail again. For, though this claim about Freud's historical influence may well be correct, his new and fresh way of making us 'see' human nature is not self-guaranteeing. It has to be established. Nor can the impact of psychoanalysis on our culture be justified on the ground that it uses a method of exploration into human nature, which is of known or established validity. On the contrary, the results of this exploration are infected with an unknown degree of uncertainty. Nor yet again can the impact of psychoanalysis be justified on the purely pragmatic ground that it works – that it is an effective method of treatment. Chapter 9 makes it evident that the case for the effectiveness of analysis is too weak to serve as a good foundation on which to base the Freudian revolution.

This negative answer at once raises further questions. Why have we in the West become the victims of this delusion? How has it happened that the stereotypical inhabitant of Hampstead, London N.W.3 carries round with him (or her) such a mistaken view about the nature of psychoanalysis? If, as we have been told, Freud is 'the presiding figure' of our culture, whose 'intellectual influence [in America today] is greater than that of any other modern thinker',[1] how has America succumbed to this delusion about Freud and analysis? However, these interesting questions take us away from our present subject into the psycho-sociology of Western culture during the middle of this century; and it is clear that we cannot do much to answer them here.

II

But if analytic theory does not offer us a reasonably secure or established body of knowledge, what sort of knowledge claims does it contain? What sort of putative, great discoveries did Freud make?

We have noted that analytic theory contains a Low Level part with a number of generalisations which have been supported by clinical and hardheaded investigation (Chapters 7 and 8). It seems safe to describe these generalisations as pointers to the truth – signposting the avenues to pursue if we wish to get at a reasonably definitive account of human nature. No doubt, they are not the precise indicators that the hard-headed man from the laboratory prefers. But this does not make them worthless. Far from it. Such imprecise or vague pointers are not uncharacteristic of the early stages of a scientific inquiry, and they may be indispensable to further advance. We also discussed (Chapter 7) the orthodox claim that psychoanalysis contributed to the discovery of the neurotic disorders; and we noted that, though this is an insecure classificatory thesis, it nevertheless seems to be indicating something authentic, which may turn out to be of scientific importance. We can say, therefore, that at least what Freud discovered, or contributed to discovering, were some pointers to the truth. On the other hand, we have noted that the Low Level theory also contains generalisations which are *not* supported at present, and still others which run *counter* to the evidence and drift of scientific inquiry, and which, therefore, point away from the truth (see Chapter 8).

The Low Level account is embraced by a High Level theory, which uses concepts from a nineteenth-century view of instinct, plus concepts about psychic energy operating in a control system. This enables analytic theory as a whole to present a comprehensive account of human development, mental functioning and malfunctioning.

It is tempting today for the man in the laboratory, or the sceptically minded philosopher, to regard this whole exercise in theory making as a piece of staggering and foolish audacity. But, given the context of the period – a romantic age when grand theorising was still an intellectually respectable enterprise, and all things were possible – it was quite natural for Freud, and other psychodynamic inquirers, to try to bring their therapeutic 'findings' together within the unified description and explanation provided by 'a theory'. Indeed, this exercise may have been psychologically necessary for psychodynamic workers at the time – in order to give them the personal confidence to proceed with the treatment of patients on the new lines they were developing. Therefore, we must put on one side our present day scepticism about grand theorising when we consider what Freud offered us.

What, then, is the standing at the present time of psychoanalytic theory as a whole?

Our examination suggests that the theory was a premature one in several ways. It was premature in that it was built upon a theory of instinct which, it turned out, would not do. This meant that the analytic account of sexuality and aggression, of pre-Oedipal and Oedipal development would not do either (Chapter 8). The theory was premature, too, in that it was built (primarily) upon a base of supposed clinical fact (Chapter 6), and this base is far too small and soft to bear the load erected upon it. So the theory suffers from over-generalisation and distortion in very important places – in the theory of dreams, of pathology, of development – showing in the last an almost total neglect of 'normal' cognitive and emotional development and functioning. One consequence of this is that even where the theory is, or may be, pointing to the truth in its low level generalisations, it does not give us the whole truth. It is an incomplete or partial account. The work surveyed in Chapter 8 makes this very obvious; and one needs only listen to a symposium of speakers from different disciplines on (say) homo-sexuality, or schizophrenia, or enuresis, to appreciate that the analyst on the platform has but a limited contribution to make. His account is also incomplete in that it does not tell us much about the ways the variables of social structure and process cooperate with those of biology and psychology in the development of the human individual, and of human disorders. The same is true, no doubt, of every other theory on the market. Neither neo-Pavlovian psychology nor behaviour theories contain at present a generally acceptable account, which integrates the interweaving contributions from the individual and from his society. Hence it is clear that the truth contained in the partial story, which analytic theory offers us, has to be fitted, in due course, into a wider and more complete account of human functioning, in which, *inter alia*, the contribution from society is given adequate recognition.

Analytic theory is also premature, in the sense that (as noted in Chapter 8) the story as a whole presents us with a vision of human nature, which runs far beyond the power of contemporary science and rational inquiry to determine how much truth it really contains.

In the history of science there are well-known examples of theories that have been premature in this sort of way. Harvey's theory of the circulation of the blood remained very unsatisfactory until the capillaries were discovered. Prout's suggestion – that the atomic weights of elements could be exhibited as multiples of hydrogen – was only taken up and appreciated later on. Newton's theory of matter (cf. Chapter 3) and his corpuscular view of light had to wait for a couple of centuries and more before they could be handled by science with some confidence. The vision that analytic theory offers us may tread this same route to a large or small degree. Naturally, at the present time we cannot tell whether this will happen or not. Analytic theory may turn out in the end to be more like Aristotle's physics or Ptolemy's astronomy than like Newton's theory of matter. We cannot tell in advance, because we cannot predict the future of science – we can only bet on it. But, since scientific discovery so often startles us with surprises, it is unwise for anyone to bet on the contribution that psychoanalysis will ultimately make to the definitive account of human functioning which we may arrive at in the course of the next few centuries – provided *Homo sapiens*, and his enterprise of scientific and rational inquiry, manage to survive for this length of time.

There are some lessons that follow at once from these conclusions.

In the past, critics of analysis have argued (Chapter 3) that analytic theory cannot be tested or validated. It is clear now that this argument is even *more* misleading than we have found it to be so far. For it induces us to overlook that the theory may stand to science as an account which is open to incorporation. Again, this is not an unfamiliar theme in the history of science. Consider a well-known example – Lavoisier's theory of combustion. In one sense, it is a mistake to say that this was ever tested and confirmed. For his concept of oxygen was not the concept that came to be employed in the nineteenth-century theory of the chemistry of combustion. His concept had to be *modified* before his theory of combustion could be incorporated into the corpus of established scientific knowledge. So in one sense the theory that was accepted was not really Lavoisier's; but in another sense it obviously was his account, and no one else's.

Now if the truth in the partial account, which analytic theory offers, is to be fitted into a corpus of scientific knowledge, it is very likely that this incorporation can, and will, only take place by modifying, or transforming, the concepts of the theory. Herein lies the important element of truth in Popper's remark that psychoanalysis contains 'most interesting ... suggestions, but not in a testable form.[2] The more this is true, the more will the concepts of analysis probably have to be transformed into precise tools. At this future time we could then say that it was *not* analytic theory which was tested and confirmed, and which has become part of scientific knowledge; or we could say that it *was* analytic theory which was studied, transformed, and confirmed and so incorporated into science. As long as we are clear what we are saying then and now, what we do say in this respect about analytic theory is a purely verbal matter. But all this does explain why the present emphasis on testability and validation is even more out of place than we have hitherto suggested. What we really need are studies which will show us whether, and how, we can incorporate the pointer generalisations of the theory into science, or whether we should discard them.

It has also been suggested (see Medawar's remark, Chapter I) that psychoanalysis is 'something akin to a dinosaur ... in the history of ideas – a terminal product with no posterity'. It should be obvious by now that this remark is not just a mistake; it is something akin to a howler. For analytic theory is *not* one big thing, like a dinosaur or zeppelin; it is differentiated, in relevant respects, into parts and has internal ramifications (Chapter 3). Moreover, the Low Level part contains some general statements which seem at present to be pointing to the truth; and a plausible case can be made for the claim that the High Level part embodies a theory and a vision of promise, and hence, probably, a posterity of some note. Of course, if Medawar's remark is restricted to the High Level part, then it *may* be correct. But no one can *show* that it is; and at the present time the betting seems to be that the remark is wrong, even when it is restricted in this way. So we would be quite mistaken at present to throw analytic theory *as a whole* into the wastepaper basket of human aberration, along with phrenology, mesmerism, and other discarded ideas.

III

The premature and incomplete nature of the theory does not make up the whole picture. The theory is also a comprehensive one. It does not only cover the nature of human development, mental functioning and malfunctioning, on which we have been concentrating. The theory can also be used to describe, and to explain, a wide variety of other phenomena right outside the clinical and therapeutic fields. For example, the work of the artist, religious belief, the character of Hamlet, and the nature of groups and their leadership. Indeed, it has been maintained, the fact that the theory, which was designed primarily to order and explain therapeutic material, can *also* be used to cover a whole range of non-therapeutic phenomena is an argument in favour of the authenticity of the theory. This circumstance supports the claim that the theory is, in some degree at least, pointing to the truth.

How much does the great scope of analytic theory do to improve its standing? There seems to be no clear answer to this question.

There is one place where the argument from scope *does* seem to have considerable strength. In our survey of scientific studies (Chapter 8) we met several examples, in which the support that findings appeared to lend to the theory was questioned on the ground that the findings could be explained equally well in some other, non-analytic way. But we also noted that these *other* ways of explanation were apt to be *ad hoc* in character; and this obviously weakens the doubts that they throw on the analytic explanation of the findings. In contrast, the psychoanalytic account was constructed in advance; it has a scope that the *ad hoc* accounts do not seem to possess; and this enables us to use it to explain a variety of novel findings. The fact that it can be used in this way lends additional weight to the analytic concepts and generalisations, from which these explanations can be obtained; and this, in turn, lends additional weight to a particular psychoanalytic explanation of a given group of findings about, say, castration fears, or dreaming, or whatever it may be. No doubt, we can in principle set about constructing an alternative theory with a scope which could give us findings of the same, or similar, scope to that which we can obtain from analytic theory. In Chapter 8, Section III, we hinted at one way in which this seemed quite possible for at least some of the central findings of scientific inquiry. But, in actual fact, no such alternative seems to have been constructed at the present time. Hence, the scope of analytic theory does lend to it some added and considerable weight in respect of these scientific findings; and this was insufficiently emphasised in Chapter 8.

Now it seems that it is the scope of the theory, plus the apparent difficulty about testing it, that has led some of us to exaggerate Freud's achievement by drawing a favourable comparison between his theory and Darwin's theory of evolution. This comparison is a very feeble one. It may be that the chief support for Darwin's theory lay in the comprehensive character of the explanation it provided of the facts. Our examination of analytic theory in earlier chapters makes it clear that we can hardly claim that the chief support for the Low Level theory is to be found in its comprehensive character; and the High Level one is still only a promise. Then, the facts or data that Darwin explained were hard, unlike Freud's, which were soft and artefact-infected (Chapters 4 and 6). The facts in Darwin's case are such that it was possible to deal with the chief objections to his account – difficulties stemming from Mendel's work – by showing how it was possible to synthesise a Darwinian type of theory with modern genetical theory.[3] Nothing like this is true of, or has happened to, analytic theory. Hence, it is just very confusing to describe Freud as the Darwin of the human mind, and to use the argument from scope to support this view.

On the other hand, the scope of the analytic story – covering as it does both therapeutic and non-therapeutic material – does obviously itself lend *some* further weight to the theory. The critical questions we have to ask here are two. (*a*) How far does this coverage enable us to see the non-therapeutic material in a fresh light? How illuminating is it? (*b*) How far does analytic theory and its covering language also help us to explain this material? Unfortunately, (*a*) is a very vague question which opens the floodgates to personal predilections; and (*b*) plunges us into controversy and doubt. For example, how far does Freud in his account of Leonardo *really* explain his artistic and scientific work? It is easy to argue that Freud does not do much.[4] So it is quite uncertain at present how much weight we can place on the argument from scope; and how far, therefore, this aspect of the theory really improves its standing. The whole problem raised by the scope of *any* theory is difficult enough as it is. When we raise it about analytic theory – with all its own peculiar and manifold complications – the problem seems to become unmanageable.

IV

What does certainly improve the standing of the theory is a feature of a very different character, which we are apt to overlook.

In Chapter 2 the theory was presented in a way which makes it look like a prospective scientific theory, and like *this alone*. The exposition there makes it seem as if the intellectual capital of analysts (and their colleagues in psychodynamic and clinical psychology) is completely contained within the confines of the theory presented in that chapter, or in related theories (such as those mentioned there). Our survey of empirical inquiries (Chapter 8), and the admirable surveys presented by Kline and by Fisher and Greenberg also encourage us to adopt the same view.

But this is a mistake. The fact is that the psychodynamic worker in psychiatry also works from a background of clinical experience, derived from his medical, psychiatric and psychoanalytic or psychodynamic training, and current practice. (The clinical psychologist works from a different but related background.) When he goes to work with a patient, he also and primarily operates from this background, not only with the particular theoretical orientation he prefers. Now, admittedly, the concept of clinical experience, in spite of its widespread use, is still obscure, and much in need of clarification. One thing, however, does seem to be fairly clear about it. Through his clinical experience, the analyst acquires the ability to notice features of the patient's personality and conduct, which others, without his experience, would probably not notice. These are features which help him to fit his own theoretical orientation to the patient, and thereby build a coherent picture of him or her. In other words, he acquires the ability to pick on features that his own theory suggests may be important, and which help him to fit together material from the patient, and so make intelligible, narrative sense out of it. The features which can be picked on in this way are endless. They are very like the sort of thing that a consultant points to endlessly on his teaching ward rounds. So the analyst and fellow workers in psychodynamics acquire a skill in noticing and in narrative construction. Neither this skill nor the endless array of features it enables them to pick on are the sorts of things that can be encapsulated inside a theory. Yet the skill forms part of the analyst's intellectual capital; and, if he is able and experienced, it can give to his work a power and authority which is impressive.

What this means is that analytic theory does not stand alone. It goes along with the clinical experience of analysts and psychodynamic therapists. The intellectual capital, therefore, of the working analyst does not only consist of analytic theory, or his particular theoretical orientation, with its battery of concepts and pointer generalisations. It also consists of the ability to discriminate an indefinite range of aspects of human functioning, and to make intelligible sense out of them. None of this can be brought within analytic theory; but it gives to the theory a weight which the outsider – who does not see the theory at work – is likely to overlook.

V

Is the present standing of analytic theory good enough to give the analyst what he needs for his work?

It can be argued that, since analytic theory only contains some pointers to the truth, and is far from being an established body of knowledge, it cannot be used to give the analyst and patient the understanding and knowledge about the patient that traditionally they are supposed to need and to acquire. At best, the case material gives us some reason to believe that the narrative the analyst can spin about a patient may be an approximation to the truth (as we have seen). But since the analyst claims to arrive at understanding and knowledge and insight, he is also claiming to arrive at the truth about the patient. If he cannot reach the truth, then he cannot arrive at understanding and knowledge either. So the standing we have accorded to analytic theory is not enough for his work; and the whole enterprise seems to be in danger of collapse.

This argument is a mistake. It is the case, no doubt, that the analytic and psychotherapeutic world has traditionally supposed that, for an analyst to do his therapeutic job, it is logically necessary for him to arrive at the truth about the patient. But this widespread supposition is an error. It is quite unnecessary for the analyst to rely on it; and his actual practice suggests that, in fact, he does not do so. What the analyst is actually concerned to achieve in practice is something much more modest than the truth about the patient. He is concerned to develop a narrative – whether barely or fully articulated – which will keep things moving, and which will fit together the material about the patient in a coherent way. As such a developing narrative becomes available to him, it then becomes natural and reasonable for him to claim that this may contain some pointers to the truth about the patient; and, in consequence, that he may now have some understanding of the patient, and some insight into his condition. So the most that it is *logically* necessary for him and us to believe about his narrative is that it *may* contain some pointer(s) to the truth. It is not necessary, psychologically or logically, for the analyst to swallow his own story as the truth; and it is probably inadvisable for him to do so.

Much the same applies to the patient. What he needs in respect of himself is a narrative that he can accept as a helpful one in fitting together into a coherent pattern the material of his life and difficulties. He needs a narrative which, in this way, can make sense out of his difficulties, and which, in consequence, makes it natural for him to claim that he now has some self-understanding and insight. Moreover, this narrative *may* indeed be pointing to the truth about himself, and it is natural and reasonable for him to believe that it may be doing so. But it is very doubtful whether there is any evidence, or reason to claim, that it is desirable, or necessary, for therapy that the patient has to come to believe that the narrative *really does* contain the truth about himself. Should he come to believe this, then he may just be partially or totally mistaken (Chapter 6).

But this account and defence of analytic practice will only do if it is reasonable to construct these narratives about patients. For this to be the case, we must be able to adjudicate rationally between two alternative accounts – let us call them 'A' and 'B' – about a patient. Can we do anything to show that one account A about Joe, and his difficulties, is better than another one B? Or is one as good as any other (as Popper has implied)?

There are some rational considerations available which constrain us in our construction of Narrative A, and by reference to which we can discuss its value and comparative worth. First of all, it has to cover *all* the known material about the patient Joe – in a way which builds a coherent story out of the material, thereby making it intelligible. Next, one has to ask: how *easily* does it fit the material? It might be maintained that Narrative A achieves a better fit than Narrative B, since it is less strained, and so gives a simpler picture of Joe in consequence. One is also guided at this point by the same sorts of considerations that guide the historian when he gives an account of some character in history. How natural and plausible-sounding is A? What illumination and fresh and stimulating insight does it give us in comparison with B?

Of course, in so far as the material has been manufactured by the analysis – in so far as it is artefact-infected (Chapter 6) – then it will fit more easily the orientation and narrative of the analyst involved than some other orientation and narrative. But this is a fact about the process of psychoanalysis that it is possible to do something to discount. Thus, as we saw with the boy John, even though the material was the outcome of an interaction between Turquet – with his Kleino-Freudian outlook – and John, it is possible to argue that John is a paradigm of an Adler-Horney type of case, and, therefore, that their sort of narrative is more natural, and achieves a better and simpler fit than Turquet's.

So alternative narratives about a patient can be rationally discussed and assessed. Which one we choose is far from being just an arbitrary and purely personal preference. Still, as we have emphasised, intelligibility is one thing, truth is another. The rational considerations we can bring to bear on these narratives are not strong enough, in general, to give us a reasonably conclusive outcome.[5]

VI

Similar considerations apply to psychodynamic theories themselves, including psychoanalytic theory.

It is a clear implication of our survey in Chapter 9 that there is no way at present of establishing with reasonable assurance that one psychodynamic theory is better than another, or better than every other. But there are rational considerations available which make it reasonable to discuss the worth of these various theories. To begin with, we have to ask: where and how far do these 'competing' theories really map into one another? That is, where and how far are they mutually isomorphic, and the apparent differences between them, therefore, largely locutional in character? So the first step is to do some mutual translation, and to exhibit where, in an important sense, they are not really competing at all. With this confusion out of the way, we can ask: what is the *scope* of theory T.1 in comparison with theory T.2, and any of the others? That is to say, what range of material does T.1 purport to cover, in comparison with theory T.2, and any of the others? The larger the scope, then, prima facie, the better the theory. But how *adequately* does it cover its purported scope? Does it bring the field together well and clearly, or not? Jung's theory, for example, has great scope, but it has run into the objection that the cover it provides is defective, because it is poorly constructed – it brings the pieces of the human jigsaw together in a loose and vague way. Then we can ask: does the theory T.1 base its support primarily on a certain type of material, and T.2 on another? Or not? To this question there is a widely accepted and well-known answer. Yes, analytic theory is based primarily on the young person with difficulties of the sort Freud emphasised (Chapter 2); Jung's is based primarily on the problems presented by the person in a crisis of middle life; Adlerians obviously rely on a different type of case; contemporary Existentialist theories centre round crises of identity, and so on. This fact about these theories at once raises the further question: how far can the material on which theory T.1 is *primarily* based be used as a springboard for generalising about human functioning and malfunctioning *as a whole*?

In addition, there is the consideration that always has concerned analysts: how initially plausible or implausible is the theory? How much does it conflict with what is generally believed about human nature? Where it does conflict, analysts are apt to be worried – as Freud appears to have been about his theory of infantile sexuality, a matter on which he constantly harped in his early years in efforts to justify it. When later analysts were faced by stories about a Collective Unconscious or a Death instinct, or birth traumas, or infantile fantasy, they reacted with caution. Naturally. For though commonly accepted beliefs cannot be made the arbiter of reasonable acceptability or truth, they remain an important consideration to be taken into account.

Then, of course, there has slowly emerged in recent decades a growing body of scientific inquiry, and a drift in science (Chapter 8), which are relevant to the truth claims of the various psychodynamic theories, and to their general worth. We have noted that this scientific inquiry and drift have centred almost wholly round psychoanalytic theory; and the support they have given to it is not particularly strong. But it is clear that science gives the analytic theory more support than any other psychodynamic offering. This concentration on analytic theory by scientific inquirers may have arisen quite naturally out of current historical circumstances. On the other hand, it may just be that analytic theory has the virtue of being more stimulating scientifically, and easier to investigate, than other psychodynamic offerings; and this could be counted as a point in its favour.

These, then, seem to be the chief rational considerations in terms of which we can discuss the value of current psychodynamic theories. It is very plain that the choice between these is not just a personal matter, like the choice of the colour of one's overcoat. But, because there is no way at present of rationally establishing that one theory is better than another, it is clear that for all of us the choice between these theories is also the outcome, in part, of *personal* considerations. It is doubtful whether we know much about these. However, it would be generally agreed that, for analysts and their psychodynamic colleagues, these personal considerations are, to some degree, the result of the sort of professional training and analysis they have had. Thus, a psychoanalyst – having been trained in the Freudian tradition – will be disposed to favour a Freudian type of theory; an Adlerian – trained in another tradition – will favour a correspondingly different type of theory; and so on. This suggests that, in so far as analysts and others remain the prisoners of their own professional training, their capacity to assess these theories rationally is impaired; and that detached outsiders may be better at doing so. (Cf. Chapter 4, Section II.)

These suggestions, in turn, may incline us to look down our noses at analysts and psychodynamic workers generally. But before we succumb to this temptation, we should remember that personal predilections, and the limitations of professional training, have played a not inconsiderable role in the history of science itself. They also play a conspicuous part in the work of those supposed paragons of rationality – the professional philosophers of contemporary Anglo-American philosophy. If these are challenged to explain why they philosophise as they do, rather than (say) in an Existential-cum-Phenomenological way, then one is likely to evoke from them a reaction which is psychologically akin to that forthcoming from a group of (say) Kleino-Freudians, when these are asked why they do not treat patients in a Jungian or a Rogerian way, instead of the way they do. Philosophers, too, are liable in some degree to be the prisoners of their training. It is advisable for us not to emphasise the mote of personal predilections in the eye of others and to ignore the beam in our own.

VII

So far we have assessed the standing of psychoanalysis by reference, largely, to the nature of its theoretical achievement. But it also has to its credit some relevant *practical* achievements, which we have not yet considered.

When Freud hit upon the technique of free association, he started on the road that led to the development of psychoanalytic method. Now, whatever the defects of this method as a valid tool of research, and these are very considerable (Chapter 6), it is also evident that the rules of the method maintain an interpersonal situation which is good at getting patients to talk about and, apparently, reveal themselves. In so doing, the method contributes to produce a mass of material about patients – material which is relevant, prima facie, to the understanding and treatment of them. What happened then was that the use of this method in analysis spilled over to influence contemporary psychiatry and medicine in general. It 'sensitised' psychiatrists and doctors in various ways to the (apparent) needs of their patients and to their own relations with them. Indeed, the doctor-patient relation in the West was never the same after the influence of psychoanalysis had percolated through the medical world.

What is more, this influence was not restricted in the West to the activity of analysts, psychiatrists and medical practitioners. Its influence has percolated through to affect the training and activity of professional services and workers of various kinds: educational psychologists, services for the mentally handicapped, social workers, psychologists in the prison service, pastoral work in the churches, training for leadership and management in industry, T-groups and sensitivity training, and on and on. By this percolation, psychoanalysis has extended or widened the sensitivity of these professionals to include (alleged) aspects of human functioning that had not been noticed or emphasised before. In addition, analysis has influenced in a similar way most professionally educated people, and many others besides. It is difficult to make contact with the news and publications media in any form without being aware at once of the impact of psychoanalysis – from novelists and book-reviewers at one end to agony columnists at the other. And, no doubt, it is this percolating influence that has been primarily responsible for Freud and analysis becoming a whole climate of opinion, of which Auden spoke.

We have noted that we cannot justify this climate of opinion, and the popular belief that Freud and analysis have rightly revolutionised our view of human nature, by claiming that they really are built upon an established body of knowledge. For there is no such body. This means that we also cannot justify the extended sensitivity of doctors, or of professionals, or of the ordinary public on the ground that this sensitivity represents the existence and application of a body of established knowledge about human nature. If we are to justify it at all, we must do so in some other way.

How? It could be argued that the extended sensitivity of doctors and professional workers gives them certain ways of looking at and talking about problems – ways which may be new and which help the participants, in one manner or another, to deal more effectively with the problems confronting them. Of course, whether a group of professionals (for example, doctors or probation officers) really *does* do good in a certain context – and whether their psychoanalytically extended sensitivity really *does* help – all this has to be shown by empirical inquiry. In these respects the activity of professional workers is in the same logical boat as the therapy of psychoanalysts themselves.

But we need not wait for all this to be shown. For there is another justification available of this extended analytic sensitivity – a justification which holds for doctors, professionals and for the educated public alike. It is evident that to acquire this sensitivity we must, *inter alia*, improve our capacity to empathise; to look for clues which will help us fit our extended ways of talking to the other person, and so give some 'understanding' of him or her; to learn to control the destructive emotions of anger, and so forth, in oneself, and to foster the constructive emotions instead. Now it seems reasonable to claim that to achieve all this, on a widespread scale, is to humanise the community concerned, to make it a more kindly and more civilised place, where the needs and difficulties of the individual are more likely to be noticed and cared for. And this is an intrinsically desirable state of affairs.[6] A community in which this extended sensitivity is widespread contrasts, some would argue, with a community such as the Soviet Union, where it is not widespread or influential, and where, in consequence, a variety of human problems and sufferings are not noticed, but are neglected and uncared for in a somewhat unfeeling and brutal way.[7]

However, this extended sensitivity has its dangers. Though it helps to constitute and to justify the favourable climate of opinion towards psychoanalysis in the West, it also helps to corrode and undermine its standing there by getting out of control. For it is very unclear just what extended sensitivity analytic theory legitimises, and what it does not. Outside the contexts of professional training, it has been impossible to control the spread of analytically influenced sensitivity. And among the large middle classes in the United States, it seems to have gone quite wild – with expected results. Thus, for example, analytic theory does indeed say a great deal about human development and the growth of human difficulties. But it does not legitimise any manual of child rearing, whether by Dr. Spock or anyone else. If a writer claims "to base" his manual on analytic theory, he is being quite misguided. But, naturally, when the volatile American public comes round to criticising or rejecting the manual, it will also then go on to hurl corresponding brickbats at analytic theory. And it will be quite wrong in doing so.

VIII

It is tempting to maintain that, even when we allow fully for the practical achievements of psychoanalysis, our review of the standing of psychoanalysis adds up, as a whole, to a depressing picture of the subject. In the theory, we have a premature production which, though comprehensive, is also partial or incomplete. Though this theory has been, and still is, of considerable heuristic value to science, it contains at best – in its Low Level part – only pointers to the truth; and – in its High Level part – a theory of great promise, which offers a vision of human nature that goes far beyond our present powers of empirical validation and incorporation into the corpus of scientific knowledge. In psychoanalysis as a tool of inquiry, we have a method which seems to have reached the state of poor returns – it brings forth little, or no, new or fresh material. In psychoanalysis as a treatment, we have a method which produces modest results, but which is very costly in human resources, and which seems on the verge of being superseded by other more efficient methods.

Does this view of psychoanalysis justify us in feeling depressed about the subject as a whole?

It does *not* justify us in feeling depressed about the *theory*. When we put on realistic spectacles, we can see at once that what, in effect, psychoanalysts have been trying to do is 'to crack the code' of human nature. But this nature is a manifestation of the nervous system at work; and this system is the most difficult terrain in the world – one which science still has not got anywhere near conquering. Why then feel depressed because psychoanalysis has not managed to do the job of understanding human nature, all on its own, in the course of a mere eighty years? It is plainly silly to imagine that it should, and would, do so. Psychology has not yet managed to do the job either; and psychologists are also apt to go through bouts of understandable, but unwarranted, depression when they contemplate their own achievements. Given the intrinsic nature of the subject, it could be maintained that psychoanalysis has done remarkably well in the course of its very short history. In its Low Level theory, it reports exploratory achievements of interest and importance. In its High Level part, analysis suggests that it may be in a position historically like that which surrounded Newton's theories of matter and light. And it may be just a measure of Freud's genius that his High Level theory does run so far ahead of possible incorporation into science.

But, even when we recognise that we are not justified in feeling depressed about the theory, the fact is that it still leaves us feeling very uncomfortable. For it is surrounded by serious uncertainties, which, apparently, will be very difficult to dispel. It looks as if we shall have to traverse long corridors of time – perhaps several centuries – before we come to know how much truth there is in analytic theory, and how, therefore, to incorporate it into science. During this long period, we are doomed to uncertainty about the theory, and we will just have to learn to tolerate the ambiguities it poses for us.

Still, none of us likes uncertainty – and this includes the analysts. Some of them may be tempted to deal with it – and with all the doubts and difficulties we have raised about analytic theory – by the simple expedient of repudiating the whole problem we have been examining in this book. They do this by claiming that psychoanalytic theory is only of *historical* interest at the present time, and simply not worth the attention we have been giving it. There is no need, therefore, to be troubled by the uncertainties that surround the theory. The fatal objection about this escape route is that, if contemporary analysts and others are concerned about the nature and standing of their *own* doctrines, then it is false to say that psychoanalytic theory is *only* of historical interest. For the character and logic of psychodynamic doctrines, past and present, have much in common with that of analytic theory. If contemporary analysts wish to settle the standing of their own doctrines, then it is very advisable for them to try to settle the standing of the founding doctrine itself, psychoanalytic theory. Therefore, they cannot escape the uncertainties of the latter by just dismissing it as *passé*.

Some other analysts – apparently based for the most part in Britain – tend to take a more radical stand. They tend not only to regard analytic theory as *passé*, but also to be uninterested in, and apparently uncommitted to, *any* theory at all, high or low. They are quite happy to offer reports of their clinical experience with various cases. Occasionally, they do venture some general remarks about development, or the connection between early experience and adult personality and difficulties. But for the most part these analysts tend not to offer us what can reasonably be described as general discoveries, or a theory of development or psychopathology, or anything else. So they appear to have no theory about which they can be uncertain.

It is clear that this a-theoretical stance, if consistently maintained, would make the work of these analysts very uninteresting indeed. They would become mere operators *ad personam*. But it is very doubtful whether they do, and can, maintain it consistently. For it is difficult to see how they can make sense out of their case material without the use of general psychodynamic considerations; and these embody their concealed theory (cf. Chapter 4, Section VIII). Therefore, their a-theoretical stance is self-deceptive and misleading; and it fails to save them from the sort of uncertainties that afflict psychodynamic doctrines in general, and psychoanalytic theory in particular.

There is another way in which we are apt to try to reduce, or to escape from, uncertainty. We succumb to the delusion that thought is omnipotent. So we think up some new way of talking about psychoanalysis, which we hope will do the trick for us, at least in part. These new ways are a familiar feature of the analytic landscape. Thus, Bowlby has suggested a revision of analytic theory which discards its stories about instinct and energy, and yet keeps and emphasises the parts of the theory which speak of the human being as a control system. This proposed revision has its value in, for example, bridging the chasm between analysts and the scientific students of behaviour. But, *qua* revision, it is incoherent. One cannot postulate that Smith embodies a control system which manages somehow to run without the use and expenditure of energy. This sort of talk will not do much to bring psychoanalysis into science. Again, as we have seen (Chapter 2), several analysts have extended analytic theory by developing it into an Ego psychology. This work has done something, at least, to meet the reasonable objections from Pavlovian and Soviet psychologists, as well as from cognitive psychologists in the West, that analytic theory does not, and cannot, deal with normal, cognitive, and rational and conscious functioning. But it is very doubtful whether this development is much more than a linguistic and conceptual extension of analytic theory (Chapter 8). So, though this extension of analytic theory may do something to reassure cognitive psychologists, and others, about analytic theory and its prospects, it does little to bring it any further within the fold of established knowledge.

What is needed, as we have emphasised, to sift the grain from the chaff in analytic theory is further scientific inquiry – piecemeal, incomplete and disappointingly thin though this may be at any one time. Chapter 8 makes it plain that scientific work has been, and still is, very active indeed; and this springs to a large degree from analytic theory itself. But, as science is an enterprise whose branches intermesh, and whose future usually holds surprises for us, the relevant progress in our knowledge may emerge from quite unexpected places, *not* only or chiefly from the work we have looked at in Chapter 8. Apart from prosecuting scientific inquiry, and clarifying the nature of the whole problem (which is what we have been trying to do in this book), there seems to be little else we can do to hasten the incorporation of what is authentic in analytic theory into the corpus of scientific knowledge.

But what of psychoanalytic method – both as a tool of inquiry and as a therapy? Are we justified in feeling depressed about these?

When new methods of exploration and discovery are first developed, it is typical of their pioneers and promoters to exaggerate their strength and value. It is also not unusual for a new method – if it has any value at all – to begin its life with a high rate of return. After a time, the rate falls; the method may even exhaust its utility altogether and be discarded; and the real strength and value of the method can then be assessed. What possible reason can we have for expecting psychoanalysis to be any different from other methods of inquiry? The optical telescope does not yield the dividends today that it did in the days of William Herschel. Why should analysis be any different? There seem to be no reasons to warrant making an exception of it. On the contrary, the method just seems to have gone through a history which is typical of other methods of exploration.

When in the past a new method of healing or treatment was developed, it was liable to be presented in the market-place with a flourish of high hopes and expectations, and backed by the confidence and optimism of its promoters. When, after a time, experience of the new method was gained, it was possible to arrive at a realistic judgement of its value. It is by no means unknown for the medical world to decide after a time that a new method is of little, or no, therapeutic value. Again, why should analytic method be any different? This method seems to have gone through a history which is similar to that of some other therapies in ordinary and in psychological medicine. There seems to be nothing special about psychoanalysis which should make it an exception to this familiar pattern in medical history.

We are not justified, therefore, in being depressed about psycho-analytic method. This mood is inappropriate. Of course, it is disappointing to find that the method is of doubtful and limited value as a tool of exploration and discovery. It is equally disappointing to find that it is also of limited worth as a therapy. This is especially so after the great hopes that were entertained in the early years of analysis. However, the history of the method makes it clear that the appropriate mood for us is not one of depression, but one of sobriety and realism.

IX

Yet, even when we recognise and fully accept that depression about analysis is out of place, we may still feel doubtful about it for quite a different reason. When we look at what analysis has actually achieved in the course of its life – at the uncertainties surrounding the theory, and at the limitations of the method; and when we also bear in mind the current state of play in psychology and in mental therapy, we are naturally tempted to ask some very obvious questions. Why should we learn to tolerate the uncertainties which surround the subject? For is there any reason why we should keep analysis alive any longer? Should scarce public funds be spent on preserving the institution of psychoanalysis? Or should we cease bothering to try to maintain it, now that it seems to have done its job?

Unlike some questions we have discussed in this book, these ones are fairly easy to answer. It is generally accepted that the weapons of treatment available in the psychiatric armoury are not anything like as powerful and efficient as we should like them to be. It is essential, therefore, for the psychiatric profession to keep in being any method of treatment for which a reasonable case can be made out, just as it is essential for the profession to be on the constant lookout for new and better methods. It is clear that a limited but reasonable case can be made out for psychotherapy and the analytic forms of it (Chapter 9). It may well be the case that when the fundamental sciences decipher the code of brain functioning, new and simpler methods of treatment will emerge that will render psychoanalysis quite *passé*. But that day has not yet arrived, and it is obviously desirable that for the present psychiatrists should retain analysis as one weapon in their armoury.

But quite apart from the question of mental treatment, we are confronted by the whole problem of how much of the theory will eventually be incorporated into science, and in what ways. It is necessary, therefore, to keep the theory alive. But to do this requires us to maintain in being the case material, by reference to which the central concepts of the theory can be explained and mastered. This material can only be produced by analysts and cognate workers. Hence during this whole historical period – the period of transition from early theory building by analysts to incorporation into science – we need the presence of analysts, so that they can go on producing the case material that is central to the whole problem. It may well be that, when in the future the chaff and the grain in analytic and psychodynamic theories have been distinguished, and the grain incorporated into a body of established knowledge, the intellectual and therapeutic scene may then be so transformed that analytic theory and analysis as a profession will be transmogrified into archaic and historical curiosities. They may then look like alchemy and alchemists. But for the present, and the forseeable future, we need analysts and their work, if we are to make scientific progress in this field. For this reason alone, it is fitting that public funds should contribute to maintain the profession and its work. How large or small this contribution should be, and the exact form it should take are obviously matters to be settled in the light of the detailed circumstances prevailing in each particular country.

X

Where, then, does psychoanalysis stand in respect of related disciplines?

History

The psychoanalyst or psychodynamic worker is concerned in particular to try 'to understand' his patient or analysand. A historian of (say) Queen Elizabeth I is also concerned 'to understand' his subject.

The historian goes to work (to put it summarily) by using the generally accepted concepts and beliefs of common sense, plus the generalisations and concepts and particular propositions of established scientific knowledge, where relevant. He applies these to the material contained in the documents and other records of Elizabeth's life and times. He develops a narrative about her, in which he fits the material together in a coherent way, and which will help us to understand, for example, why she never married, why she resisted executing Mary, and so on. If his narrative satisfies the strict standards of contemporary historical scholarship, it will probably be accepted as a piece of good history; and in so far as it throws light on dark places not previously understood, it will be accepted as making a contribution to the subject.

The psychoanalyst is in a very different position. He makes use, in particular, of the special notions and generalisations of the version of analytic theory he prefers, plus common sense. He uses these in the analysis itself to help to produce the case material (Chapters 5 and 6); and to spin a coherent narrative about it – which will help him 'to understand' the analysand. But his psychoanalytic concepts and generalisations are not generally accepted as true, unlike the common sense equipment of the historian. Hence, though a narrative of his may spin a coherent tale, it is not acceptable *ipso facto* as a contribution to the truth. Therefore, his narrative is not as strong as the historian's. The analyst has tried to use the case material to bridge the gap between intelligibility and truth. For psychoanalysis is a generalising enterprise (quite unlike history), and analysts have attempted to use the case material to support the general claims of the theory. We have seen that these attempts have not been particularly successful, and that it is advisable, and sufficient, for the analyst to be more modest and to rest content with a coherent story about an analysand that *may* contain pointers to the truth about him or her (pages 197–198).

In recent years some students of history – especially in the United States – have been confused by psychoanalysis into overlooking the severe limitations of narrative explanation by analysts. They have tried to use analytic theory and psychodynamic theories to explain historical characters and events, and thereby supplement traditional historical studies and methods. This is clearly a hazardous enterprise with very severe limitations. It can be fruitful only when the characters or events pose questions that common sense and science are not strong enough to answer; and when the information available closely resembles psychoanalytic case material. This second condition is very difficult to satisfy. Naturally. Elizabeth I has left us a lot of records, but, alas, not the tape records of her psychoanalysis, or anything remotely resembling them. If, therefore, the available information in any instance is very different from the analytic material, and if we then proceed to develop a psychoanalytic narrative about the information, we are in grave danger of abandoning our strict standards of historical scholarship. We are liable to take flight into the fantasy of a psychoanalytic novel. This novel may represent a plausible application of some psychoanalytic orientation to the given historical material. But we are not likely to have any *independent* reason for believing it. This is the central objection to, for example, a work in psycho-history which is much esteemed in psychoanalytic circles, namely *Young Man Luther* by Erik Erikson.[8] It is small wonder, therefore, that the distinguished Cambridge historian, G. R. Elton, can say that he does not find this work 'contributes anything of value to an understanding of either Luther or his age.'[9]

Of course, it is generally agreed that history can be written under the strong influence of certain guiding ideas. A historian who has assimilated Marx's thought, for example, may write reputable history which is obviously post-Marx in character. Whether there are historians who have assimilated Freud and produced reputable post-Freudian history is a matter for the historians themselves to decide. But it would seem that psycho-historians have been misled into supposing that, when they write psycho-history, they are *ipso facto* writing reputable post-Freudian history as well. The confusion of these two tasks has helped to give rise to the current misuse of psychoanalysis in historical studies.[10]

Psychiatry

What of the present and future relations of psychoanalysis to psychiatry?

If we put on one side the existence of those few analysts who are not medically trained (known as 'lay' analysts), it is correct to say that psychoanalysis has been, and still is, a speciality inside psychiatry. It is one which concentrates on the character, causes (or aetiology) and treatment of the psychoneuroses. Analytic theory also offers psychiatry a general description of, or way of talking about, most of the whole field of abnormal behaviour. The fact that analytic theory does offer this general way of talking has been a very dubious blessing. It has helped to mislead the public (especially, perhaps, in the United States) into supposing that to be a psychiatrist is to be a psychoanalyst, that psychiatry and analysis are identical disciplines. It has also helped to mislead some psychiatrists themselves. The fact that analytic theory can be used to cover a large part of the psychiatric field appears to make analytic theory a story of very great scope, which adds to its strength. But this feature of its scope is misleading (cf. above page 195 ff.). In reality analytic theory only provides a general way of talking which some workers may find convenient; but which is far from being obligatory.

On the other hand, in dealing with patient Joe or Sue, the psychiatrist is aware that there is 'something the matter with', or 'something wrong with', Joe or Sue. If Joe's erratic aggression is 'due to' a front temporal tumour, then he knows, in part, what is wrong with Joe. But if Joe's aggression is 'not organic' in origin, he then inclines to say that there is something *psychologically* the matter with him. Here analytic theory steps in to tell us what this psychological matter is. It gives psychiatry a general psychopathology, and to a lesser exent an aetiology of psychoneurotic disorders. In these respects analytic theory makes a contribution to contemporary psychiatry.

But, again, this psychopathology and aetiology are not obligatory upon us. The 'model' offered us is not a compulsory one. There are other candidates around. Thus, it is logically possible to speak in, for example, neo-Pavlovian terms about Joe's neurotic behaviour, or in terms of operant conditioning, or social learning. No doubt, the differences between these various theories, or 'models', appear to be somewhat greater than they really are, since locutional and related differences conceal that the theories are partially isomorphic. But there *are* genuine differences between them, and these may be important. In particular, analytic theory directs our attention to what was, and is (allegedly), the case *inside* the psychic system, and how it functions. This is an 'intra-psychic model', to use current jargon. Some other competing models direct our attention 'outside' – to the observable behaviour of the person (for example, phobic responses, obsessive and compulsive behaviour, defective social skills). By attending to the behaviour of patients, and its 'external' determiners, it has been possible to develop new methods of treatment that are very promising (for example, desensitisation, operant conditioning, social skills training); and further inquiry on these lines is clearly desirable. In contrast, by concentrating on what is going on 'inside' the person, it may turn out that the psychoanalytic intra-psychic story is leading us therapeutically up an unrewarding and ultimately blind alley – in spite of the case which can be made for analytic treatment at the present time (cf. Chapter 9).

As a psychiatric speciality, the future of psychoanalysis depends on the future of psychiatry itself. This medical discipline is still at the clinically descriptive stage of its development. If we accept the analogy with the history of general medicine, then it is reasonable to maintain that the development of psychiatry depends on the development of the sciences fundamental to it – namely, those concerned to unlock the neuro chemical machinery of the nervous system. As and when this comes about, a psychiatrist *will* then come to know what is 'the matter with' mental patient Joe. This will transform the place of psychoanalysis in psychiatry. For the development of the sciences fundamental to this subject will also, *ipso facto*, have the result of helping to incorporate whatever is of value in psychoanalysis into science. This whole development will also probably determine the future place of analytic treatment. It is not worth speculating on the shape of the *theoretical* scene in psychiatry after the transformation in it of the place of analytic theory. But those of us who are rash may be ready to bet that analysis as *treatment* will be replaced by cheaper and more effective *physical* methods, which will affect the functioning of the biological machinery responsible for our inner world and outer behaviour (cf. Chapters 8 and 9).

Psychology

Psychology is one of the sciences necessarily involved in developing those areas which are fundamental to psychiatry, and in incorporating the valuable in analytic theory into the corpus of science as a whole. Such developments will also involve the large branch of psychology known as 'social psychology', if only because analytic theory is concerned with the development of the individual, and this takes place in a social group.

When psychologists address themselves to the problem of incorporating analytic theory, it is advisable for them to be modest. Condescension is out of place, for their own subject is still in a fairly primitive and exploratory stage. They cannot boast, for example, any more than an analyst can, of possessing a single wide-ranging theory in their own subject, whose standing is secure. The doubts surrounding Piaget's theory, for example, are well known;[11] and Pavlov's general position runs into the objection that the brain just does not seem to work in the way Pavlov supposed it did.[12] At the present time we do not have an accepted explanation of even such a comparatively elementary pheno-menon as classical conditioning; and it is likely, therefore, to be a long time before psychology can present us with established theories of human development and of personality. Hence the contribution psychologists can make to resolving the uncertainty about analytic theory is likely to be a modest one in the foreseeable future.

In the meantime, we are faced by questions of psychological fact which we cannot do much to answer. How important is the role of unconscious motives, and the like, in the ordinary life of the ordinary person – in contrast with the role of conscious motives, rational considerations, and so on? How far is his adult personality the outcome of his biological equipment intermeshing over time with the pattern of parental and family influence in his particular community? Or how far is it the outcome of social influence conveyed via the family? Even when we do begin to understand how the nervous system works (and this may happen quite soon), it will still probably be some centuries before we can get to grips with the large and awesome questions about ourselves which we would like to have answered. When we do get to grips with them, we will probably do so in a theoretical and technological landscape unimaginably different from our own at the present time.

So for the present and the future, analytic theory will not form part of the discipline of psychology. Nor will any other psychodynamic type of theory. Psychoanalytic theory is, and will continue to be, of great heuristic interest and value to psychologists – even if, in the end, not much of it remains inside our established body of scientific knowledge about human nature.

Psychoanalytic Education

Some light can usually be thrown on the standing of a subject in a community by looking at its place in the educational system. How do analysts and related colleagues receive their education in analysis? How do psychologists and the ordinary public learn about it? The uncertainty and uneasiness surrounding analysis comes out in the way it fits into the educational system.

The training of professional analysts is in the hands of the respective analytic organisations in each country. That is to say, the trainee is taught by the particular institution – Freudian, Jungian, or whatever it may be – that has accepted him; and a full psychoanalysis is a necessary part of his training. It is manifest at once that a course of training of this type is deeply unsatisfactory as a professional education. Self-contained, institutional training under tutors who have like-minded views, plus a psychoanalysis from an analyst of a kindred orientation – all this reads like a recipe for disaster; and it is a tribute to the resilience of the human mind that so many analysts have managed to recover so well from the evils of their education. Obviously, what is required for their own professional health is that their education should be absorbed into adequately designed courses of university instruction.

But this requirement runs slap into irremovable opposition from the analysts themselves. The reason is obvious. Absorption into university life can only be achieved if analysts are prepared as a group to open up their own theoretical and practical work to the salubrious and bracing winds of fundamental criticism and scepticism, which are essential to the life of scholarship and the advance of knowledge. Now the development of tape recording since the Second World War has made it quite possible to reconcile the requirement that the analyst's work be presented to psychiatric colleagues and students for fundamental examination with the need to secure the confidentiality of the material from patients. But analysts in general are still very unwilling to cooperate with others, and to submit their work to public scrutiny. The sources of their unwillingness are mixed, no doubt, and by no means wholly unreasonable. Unhappily, however, they lay themselves open to the suspicion, owing to the way they are apt to handle the problem, that their unwillingness to cooperate stems in part from their own professional insecurity. They seem to fear the demystification of their own practice and subject, which would ensue if they were absorbed into the organisation and ethos of university life. But unless, and until, they are prepared to accept demystification, their subject and training will remain in the shadows; and there is little that their friends in the learned world can do for them.

What of psychiatrists who are not analysts, of psychologists and the general public? In general, they are given little formal education in analytic concepts and practice. They tend to 'pick up' their knowledge of psychoanalysis (Chapter 4). Obviously, the results of this can be unfortunate or even bizarre. It is not unknown for non-analytic psychiatrists to be as full of misconceptions about analysis as the man on the Clapham omnibus.[13] In recent years analysts have been trying to remedy this situation by running courses themselves – for instance, groups for sensitivity training, seminars and lectures with case reports for members of other professions, for example, doctors, business managers, and clergy interested in pastoral work. Admirable and helpful though these efforts are, they run into the basic objection that they amount, in effect, to an apprenticeship training. They do not enable, or even encourage, the students to raise the fundamental questions about psychoanalysis that should be raised of it, as of any other subject. A critic could protest that these courses are, in part, subtle exercises in psychoanalytic propaganda by example – the teachers saying indirectly: 'Go and do thou likewise'.

Some universities and colleges, however, *do* give *explicit* instruction in Freudian theory and other psychodynamic theories. This instruction is a notable feature in psychology courses in colleges and textbooks in the United States of America. But, as far as one can discover, this instruction is largely second-hand. The student gets the material out of lectures and textbooks; and does not have independent access to it. This contrasts sharply with psychology courses in (say) animal learning, where the student *does* have independent access to the behaviour of rats in a Skinner box. This position contrasts, also, with the psychology syllabus at the University of Oxford, which contains no reference to Freud or psychoanalysis, and which cannot do so, if only because it is not possible in Oxford to ensure independent access to the analytic material.[14]

The second-hand education in psychoanalysis which seems to be meted out to college students in the United States can be accused of being responsible, in part, for producing a large population of graduates with little real idea of what analysts are up to, and who accord to psychoanalysis an inflated status it does not deserve. But this graduate population – believing that it *has* been taught about psychoanalysis – obviously encourages the large educated classes in the U.S. to bandy psychoanalytic concepts about in relatively unrestrained freedom. This in turn helps to debase their extended psychoanalytic sensitivity, and to turn it into the wild, unthinking application of jargon. Analysis may have 'captured' the great American public; but it has paid a considerable price in doing so.

Common sense

It is evident from all this that, whatever its therapeutic value, psychoanalysis has its dangers – for the analytic profession itself, and related professions, as well as for the outside public. One of the things that helps to make it a dangerous enterprise is that it appears to encourage analytic and psychodynamic practitioners to overlook the place and great importance of ordinary common sense.

In contrasting psychoanalysis with common sense, we must not fall into the trap of supposing that there is a sharp line between them. Far from it. Common sense has been very familiar for centuries with the idea that there are aspects of personality, involving both dispositions and motives, of which a person may be unaware, and by reference to which we can explain his conduct. In other words, common sense makes use of the ideas contained in Regulative principles 2 and 3 (Chapter 2). It has also been very familiar for centuries with ideas connected with human beings having impulses, growing up to deal with the world, developing a conscience, learning and losing self-control, with feelings of guilt and shame, and so on. In other words, common sense is familiar with those aspects of human functioning which the concepts of Id, Ego and Super-Ego cover in their low level use. Consequently, it is reasonable to maintain that, far from there being a sharp line between commonsense psychology and that of psychoanalysis, the latter is an extension and development out of the former.

Where psychoanalysis differs from common sense is, in the first place, in the very great emphasis it places on the ideas embodied in principles 2 and 3 about goal direction, unconscious motives, and the rest. It gives these ideas a pervasive importance not found in common sense. Psychoanalysis also differs from the latter in the *sort* of unconscious motives, purposes and states it ascribes to human beings. It claims, for example, that boys develop an unconscious libidinal interest in the mother, that compulsion neurotics are in fundamental conflict between hating the parental figures and fear of giving way to this hatred (Chapters 2 and 7). Common sense does not contain these ideas about unconscious motives, and the like; nor many others which are characteristic of, and central to, psychoanalytic theory (cf. Chapter 2). In addition, of course, common sense does not contain any High Level theory at all.

But in spite of these very large differences between the psychology of psychoanalysis and that of common sense, it is very important for us all – and especially for analysts themselves – to be aware of the existence of common sense and of the role it can, and does, play.

It provides analysts with logical and complementary support. The fact is that, where Joe and Sue are not in great psychological difficulties, it is not logically possible for an analyst to use analytic theory to construct a complete narrative about them – without making extensive use of common sense and the ordinary psychological notions embodied in it. If Joe has a great interest in drawing and music, which leads him to neglect his school work, or if Sue has a passionate interest in science and its possible benefits for the Third World, we (probably) cannot give an adequate description and account of them without appealing to considerations which are commonsensical in character and outside analytic theory. But even where Joe *is* in great difficulties, it is not possible to construct an adequate narrative without making *some* use of common sense. For Joe's unconscious conflicts and difficulties go along with the workings of Joe's beliefs, the considerations he rationally entertains, the decisions he makes, the intentions he forms, and so on. We have to resort to common sense to bring these into an adequate picture of Joe. All this, of course, would be no surprise to (say) an historian. But it is apt to surprise analysts, because they are inclined to overlook the use they make, and have to make, of common sense. It is apt to be especially surprising, perhaps, to an Ego-Psychoanalyst. For though he is ready to purloin the offerings of common sense, he is liable not to notice he is doing so, because of his propensity to disguise his thefts in the clothing of his favourite psychoanalytic language.

Psychoanalysis, therefore, is logically dependent on the psychology of common sense. It will remain so theoretically, until developments in psychology allow us to incorporate reasons, intentions, etc. in the cumbersome jargon which will be invented in the future to incorporate reasons, and so on, into science.

In overlooking common sense, analysts are also overlooking one of their safeguards against the troubles and dangers that beset them. It is well-known that analysts lead difficult lives, personally and professionally. When they forget common sense, or allow its hold on them to loosen, they make matters worse. They are then liable to forget that, whereas it is essential and appropriate to exercise their professional sensitivity when treating a patient, it is not essential and not necessarily appropriate for them to do so when conducting committee meetings, or running their own families. In these circumstances an analyst is liable to exhibit a tortuous, sticky, self-conscious over-sensitivity, which will prevent him from being appropriately direct, straightforward and natural. He will be liable to treat his own children as patients, or prospective ones, and so be ready to pack off his own little, pre-school Sue for child psychoanalysis at the first glimpse of quite ordinary and normal childish difficulties.

If the outside public forgets its common sense, then, lacking the constraints which this provides, the public is liable to allow its extended analytic sensitivity to go wild and to be debased. Of course, if the public is not given a good education in its common tongue, it will be somewhat unaware of the resources the tongue opens up to us; and this may prevent the growth and influence of commonsense beliefs and notions.

If, furthermore, the population and social structure are relatively mobile and fluid, the social circumstances may not be present for the growth of a common sense which is widely accepted and influential. Where these circumstances hold, the public may lie open to seduction by a technical discourse, such as psychoanalysis, which purports to give a general account of human nature, and which seems to contain a ready answer to most questions about human difficulties. A critic could argue that these two social circumstances – an inadequate education in English, and a fluid population and social structure – have been conspicuously present in the United States of America for some time. If so, then these circumstances may also help to account for the widespread acceptance of psychoanalytic discourse in that country, the inflation of Freud, and the debasement of analytic sensitivity that seems to be present there.

So, however feeble the psychology of common sense may be, it still has its uses. When Jane Austen makes us look at Darcy from a different angle, then his pride takes on quite a different appearance. When we hear about the expectations which Wickham developed as a youth, then we learn that he is a bit of a smooth rogue and why. Because Elizabeth was attracted by Wickham's attentions, she was blinded into not noticing his improprieties; and only later on was she able to recognise her prejudice and admit that 'till this moment she never knew herself'. We do not need to take flight into the fanciful or the extravagant or the odd to understand what is going on. Indeed, when Catherine Morland does this very thing, she is gently laughed at and brought back to earth.[15] Austen is limited, of course, by her own outward-looking vision and in other respects. But in spite of her limitations, she shows us how common sense can be shrewdly and perceptively used to highlight features of the human scene in interesting and amusing ways. She shows us how it can be used to describe and to help explain conduct by means of the most ordinary and familiar of human wishes, aspirations, dispositions and the like. Her work gives rise inevitably to the thought that, for much of ordinary life, it is sufficient to rely on the sense and sensitivity of common sense, when exercised with sympathy and kindness. For much of ordinary life, it is quite unnecessary to bother ourselves about psychoanalysis, or any of the other psychodynamic psychologies that are on sale in the market-place. The path of wisdom – for most of us most of the time – is to forget about them.

Chapter references

Chapter 1

1. Austen, J. (1813) *Pride and Prejudice* (T. Egerton: London).
2. Kraepelin, E. (1905–6) *Lectures on Clinical Psychiatry*, 2nd ed., authorised trans. by T. Johnstone (Bailliere, Tindall and Cox: London).
   Henderson, D. K. and Gillespie, R. D. (1927) *Textbook of Psychiatry* 1st ed., (Oxford, London and New York).
3. Cf. Ferrier, D. (1886) *The Functions of the Brain* (Putnam: London); Ferrier, D. (1890) *Cerebral Localization* (Smith Elder & Co.: London).
4. Breuer, J. and Freud, S. (1895) *Studies on Hysteria* in Freud, S. *Standard Edition* (1953, 55, 57), (see note 8 below.) ed. James Strachey, vol. 2. (Hogarth: London).
5. On this whole history, see Ellenberger, H. F. (1970) *The Discovery of the Unconscious* (Basic Books: New York).
6. Whyte, L. L. (1962) *The Unconscious before Freud* (Tavistock: London).
7. Auden, W. H. (1940) 'In Memory of Sigmund Freud' *Another Time* (Faber and Faber: London).
8. Medawar, P. B. 'Victims of Psychiatry' *New York Review of Books*, 23 Jan., 1975.
9. For Freud's work, see *Standard Edition*, (1953–74) of The Complete Psychological Works of Sigmund Freud, ed. J. Strachey, (Hogarth: London). For a guide to his work, see Jones, E. (1953, 1955, 1957) *Freud: Life and Work*, vols. 1, 2 and 3. (Hogarth: London).

Chapter 2

1. Freud, S. *Civilization and its Discontents* (1930), *Standard Edition* (1961), vol. 21 (Hogarth Press: London).
2. Jung, C. G. *Collected Works* (1953–), (Routledge, Kegan Paul: London).
   Fordham, F. (1953) *An Introduction to Jung's Psychology*. (Penguin: London).
3. For Adler, see in particular the following:
   Adler, A. (1907) *A Study of Organ Inferiority and its Psychical Compensation*. Nervous and Mental Diseases Monog. Series. no. 24, English trans. 1917, (New York); *The Neurotic Constitution* (1912), English trans. 1917 (Routledge, Kegan Paul: London); *Understanding Human Nature* (1921), English trans. 1928 (Allen and Unwin: London); Lewis Way (1956) *Alfred Adler: An introduction to his Psychology* (Penguin: London).

4. See, e.g.

Horney, K. (1937) *The Neurotic Personality of Our Time* (Norton: New York).

Horney, K. (1939) *New Ways in Psychoanalysis* (Norton: New York).

Sullivan, H. S. (1955) *The Interpersonal Theory of Psychiatry* (Tavistock: London).

5. Freud, A. (1936), English trans. 1937 *The Ego and the Mechanisms of Defence*, (Hogarth: London).

Hartmann, H. (1931) 'Ego Psychology and the Problem of Adaptation' in D. Rapaport *Organization and Pathology of Thought*, (Columbia: New York).

Hartmann, H. (1964) *Essays on Ego Psychology*, (Intern. Univ. Press: New York).

6. Klein, M. (1932) *The Psychoanalysis of Children* (Hogarth: London).

Klein, M. (1948) *Contributions to Psycho-Analysis* (Hogarth: London).

7. Rank, O. (1929) *The Trauma of Birth* (Harcourt Brace: New York).

8. Reich, W. (1933) *Character Analysis*, 2nd ed. 1945, (Organe Inst. Press).

9. Fromm, E. (1942) *The Fear of Freedom* (Routledge, Kegan Paul: London).

Fromm, E. (1948–9) *Man for Himself* (Routledge, Kegan Paul: London).

10. A recent review of the field has listed about fifty therapies and theoretical positions. See Karasu, T. B. (1977) 'Psychotherapies: An overview'. *The Amer. J. of Psychiatry*, *134*, no. 8, 851–863.

Chapter 3

1. Sutherland, S. (1976) *Breakdown* (Weidenfeld and Nicolson: London).

2. Popper, K. R. (1955) 'Philosophy of Science: A personal report' in *British Philosophy in Mid Century*, ed. C. A. Mace (Allen and Unwin: London).

3. The literature on this topic is large. See, for example, Hempel, C. G. (1965) *Aspects of Scientific Explanation* (Collier; Macmillan: London).

4. For example, Gesell, A. and Ilg. F. L. (1942) *Infant and Child in the Culture of Today* (Hamish Hamilton: London).

5. Nagel, E. (1959) 'Methodological Issues in Psychoanalytic Theory' in *Psychoanalysis Scientific Method and Philosophy*, ed. S. Hook (New York Univ. Press: New York).

For a discussion of issues discussed in this chapter, and elsewhere, see:

Thomä, H and Kächele, H (1975) 'Problems of Metascience and Methodology in Clinical Psychoanalytic Research', *Annual Rer. of Psychoanalysis*, *III* (Intern. Univ. Press: New York).

Grünbaum, A. (1979) 'Is Freudian Psychoanalytic Theory Pseudo-scientific by Karl Popper's Criterion of Demarcation?' *Amer. Phil. Quarterly*, *16*, no. 2.

6. Nagel, E. *op. cit.*

7. Nagel, E. *op. cit.*

8. Bruner, J. S. and Postman, L. (1949) 'Perception Cognition and Behaviour' *J. Personality*, *18*, no. 1, p. 14.

9. Hall, C. (1963) 'Strangers in Dreams: An empirical confirmation of the Oedipus complex', *J. Personality*, *31*, 336.

10. Jeans, J. (1940) *An Introduction to the Kinetic Theory of Gases* (Cambridge).
11. Harré, R. (1972) *The Philosophies of Science* (Oxford: London).
12. Cf. Miles, T. R. (1966) *Eliminating the Unconscious* (Pergamon: Oxford).
13. Cf. the relation of inductive support in Hempel, C. G. (1965), *op. cit.* Ch. 12.
14. Newton, I. *Opticks* 4th ed. (1730), republished Dover Publ. (Constable: London).
15. Martin, M. (1970) 'An Explicative Model of Theory Testing', *Zeitschrift für Allg. Wissenschafts theorie*, Band I, Heft. 2. On tendency generalisations, see Braithwaite, R. B. (1953) *Scientific Explanation* (Cambridge).

Chapter 4

1. Sartre, J–P. (1939) *Sketch for a Theory of the Emotions*, trans. P. Maigret (Methuen: London, 1962).
   Sartre, J–P. (1943) *Being and Nothingness*, trans. H. E. Barnes (Methuen: London, 1957).
   Habermas, J. (1968) *Knowledge and Human Interests*, trans. J. Shapiro (Heinemann: London, 1972).
   Ricoeur, P. *Freud and Philosophy*, trans. D. Savage (Yale: New Haven 1970).
2. For a discussion of some of these problems, see:
   Cioffi, F. and Alexander, P. 'Wishes, Symptoms and Actions' (1974) *Proc. Arist. Soc. Suppl. vol.* 48 (Methuen: London).
3. For an analyst who *is* troubled, see Schafer, R. (1976) *A New Language for Psychoanalysis* (Yale: New Haven).
4. In view of the emphasis Freud gave to forgetting, slips of the tongue in everyday life, and the like, the ordinary person may be inclined to think that these facts lend considerable support to psychoanalytic theory. This is not so. As we shall see below (Chapter 5), a psychoanalytic interpretation of an item in the psychoanalytic session gets its backing from the context in which it occurs. When a psychoanalytic interpretation is given of an item *in everyday life*, it generally lacks the contextual backing required to give it much weight. These items, therefore, lend only very feeble support to psychoanalytic theory, and we shall pass them by.
5. Freud, S. (1909) *Standard Edition* vol. 10 (Hogarth: London 1955).
   Cf. Sherwood, M. (1969) *The Logic of Explanation in Psychoanalysis* (Academic Press: New York, London).
   On the issues discussed in this chapter, and elsewhere, see:
   Grünbaum, A (1980) 'Epistemological Liabilities of the Clinical Appraisal of Psychoanalytic Theory' *Nous, 14* (in press).
6. Rogers, C. R. (1942) *Counseling and Psychotherapy* (Houghton Miflin: Cambridge).
   Wolberg, L. R. (1954) *The Technique of Psychotherapy* (Grune and Stratton: New York).
   Farrell, B. A. (1962) 'The Criteria for a Psychoanalytic Interpretation', in *The Philosophy of Mind* (1976) ed. J. Glover (Oxford).
7. For a criticism of 'the informal case study method' in analysis see:

Wallerstein, R. S. (1975) *Psychotherapy and Psychoanalysis*, (Intern. Univ. Press: New York).

Shakow, D. (1960) 'The recorded psychoanalytic interview as an objective approach to research in psychoanalysis', *Psychoanalytic Quarterly, 29*; 82–97.

8. Rosen, G. (1972) 'Freud and Medicine in Vienna' in *Freud*, ed. J. Miller (Weidenfeld and Nicolson: London).

Jones, E. *op.cit., passim.*

9. Rapaport, D. (1959) 'The Structure of Psychoanalytic Theory: A Systemizing Attempt' in *Psychology: A Study of A Science*, vol. 3, ed. S. Koch (McGraw-Hill: New York).

Sarbin, T. R. and others (1960) *Clinical Inference and Cognitive Theory* (Holt Rinehart and Winston: New York).

Stein, M. (1961) (ed.) *Contemporary Psychotherapies* (The Free Press: New York).

Frank, J. D. (1961) *Persuasion and Healing* (Oxford).

Levy, L. H. (1963) *Psychological Interpretation* (Holt Rinehart and Winston: New York).

Bergin, A. E. and Garfield, S. L. (1971, 1978) (ed.) *Handbook of Psychotherapy and Behavior Change, passim.* (Wiley: New York).

10. Fisher, H. A. L. (1912) *Napoleon* (Home Univ. Lib.: London).

11. Popper, K. R. (1955) *op. cit.*

12. Cf. Rycroft, C. (1966) 'Introduction: Causes and Meaning' in *Psychoanalysis Observed*, ed. C. Rycroft (Constable: London).

Storr, A. (1966) 'The concept of Cure' in Rycroft, C. (ed.) *op. cit.*

Chapter 5

1. Freud, S. 'Leonardo da Vinci and a Memory of his Childhood', *Standard Edition* (1957), *op cit.*, vol. 11.

2. Fenichel, O. (1945) *The Psychoanalytic Theory of Neurosis* (Routledge, Kegan Paul: London).

In general, cf. Paul, L. (ed) (1963) *Psychoanalytic Clinical Interpretation* (Free Press of Glencoe, Collier-Macmillan: London).

3. Wisdom, J. O. (1962) 'Criteria for a Psychoanalytic Interpretation', *Proc. Aristot. Soc. Suppl. Vol. 36* (Harrison: London).

4. Freud, S. (1937) 'Constructions in Analysis', *Standard Edition* (1964) *op. cit.*, vol. 23 (Harvester Press, Basic Books).

5. Cf. Fisher, S. and Greenberg, R. P. (1977) *The Scientific Credibility of Freud's Theories and Therapy*.

These authors say that Freud, at one stage at least, 'indicated that any patient response to an interpretation ... could be taken as evidence of its validity'. This, they argue, is 'equivalent to saying that patient responses may play little role in determining the direction of the analyst's interpretations' (p. 367).

6. See, e.g. Erikson, E. (1958) 'The nature of clinical evidence', *Daedelus, 87*, no. 4.

Wisdom, J. O. (1966) 'Testing a psychoanalytic interpretation', *Ratio*, 8.

7. Luborsky, L. and Spence, D. P. (1978) 'Quantitative Research on Psychoanalytic Therapy', in *Handbook of Psychotherapy and Behavior Change* 2nd ed., eds. Garfield, S. L. and Bergin A. E. (Wiley: New York).

8. Farrell, B. A. (1976) 'Criteria for a Psychoanalytic Interpretation' in Glover, J. (ed) *op. cit.* Ch. 4.

   Cf. Turquet, P. M. (1962) *Proc. Aristot. Soc. Suppl.* Vol. 36. This seems to be the only place where Turquet has offered us his views on the questions we are raising.

9. There are studies into what analysts and psychotherapists report what they do, and these raise doubts about the general assumption that psychoanalysts do in fact practise a common method.

   Cf. Glover, E. (1955) *The Technique of Psychoanalysis*. (Balliere Tindall and Cox: London).

   Lennard, H. L. and Bernstein, A. (1960) *The Anatomy of Psychotherapy* (Columbia Univ. Press: New York).

   Sklansky et al. (1966) *Arch. Gen. Psychiat.*, *14*, 158–170.

10. Cf. Seitz, P. F. D. (1966) in *Methods of Research in Psychotherapy* eds. Gottschalk, L. A. and Auerbach, A. H. (Appleton: New York). This study suggests that it is not possible in practice for analysts to arrive at a consensus in their work of interpretation.

    For other studies bearing on this and related issues, see Fisher and Greenberg, *op. cit.*

11. Cf. Farrell, *op. cit.* for a discussion of some of these differences.

Chapter 6

1. Erikson, E. (1958) 'The Nature of Clinical Evidence', *op. cit.*

2. Forer (1949) 'The fallacy of personal validation: A classroom demonstration of gullibility' *J. Abn. Soc. Psychol.*, *44*, 118–123.

   Sundberg, N. D. (1966) 'The acceptability of "fake" versus *bona fide* personality test interpretations' *J. Abn. Soc. Psychol.* *50*, 145–147.

   O'Dell, J. W. (1972) 'P. T. Barnum explores the computer' *J. Consult. and Clin. Psychol. 38*, 270–273.

   Dmitruk, V. M., Collins, R. W. and Clinger, D. L. (1973) 'The Barnum Effect and acceptance of negative personal evaluation' *J. Consult. and Clin. Psychol. 41* (1973) 192–4.

3. Glover, E. (1955) 'The therapeutic effect of inexact interpretation: a contribution to the theory of suggestion', in *The Technique of Psycho-analysis* (Balliere Tindall and Cox: London).

   Mendell, W. (1964) 'The phenomenon of Interpretation' *Amer. J. of Psychoanal.*, *24*, 184–189.

4. Eysenck, H. J. (ed.) (1960) *Behaviour Therapy and the Neuroses* (Pergamon). Beech, H. R. (1969) *Changing Man's Behaviour*: (Pelican).

   Bergin, A. E. and Garfield, S. L. (ed.) (1971) *Handbook of Psychotherapy and Behaviour Change*, Part III (Wiley: New York).

Fisher, S. and Greenberg, R. P. (1977) *op. cit.*

5. For a recent review, see Fisher, S. and Greenberg, R. P. *op. cit.*, Ch. 8. Cf. also Ch. 10.

6. Erikson, E. *op. cit.*

7. Skinner, B. F. *Science and Human Behavior* (Macmillan: New York).
Greenspoon, J. (1962) 'Verbal Conditioning' in Bachrach, A. J. (ed.) *Experimental Foundations of Clinical Psychology* (Basic Books: New York).
Krasner, L. (1971) 'The operant approach in Behavior therapy' in Bergin and Garfield, *op. cit.*

8. Adams, H. E., Butler, J. R. and Noblin, C. D. (1962) 'Effects of psycho-analytically derived interpretations: a verbal conditioning paradigm?' *Psychol. Reports, 10*, 691–694.
Adams, H. E., Noblin, C. D., Butler, J. R. and Timmons, E. O. (1962) 'Differential effect of psychoanalytically derived interpretations and verbal conditioning in schizophrenics' *Psychol. Reports, 11*, 195–198.
Noblin, C. D., Timmons, E. O. and Reynard, M. C. (1963) 'Psychoanalytic interpretations as verbal reinforcers: Importance of interpretation content' *J. Clin. Psychol. 19*, 479–81.

9. Shapiro, A. K. and Morris, L. A. (1978) 'The Placebo Effect in Medical and Psychological Therapies', Ch. 10, in Garfield, S. L. and Bergin, A. E. (ed.) *Handbook of Psychotherapy and Behavior Change: An Empirical Analysis*, 2nd ed. (Wiley: New York).

10. Frank, J. D. (1961) *Persuasion and Healing* (Johns Hopkins: Oxford).

11. Blake, R. R. and Mouton, J. S. (1961) 'The Experimental Investigation of Interpersonal Influence' in *The Manipulation of Human Behavior*, Biderman, A. D. and Zimmer, H. (eds.) (Wiley: New York. London).
Lifton, R. (1961) *Thought Reform and the Psychology of Totalism.* (Gollancz: London).
Frank, J. D. (1961) *op. cit.*
Krasner, L. (1966) 'Behavior Modification Research and the Role of the Therapist' in Gottshalk, L. A. and Auerbach, A. H. (eds.) *Methods of Research in Psychotherapy* (Appleton Century: New York).
Strupp, H. H. (1973) *Psychotherapy: Clinical, Research and Theoretical Issues*, esp. Chs. 3, 5 and 23 (Jason Aronson Inc.: New York).
Garfield, S. L. and Bergin, A. E. (1978), esp. Chs. 7, 8 and 17 *op. cit.*

12. Freud, S. (1937) 'Constructions in Analysis' in *Standard Edition* vol. 23, 255–269, 1964.

13. Pfeffer, A. Z. (1959) 'A procedure for evaluating the results of psycho-analysis', *Amer. J. of Psychoanal.* July, no. 3, 418–58.

14. See, in particular, Horney, K. (1946) *Our Inner Conflicts* (Routledge and Kegan Paul: London).

15. Lifton, R. J. (1961) *op. cit.*
Farrell, B. A. (1972) 'The validity of psychotherapy', *Inquiry, 15*, 146–70.

16. Palmer, L. R. and Boardman, J. (1963) *On the Knossos Tablets*, (Clarendon: Oxford).

17. Rosenthal, R. (1966) *Experimenter Effects in Behavioral Research*, (Appleton Century: New York).

18. Farrell, B. A. (1972) *op. cit.*
For a penetrating examination of the problem, see Cheshire, N. M. (1975) *The Nature of Psychodynamic Interpretation*, esp. Ch. 4 (Wiley: New York).

Chapter 7

1. Eysenck, H. J. (1960) 'Classification and the Problem of Diagnosis' in Eysenck, H. J. (ed) *Handbook of Abnormal Psychology* (Pitman Med. Publ.: London).
Kendell, R. E. (1975) *The Role of Diagnosis in Psychiatry* (Blackwell: Oxford and London).
Shepherd, M. (1978) 'Psychological Medicine' sect. 18, in *Price's Textbook of Practical Medicine* 12th ed., ed. Scott, R. B. (Oxford).
2. Kraepelin, E. (1896) *Clinical Psychiatry* Abs. and adapted from 6th ed. of *Lehrbuch der Psychiatrie*, by A. Rose Defendorf (Macmillan: New York and London, 1902).
Henderson, D. K. and Gillespie, R. D. (1927) *op. cit.*
3. Kraepelin, E. (1913) *Manic-Depressive Insanity and Paranoia* Trans. from 8th ed. of *Lehrbuch der Psychiatrie*. by Barclay, R. M. Livingstone (Edinburgh: 1921).
Lewis, A. J. (1934) 'Melancholia: a historical review. *J. Ment. Science, 80,* 1–42.
Lewis, A. J. (1934) 'Melancholia: a clinical survey of depressive states'. *J. Ment. Science, 80,* 277–378.
Beck. A. T. (1967) *Depression: Clinical Experimental and Theoretical Aspects* (Harper and Row: New York. London).
Kendell, R. E. (1968) *The Classification of Depressive Illnesses* (Oxford: London).
Shepherd, M. (1978) *op. cit.*
Henderson and Gillespie's *Textbook of Psychiatry* (1969) 10th ed., revised by Batchelor, I. R. C. (Oxford Med. Publications: Oxford).
4. Freud, S. (1935) *An Autobiographical Study*, 2nd ed. (Hogarth: London). *Standard Ed. op. cit. 20.*
5. Freud, S. (1887–1902) *The Origins of Psycho-Analysis*: Letters to Wilhelm Fliess. no. 69. ed. Bonaparte, M., Freud, A. and Kris, E. Imago. London 1954. From letter 69 it would seem that the chief considerations which moved Freud were commonsensical: the stories were just too unbelievable to be true.
6. Jung, C. (1943) 'Two Essays on Analytical Psychology', Ch. 3 in *Collected Works*, (1953), vol. 7.
7. Glover, E. (1955) *op. cit.*
8. Wallerstein, R. S. (1975) *op. cit.*
9. Glover, E. (1952) 'Research Methods in Psycho-analysis' *Intern. J. of Psychoanalysis, 33,* 403–9.
10. Jones, E. (1953–57) *op. cit.*
11. Bibring, E. (1953) 'Mechanism of Depression' in *Affective Disorders*, ed. Greenacre, P. Intern. Univ. Press: New York.

12. Klein, M. (1948) *op. cit.*
13. Kuhn, T. S. (1962) *The Structure of Scientific Revolutions* (Univ. of Chicago Press: Chicago).
14. Freud, S. (1913) 'The Predisposition to Obsessional Neurosis', *Standard Edition, 12,* 317–326.
15. For the formulation of these two instances, see Fenichel, O. (1945) *op. cit.*
16. The formulation of these two instances was suggested by Dicks, H. V. (1947) *Clinical Studies in Psychopathology* (Arnold: London).

Chapter 8

1. I am greatly indebted to two recent reviews of this work. Kline, P. (1972) *Fact and Fantasy in Freudian Theory* (Methuen: London).
   Fisher, S. and Greenberg, R. P. (1977) *The Scientific Credibility of Freud's Theories and Therapy* (Harvester Press, Basic Books).
   I have also been helped by the scepticism to be found in the editorial comments in Eysenck, H. J. and Wilson, G. D. (ed.) (1973) *The Experimental Study of Freudian Theories* (Methuen: London).
   For useful collections of scientific papers, see Fisher, S. and Greenberg, R. P. (ed.) (1978) *The Scientific Evaluation of Freud's Theories and Therapy* (Harvester Press, Basic Books); and Eysenck and Wilson, *op. cit.*
2. See Shakow, D. and Rapaport, D. (1968) *The Influence of Freud on American Psychology* (World Pub.: Cleveland).
   The translation was done by Dr. Rosenzweig with the help of Dr. E. Erikson. The original letter runs as follows.

   Sehr geehrter Herr,
       Ich habe Ihre experimentellen Arbeiten zur Prüfung psychoanalytischer Behauptungen mit Interesse zur kenntnis genommen. Sehr hoch kann ich diese Bestätigungen nicht einschätzen, denn die Fülle sicherer Beobachtungen auf denen jene Behauptungen ruhen, macht sie von der experimentellen Prüfung unabhängig. Immerhin, sie kann nicht schaden.

   Ihr ergebener
   Freud.

3. Berkowitz, L. (1962) *Aggression* (McGraw Hill: New York).
   Feshbach, S. 'Aggression' (1970) ed. P. H. Mussen vol. 2,
   Carmichael's *Manual of Child Psychology*, 3rd edn. (Wiley: New York).
4. Hinde, R. A. (1966, 1970) *Animal Behaviour* (McGraw-Hill: New York).
5. Tinbergen, N. (1951) *A Study of Instinct* (Oxford).
   Hess, E. H. 'Ethology and Developmental Psychology' ed. P. H. Mussen, *op. cit.*, vol. 1.
6. Feshbach, S. *op. cit.*
7. E.g. Klein, M. and others (1952) *Developments in Psycho-Analysis* (Hogarth: Inst. of Psycho-analysis: London).
8. E.g. Schwartz, M. D. (1973) *Physiological Psychology* (Prentice Hall: Englewood Cliffs, N. J.).

9. E.g. Harlow, H. F. and Harlow, M. K. (1965) 'The Affectional systems' in Schrier, A. M., Harlow, H. F. and Stollnitz, F. *Behavior of Non-Human Primates* vol. 2 (Academic Press: London).

10. Maccoby, E. E. and Masters, J. C. (1970) 'Attachment and Dependency' Ch. 21 ed. P. H. Mussen, *op. cit.*

11. Gesell, A. et al. (1942) *op. cit.*

12. Kline, *op. cit.* Ch. 5. For a negative view, see Feshbach, *op. cit.*

13. Koch, H. L. (1935) 'An analysis of certain forms of so-called 'nervous habits' in young children', *J. Genet. Psychol.*, 46, 139–170.

14. Freud, S. (1905) 'Three Essays on The Theory of Sexuality', *Standard Edition*, vol. 7.

15. Harlow, H. F. and Harlow, M. K. *op. cit.*

16. 'Of or pertaining to the sexual passion; treating of love; amatory' *Shorter Oxford Engl. Dict.* Corrected and revised 1955/6.
Cf. Klein, G. S. (1970) 'Freud's Two Theories of Sexuality', Ch. 5 in *Clinical Cognitive Psychology: Models and Integrations* (Prentice Hall: New York).

17. Friedman, S. M. (1952) 'An empirical study of the castration and Oedipus complexes' *Genet Psychol. Monogr.*, 46, 61–130.

18. Mischel, W. (1970) 'Sex typing and Socialization' Ch. 2, ed. P. H. Mussen, vol. 2, *op. cit.*

19. Sarnoff, I. and Corwin, S. M. (1959) 'Castration Anxiety and the fear of Death' *J. Personality*, 27, 374–385.

20. Cf. Fisher and Greenberg, *op. cit.*

21. Millar, S. (1966) *The Psychology of Play* (Penguin: London).

22. Hall, C. S. (1963) 'Strangers in Dreams: an experimental confirmation of the Oedipus complex', *J. Personality*, 31, (3) 336–45.
Kline, P. *op. cit.*

23. Stephens, W. N. (1962) *The Oedipus Complex Hypothesis: Cross cultural evidence* (Free Press, New York).
Whiting, J. W. M. and Child, I. L. (1953) *Child Training and Personality* (Yale Univ. Press: New Haven).

24. Young, F. W. and Bacdayan, A. A. (1965) 'Menstrual Taboos and Social Rigidity', *Ethnology 4*, (2), 225–240.

25. Levine, R. A. (1970) 'Cross Cultural Study in Child Psychology', Ch. 26 in Mussen (ed) *op. cit.*
For a more favourable view of these studies than the one presented in the text, see Kline, P. (1977) 'Cross Cultural Studies and Freudian Theory', Ch. 2 in Warren, N. (ed.) *Studies in Cross Cultural Psychology*, vol. 1 (Academic Press: London).

26. Fisher, S. and Greenberg, R. P. Ch. 4, *op. cit.*

27. See Fisher and Greenberg, Ch. 4, *op. cit.* for the relevant studies.

28. Fisher, S. (1970) *Body Experience in Fantasy and Behavior* (Appleton Century: New York).

29. Fisher, S. (1973) *The Female Orgasm* (Basic Books: New York).

30. Millar, S. *op. cit.*

31. Ford, C. S. and Beach, F. A. (1952) *Patterns of Sexual Behaviour* (Eyre and Spottiswoode: London).

Beach, F. A. (ed.) (1976/7) *Human Sexuality in Four Perspectives:* (Johns Hopkins: Baltimore, London).
Mischel, W. *op. cit.*

32. Farrell, B. A. (1979) 'Mental Illness: A Conceptual Analysis' *Psychological Medicine 9*, 21–35.

33. Kline, P. *op. cit.*

34. Mischel, W. *op. cit.*; Kline, *op. cit.*

35. Levinger, G. and Clark, J. (1961) 'Emotional factors in the forgetting of word associations' *J. Abn. Soc. Psychol. 62*, 99–105.

36. Kline, P. *op. cit.*

37. E.g. Dixon, N. F. (1958) 'Apparent changes in the visual threshold as a function of subliminal stimulation' *Quart. J. Exp. Psychol. 10*, 211–215.

38. Dollard, J. et al. (1939) *Frustration and Aggression* (Yale: New Haven).

39. Miller, N. E. (1948) 'Theory and experiment relating psychoanalytic displacement to stimulus-response generalisation' *J. Abn. Soc. Psychol. 43*, 155–173.

40. Hinde, R. A. *op. cit.*

41. Fisher, S. and Greenberg, R. P. *op. cit.* Ch. 2 for the references, and their review of the field.

42. Fisher, S. and Greenberg, R. P. *op. cit.*

43. Goldman-Eisler, F. (1948) 'Breast-feeding and character formation 1' *J. Personality, 17* 83–103.
Goldman-Eisler, F. (1950) 'Breast-feeding and character formation 2' The aetiology of the oral character in psychoanalytic theory *J. Personality, 19*, 189–196.
Goldman-Eisler, F. (1951) 'The problem of "orality" and its origin in early childhood' *J. Ment. Sci., 97*, 765–82.
Lazare, A. et al. (1966) 'Oral, obsessive and hysterical personality patterns: and investigation of psychoanalytic concepts by factor analysis' *Arch. Gen. Psychiat. 14*, 624–30.
Fisher, S. and Greenberg, R. P. *op. cit.*
Kline, P. *op. cit.*
Kline, P. and Storey, R. (1977) 'A factor analytic study of the oral character' *Br. J. Soc. Clin. Psychol. 16*, 317–328.

44. Beloff, H. (1957) 'The structure and origin of the anal character' *Genet Psychol. Monogr. 55*, 141–72.
Fisher, S. and Greenberg, R. P. *op. cit.*, Ch. 3.

45. Biller, H. B. (1971) *Father, Child and Sex Role* (Heath: Lexington).
Kokonis, N. (1972) 'Sex-role identification in Neurosis: Psychoanalytic, developmental and Role theory predictions compared' *J. Abn. Psychol. 80*, 52–57.

46. Kline, P. *op. cit.*
Cf. Eysenck, H. J. and Wilson, G. *op. cit.*, Parts 5 and 6.

47. See Fisher, S. and Greenberg, R. P. *op. cit.*, Ch. 5, for an admirable review of the work on this subject.

48. Freud, S. 'Leonardo da Vinci and a memory of his childhood' *Standard Edition*, vol. 2.

Farrell, B. A. (1963) Introduction to *Leonardo*, by Freud, S., p. 11–88. (Pelican Books: London); reprinted in Morris Philipson (ed.) (1966) *Leonardo da Vinci: Aspects of the Renaissance Genius* (1966) ed. Morris Philipson, pp. 224–275 (George Braziller: New York).

49. Cf. Fisher, S. and Greenberg, R. P. *op. cit.* and Kline, P. *op. cit.*

50. Eysenck, H. J. and Wilson, G. *op. cit.*

51. Freud, S. *The Ego and the Id, Standard Edition*, vol. 19; *New Introductory Lectures* Lect. 34. *Standard Edition*, vol. 22.

52. Hebb, D. O. (1955) 'Drives and the C.N.S. (Conceptual Nervous System)' *Psychological Review 62* (4), 243–54.

    Deutsch, J. A. (1960) *The Structural Basis of Behaviour* (Cambridge: London).

    Gray, J. (1971) *The Psychology of Fear and Stress* (Weidenfeld and Nicolson: London).

    Farrell, B. A. (1968) 'Some Thoughts on the Use of Models in Psychology', in B. Van Rootselaar and J. F. Staal (ed.) *Logic, Methodology and Philosophy of Science 3* (North Holland Pub. Co: Amsterdam).

53. For some of the problems involved, see Farrell, B. A. (1972) 'Clothing the Freudian Model in a Fashionable Dress' *Monist, 56* (3), 343–360.

54. Cf. McFarland, D. J. (1971) *Feedback Mechanisms in Animal Behaviour* (Academic Press: London).

55. Pribram, K. (1969) 'The Foundation of Psychoanalytic Theory: Freud's Neuropsychological Model' Ch. 18 in Pribram, K. H. (ed.) *Brain and Behaviour 4* (Penguin: London).

56. Bowlby, J. (1951) *Maternal Care and Mental Health* (Geneva: WHO).

    Bowlby, J. (1970) *Attachment* vol. 1 (Hogarth: London).

57. Rutter, M. (1972) *Maternal Deprivation Reassessed* (Penguin: London).

    Bowlby, J. (1973) *Separation: Anxiety and Anger* vol. 2. (Hogarth: London).

    Clarke, A. M. and Clarke, A. D. B. (1976) *Early Experience* (Open Books: London).

    The relevance and complications of animal work can be seen in Hinde, R. A. (1977) 'Mother-infant separation and the nature of inter-individual relationships: experiments with rhesus monkeys' *Proc. R. Soc. Lond. B. 191*, 29–50.

Chapter 9

1. Eysenck, H. J. (1973) 'Comment' in Ch. 21 in Eysenck, H. J. and Wilson, G. D. (ed.) *op. cit.*

2. Eysenck, H. J. (1952) 'The Effects of Psychotherapy: An Evaluation' *J. Consult. Psychol. 16*, no. 5, 319–24. Reprinted as Ch. 21 in Eysenck and Wilson, *op. cit.*

3. Landis, C. (1937) 'A statistical Evaluation of Psychotherapeutic Methods' in Hinsie, L. E. (ed.) *Concepts and Problems of Psychotherapy*. (Columbia Univ. Press: New York.)

4. Denker, P. G. (1946) 'Results of Treatment of psychoneuroses by the general practitioner' *New York State J. of Medicine, 46*, 2164–2166.

5. See, Bergin, A. E. (1971) Ch. 7 'The Evaluation of Therapeutic Outcomes' in Bergin, A. E. and Garfield, S. L. (ed.) *op. cit.*

6. For recent discussions of this issue, see Fisher, S. and Greenberg, R. P. (1977) *op. cit.* Ch. 8; Kline, P. (1972) *op. cit.* Ch. 11; Bergin, A. E. and Lambert, M. J. 'The Evaluation of Therapeutic Outcomes' Ch. 5 in Garfield, S. L. and Bergin, A. E. (1978) *op. cit.*
   Cf. also Malan, D. H. (1973) 'The Outcome Problem in Psychotherapy Research' *Arch. Gen. Psychiat.* 29, 719–729.

7. Malan, D. H. (1975) 'Psychodynamic Changes in Untreated Neurotic Patients' *Arch. Gen. Psychiat.* 32, 110–126.

8. For a pessimistic view, see Eysenck (1960) 'The Effects of Psychotherapy' Ch. 18 in Eysenck (ed.) *Handbook of Abnormal Psychology* (Pitman Med Publ.: London); and Rachman, S. (1971) *The Effects of Psychotherapy* (Pergamon: Oxford).
   For other and more optimistic views, see:
   Malan, D. H. (1973) and (1975) *op. cit.*
   Bergin, A. E. and Lambert, M. J. (1978) *op. cit.*
   Shapiro, D. A. (personal Communication).

9. Smith, M. L. and Glass, G. V. (1977) 'Meta-Analysis of psychotherapy outcome studies' *American Psychologist*, 1977, 32, 752–60.

10. Cf. Malan, D. H. (1973) *op. cit.*, for a list of the few acceptable studies.
    Fisher and Greenberg (1977) *op. cit.* for an overlapping list.

11. Schjelderup, H. (1955) 'Lasting Effects of Psychoanalytic Treatment' *Psychiatry*, 18, 103–133.

12. Orgel, S. Z. (1958) 'Effect of Psychoanalysis on the Course of Peptic Ulcer' *Psychosomatic Medicine*, 20, 117–123.

13. Cappon, D. (1964) 'Results of Psychotherapy' *Brit. J. of Psychiatry*, 110, 35–45.

14. Shapiro, D. A. (op. cit.)
    Schapiro, A. K. (1971) 'Placebo Effects in Medicine, psychotherapy and Psychoanalysis' Ch. 13 in Bergin and Garfield (ed.) *op. cit.*
    Schapiro, A. K. and Morris, L. A. (1978) 'The Placebo Effect in Medical and Psychological Therapies', Ch. 10, in Garfield and Bergin (ed.) *op. cit.*

15. Fisher and Greenberg (1977) *op. cit.*
    Malan (1973) *op. cit.*

16. The information given here about John comes from the unpublished material of his case record.

17. John's father in interview (with B.A.F.) after treatment had ended.

18. Fisher, S. and Greenberg, R. P. (1977) *op. cit.*

19. Smith and Glass (1977) *op. cit.*, p. 760.

20. Marks, I. (1978) 'Behavioral Psychotherapy of Adult Neuroses', Ch. 13 in Garfield and Bergin (ed.) *op. cit.*
    Trower, P., Bryant, B., and Argyle, M. A. (1978) *Social Skills and Mental Health* (Methuen: London).

21. Gelder, M. G. and Marks, I. (1966) 'Severe Agoraphobia: A controlled Prospective Trial of behaviour therapy'. *Brit. J. of Psychiatry*, 112, 309–319.

Gelder et al. (1967) 'Desensitization and Psychotherapy in the treatment of Phobic states: a controlled inquiry'. *Brit. J. of Psychiatry, 113*, 53–73.

Cf. Sloane, R. B. et. al. (1975) *Psychotherapy versus Behavior Therapy*, a Commonwealth Fund Book (Harvard Univ. Press and London).

22. Marks, I. (1978) *op. cit.*

23. For these large topics, see, e.g. *Lithium Research and Therapy* (1975) ed. F. N. Johnson (Academic Press: New York, London).

    Leff, J. P. and Wing, J. K. (1971) 'Trial of Maintenance Therapy in Schizophrenia', *Brit. Med. J.*, 11 Sept., 599–604.

    Hirsch, S. R. et al. (1973) 'Outpatient Maintenance of Chronic Schizophrenic patients with long acting fluphenazine' *Brit. Med. J., 1*, 633–637.

    d'Elia, G. and Raotma, H. (1975) 'Is unilateral ECT less effective than bilateral ECT?' *Brit. J. Psychiatry, 126*, 83–89.

24. Cooper, D. (1967) *Psychiatry and Anti-Psychiatry* (Tavistock: London).

    Laing, R. D. (1967) *The Politics of Experience and the Bird of Paradise* (Penguin: London).

    Farrell, B. A. (1965) 'The Logic of Existential Psychoanalysis' *New Society*, 21 Oct.

Chapter 10

1. Rieff, P. (1961) *Freud, the mind of a moralist* (Anchor Books: Doubleday: New York).

2. Popper, K. R. (1957) *op. cit.*

   It is unfortunate that Popper misleadingly describes these suggestions as 'psychological' only.

3. Huxley, J. (1942) *Evolution: The modern synthesis* (Allen and Unwin: London).

4. Farrell, B. A. (1963) Introduction to *Leonardo op. cit.*

5. Sherwood, M. *op. cit.*; Farrell, B. A. (1963) *op. cit.*

6. Farrell, B. A. (1979) 'Work in Small Groups: Some Philosophical Considerations' in *Training in Small Groups*. Babington Smith, B. and Farrell, B. A. (ed.) (Pergamon: Oxford).

7. Bauer, R. A. (ed.) (1962) *Some views on Soviet Psychology* (Amer. Psychol. Assoc. Inc.: Washington, D.C.).

   Allen, M. G. (1973) 'Psychiatry in the United States and the USSR: A comparison' *Amer. J. of Psychiatry, 130*: 1333–7.

   Segal, B. M. (1975) 'The Theoretical Bases of Soviet Psychotherapy' *Amer. J. of Psychotherapy, 29*: 503–523.

8. Erikson, E. H. (1959) *Young Man Luther* (Faber and Faber: London).

9. Elton, G. R. (1969) *The Practice of History* (Collins, Fontana: London).

10. For an interesting attempt to develop a post-Freudian account of a literary figure, namely T. S. Eliot, see L. Scott Frazier 'The Psychodynamics of Religion', D. Phil thesis, Oxford Univ., 1978.

11. Hunt, McV. (1969) 'The impact and limitations of the giant of developmental

Psychology' in *Studies in Cognitive Psychology*, eds. D. Elkind and J. H. Flavell (Oxford: London).

Bryant, P. (1974) *Perception and Understanding in Young Children* (Methuen: London).

12. E.g. Uttal, W. R. (1978) *The Psychobiology of Mind* (Lawrence Erlbaum Wiley: New York, London).

    Gray, J. A. (1979) *Pavlov* (Fontana).

13. As, e.g. the late Dr. H. Miller (1972) 'Psychoanalysis: A Clinical Perspective', in *Freud*, Miller, J. (ed.) (Weidenfeld and Nicolson: London).

14. A point missed by J. S. Bruner (1976) 'Psychology and the Image of Man', *Times Literary Suppl.* 17 Dec. Also in *Herbert Spencer Lectures 1976* (1979) ed. H. Harris (Oxford)

15. Austen, J. (1818) *Northanger Abbey* (John Murray: London).

Suggestions for further reading

Freud, S. (1917/22) *Introductory Lectures on Psycho-analysis* (Pelican Freud Library, vol. 1). *Standard Edition* vols. 15 and 16, ed. James Strachey (Hogarth: London).

Freud, S. (1910) 'Five Lectures on Psycho-analysis' in *Two Short Accounts of Psychoanalysis* (Pelican: London, 1962) *Standard Edition* vol. 11.

Wollheim, R. (1971) *Freud* (Fontana/Collins: London).

Fordham, F. (1953) *An Introduction to Jung's Psychology* (Pelican: London).

Way, L. (1956) *Alfred Adler* (Pelican: London).

Brown, J. A. C. (1961) *Freud and the Post-Freudians* (Pelican: London).

Segal, H. (1979) *Klein* (Fontana/Collins: London).

Index

Patterns of Sexuality and Reproduction

Alan S. Parkes

Can we choose the sex of our children? Why are more boys born than girls? Does the quality of intercourse affect the chance of having a baby? Human reproduction is cumbersome, prolonged, and rather messy. It is no easy task to unravel the intricate patterns of the effects of cyclic, seasonal, and social variations on our sexual activity and our ability to reproduce. This unique account of these patterns, with its clear but entertaining style, will appeal to all from the layman, whose enthusiasm is mainly practical, to the medical student and the General Practitioner, for whom the subject is of professional interest.

... [a] 'fact-packed volume, perhaps best described as a thinking man's "All you have ever wanted to know ... but wouldn't dream of asking" ... There can be few people better qualified to write such a book.'

New Scientist

Man Against Disease
Preventive Medicine

J. A. Muir Gray

Do governments spend enough time and money in the most efficient manner on the prevention of sickness? Does the individual devote enough attention to his own good health? Dr. Muir Gray considers the scope for preventing disease and premature death in both developed and underdeveloped countries, from the promotion of child health to the problems of old age.

'This is an excellent book.' *Lancet*

'There can be few people, lay or professional, who would not derive pleasure and profit from reading it.'
British Book News

How to do things with words
Second Edition

J. L. Austin

Edited by J. O. Urmson and Marina Sbisà

J. L. Austin's 1955 William James Lectures, 'a choice work by
one of the most acute and original minds that England has
produced in our time' (*Times Literary Supplement*) set out his
conclusions in the field to which he directed his main efforts for
at least the last ten years of his life. Starting from an exhaustive
examination of his already well-known distinction of
performative utterances from statements, Austin here finally
abandons that distinction, replacing it by a more general theory
of 'illocutionary forces' of utterances which has important
bearings on a wide variety of philosophical problems.

Structuralism and Since
From Lévi Strauss to Derrida

Edited by John Sturrock

France is never without one or more *maîtres à penser* those charismatic, difficult thinkers whose ideas we see as giving permanent shape to a particular intellectual epoch. Claude Lévi Strauss, Roland Barthes, Michel Foucault, Jacques Lacan, and Jacques Derrida are such figures: writers who, in their different disciplines, have made structuralism into the force that it is today. This book elucidates the structuralist phenomenon, by considering the work of these five important thinkers, and aims to establish what is of lasting worth and originality in their work. It is a reasoned and positive presentation of an important body of contemporary thought.

'John Sturrock's ... book is the best guide to its subject that has yet appeared ... Brilliantly expounded, with cracking pace and unflappable self-confidence, the book is a mine of information and an indispensable primer to anyone who comes to the subject fresh and ready to make a new conquest.'

The Voice of the Past
Oral History

Paul Thompson

'Oral history gives history back to the people in their own
words. And in giving a past, it also helps them towards a future
of their own making ... It thrusts life into history itself and it
widens its scope. It allows heroes not just from the leaders, but
from the unknown majority of the people.'

Paul Thompson argues that oral history can help to create a
truer picture of the past, documenting the lives and feelings of
all kinds of people, and that its value has been badly neglected
by conventional historians. It can juxtapose professional opinion
with interpretations of events drawn from all classes of society.
In addition, the effect of collecting oral evidence can be to bind
together communities, promote contact between generations,
and give people a sense of roots in their own historical past.

'a pioneering and valuable book' *New Society*

What is Ecology?
Second edition

D. F. Owen

Ecology has become a household word, the name of a political
party even, but what is it all about? It is concerned with the
growth of populations, plant and animal, and the resources
available to them, and with the structure of communities and
their relationship to an environment which is always in a state of
flux, not least at the hands of man. Denis Owen begins with
animals, plants, and situations that we all know – thrushes and
earthworms on the lawn, and herons and pike in the river – and
describes with great clarity (and often with humour) how they
live and why they die. He goes on to consider man as a part of
nature and explains how ecology affects us all.

'I recommend this informative book to anyone wishing to
broaden his knowledge of ecology.' *New Scientist*

A Historical Introduction to the Philosophy of Science
Second Edition

John Losee

Since the time of Plato and Aristotle, scientists and philosophers have raised questions about the proper evaluation of scientific interpretations. A *Historical Introduction to the Philosophy of Science* is an exposition of positions that have been held on issues such as the distinction between scientific inquiry and other types of interpretation; the relationship between theories and observation reports; the evaluation of competing theories; and the nature of progress in science. The book makes the philosophy of science accessible to readers who do not have extensive knowledge of formal logic or the history of the several sciences.

Urban Planning
in Rich and Poor Countries

Hugh Stretton

Whose interests are served by the new planning bureaucracies?
If some of them seem to do more harm than good, would they be
best abolished, or replaced, or reformed? Hugh Stretton suggests
that many planning projects have not been effective in practice
because they have not delved deep enough into the societies for
which they were intended. Planners must seek to understand the
complexities of societies, their economic and political structures,
he argues, and be aware of their own values and of governmental
pressure.

'remarkably well informed ... judicious and witty'
Times Educational Supplement

'There are very few books which *everyone* interested in urban
planning should read but this is one of them.'
Urban Studies